Illness
to
Wellness

A Revolutionary 11-Step Program to Conquer
Disease, Create Everyday Miracles, and
Reconnect to Your Highest Self

Dr. Jon Repole, DC, NC, HHP, CFMP

When "I" is replaced with "we," even illness becomes wellness.
-Malcolm X

I-llness to We-llness is an inspiring and essential guide for 21st century living. Drawing on insights from his decades of clinical experience, Dr. Repole teaches us how to add the heart wisdom back into the health equation in order to treat and prevent chronic disease. With empathy and clarity, *I-llness to We-llness* provides us with practical tools and methods to optimize every dimension of being. It is best summed up by the thesis running throughout the book, that doing good is good for you.

-*Will Tuttle, PhD,* a pianist, composer and former Zen monk, is the author of the acclaimed best-seller, *The World Peace Diet,* and a recipient of the *Courage of Conscience Award.*

In *I-llness to We-llness,* Dr. Jon Repole provides an expert and accessible guide to optimal health. He offers us a compass for this heroic journey of awareness, values, vision, responsibility, alignment, integration, and self-realization. This work is grounded in nature's laws and helps us find the sacred in the mundane as we take the personal focused daily steps needed to achieve miraculous healing in our lives.

-*Dr. Andrew Paul Williams,* PhD, E-RYT 500, and author of *The Space Between: Cultivating Mindfulness, Peace, and Empowerment In Your Life Through Meta-Awareness, Framing and Yoga*

As a highly-respected holistic health professional, Dr. Repole enlightens that health must be addressed on every level of existence. *I-llness to We-llness* will captivate you to contemplate the depths of life's journey. You'll be encouraged to press on to your highest Self, fulfilling life's neautiful purpose with gratitude. Nourish and flourish in fullness of insight.

-*Susanne Morrone,* natural health speaker,
author, and consultant.

Health is so much deeper than the physical, it starts with the Self. Something we've lost connection with over the years. In this insightful book, Dr. Jon Repole helps us reconnect with our roots and reestablish the lost connection to our inner knowing—where true health begins.

-*Dawn Hutchins,* plant-based lifestyle educator, plant-based chef, founder of VegeCooking.

This book is an extremely well thought out, all inclusive, multifaceted, amazing approach to health and wellness. If you want to understand how you are in charge of your health, read this book! It reframes everything you thought you knew.

-*Dr. A.J. Butler,* B.S. (Nutrition), B.S. (Anatomy), D.C., and author of the *Advanced Percussion Protocol Series (canines, felines, and equines).*

ISBN: 979-8-88759-453-8 - paperback

ISBN: 979-8-88759-454-5 - ebook

Editor: Deborrah Hoag

Illustrations: Hannah Colleen and Olga Kalinina

Disclaimer

This publication contains the opinions and ideas of the author and does not constitute any health or medical advice. The content of this book is for informational purposes only and is not intended to diagnose, treat, cure of prevent any condition or disease. The author specifically disclaims all responsibility for any liability, loss or risk, personal or otherwise, which is incurred as a consequence, directly or indirectly, of the use and application of any of the contents of this book.

Acknowledgments

I have always resonated with the Garth Brooks song "The Dance," its meaning encapsulated in the lyric, "*I could have missed the pain, but I would have had to miss the dance.*"

There are people who come in our lives for a reason, season, or lifetime. To this sentiment, I would like to recognize and give gratitude to the people and animals who have danced in and out of my life. This includes those who are no longer living, those I continue to have deep, emotional, and loving connections with, and those whose connections have been tethered or grown dim.

To the many authors, speakers, and educators who have impacted my life in profound ways, and most of whom I have never met. Their names, quotes, and insights, however, can be found in the pages to follow. Special gratitude and thanks to Jesus, Ken Wilber, Dr. Gabriel Cousens, John Robbins, Dr. Jeffrey Bland, Abraham Maslow, Dr. Will Tuttle, Eckhart Tolle, Gary Francione, and Marianne Williamson.

To my patients. You have taught me humility, patience, and more about the healing journey than any degree earned.

To my family. You have taught me the power of love, surrender, and forgiveness.

To my angelic family, especially Mom and Dad. Thanks for showering me with unconditional love and reminding me how fragile and precious this life really is. I long to remain connected and guided by your presence.

To my soul sister Heather. Thanks for beautifully shared experiences, actualizing my potential, and teaching me the power of namaste.

To my extended family at Jacksonville Health and Wellness Center. Thanks for your friendship, trust, and providing me the bedrock to live my dreams.

To my Siena and NYCC family. Thanks for building my roots, the memories, and friendships.

To my longest and most special friend Bryan. I admire your evolution, dedication to your craft, and open heart.

To my friend Deborrah Hoag. Thank you for the editing magic and your Kosmic prowess.

To my partner and love of my life, Amanda Johns. Thanks for modeling health and nonjudgement, teaching me the power of values, and sharing your heart with me. I am honored to hold your hand as we manifest our dreams into fruition.

Each dance has challenged and presented me with unique opportunities to choose between the best and worst versions of myself. Cumulatively, these relations have helped make me a better man. I continue to harness their influences, wisdom, and lessons.

It is with reverence and humility I am now able to share with you a universal message of healing—a journey to the abundant and endless love that surrounds us all.

Table of Contents

Introduction

Someone once told me the definition of hell: the last day on earth,
the person you became will meet the person you could have been.
-Anonymous

My Psychic Abilities

"Your new patient is ready," my front staff knocks on my office door
and announces. I glance down at the new patient paperwork for
Mary Jones, age fifty-five. I take a deep breath and silently muse:

> *This patient is most likely fatigued, having difficulty losing a few
> pounds, not sleeping well, lost their sex drive, struggling with
> increasing levels of job, marital, and home stress, taking anywhere
> from three to five or more medications (for high blood pressure,
> cholesterol, pain, etc.), and experiencing various emotional states
> on a continuum from anxiety and depression all the way to exis-
> tential angst for an unsatiated life void of happiness or fulfillment.*

I look down again at the patient's paperwork and, after reading
her health history and chief concerns, blurt out, "Wow, I was right.
I must be psychic!"

I stop for a moment at the section pertaining to her questions
and goals: "I want to know exactly what's wrong, find the correct

diagnoses, discuss X, Y, Z treatments, order X, Y, Z diagnostics, and know if X, Y, Z supplements will help."

I thumb to the "Diet and Lifestyle" section, and become acutely aware of the correlations between her chief concerns and the following responses: "not exercising, not eating healthy, staying up too late, drinking too much alcohol, working too many hours, unfulfilled, lack of self-esteem. "

In essence, my patients oftentimes make a list of non-nurturing and toxic actions, behaviors, emotional states, and mental constructs that are, directly or indirectly, causing harm to their most prized and precious possession—the sanctuary we call our physical body.

I ponder the following:

- Why are my patients waiting for me to tell them the specific dietary and lifestyle habits that must be stopped or started?
- Why are patients and doctors running endless batteries of testing before they feel confident in assigning culpability or responsibility for a patient's non-nurturing behaviors? Do we really have to wait to get healthy?
- And for those people who are committed to their diet and lifestyle who still do not experience health, what are the missing elements?
- And for those that feel stuck, emotionally spent, unfulfilled, lost meaning and purpose, how exactly is this affecting their health?
- Isn't it time we create a more holistic definition of health that includes the physical, emotional, relational, mental, and spiritual dimensions?
- Is there a systematic way to engage the process of health, healing, disease reversal, and the actualization of our potentials?

As the days, years, and decades flew by, I found similar stories with different faces and life experiences. To my dismay, I realized that I wasn't psychic after all. Rather, I discovered a truth hidden right in front of my eyes. Upon this realization, I traded in my "holistic pharmacy" approach (the simple act of trading a pharmaceutical for a nutraceutical) for a more nuanced understanding of health and wellness that I will unpack in the following pages.

In brief, the disease of humankind is the inability to step into the shoes and align with their most heroic Self. We are literally hypnotized as a species, focusing too much of our time on the non-essentials and settling for a life that is less than the one we are capable of living. We can live an unexamined life, a life by someone else's design, a life in self-betrayal that buries our potential, a life of quiet desperation. Or we can begin, right here and now, to construct a life of our own making—a life by design, in alignment with our highest values, dreams, goals, and in service to who and what is most important to us. At all times, we are only one decision and one miracle away from our greatest life.

Humanistic psychologist Abraham Maslow cuts to the chase: "If you plan on being less than you are capable of being, then I warn you that you'll be unhappy for the rest of your life." Ultimately, we want to avoid having to meet the person we could have been and embrace, today, the man or woman we know we must be. We must not deny our divine birthright and the magical life that awaits this recognition.

Simplicity and Complexity

The attainment of this optimal state of being lies tied up with an interesting paradox between simplicity and complexity. On the one hand, simplicity tells us that we need only step back, uncover, and recognize the great inherent power within. Complexity, on the other hand, covers up this simplistic "too good to be true" notion with years of indoctrination, programming, emotional wounds, memories, mental constructs, and more. The ego, as found in *A Course in Miracles*, keeps us forever unsatiated. Its motto is "Seek and do not find." The following Hindu legend expands on this:

> *There was once a time when all human beings were gods, but they so abused their divinity that the chief god decided to take it away from them and hide it where it could never be found. He called an elite council of the gods for advice. Opinions varied; suggestions included hiding it deep within the earth, the depths of the ocean, and the highest mountain peaks. These were all rejected, knowing that humans would one day learn ingenious and creative ways to dig, dive, and climb.*
>
> *The chief god thought for a long time and then said, "Here is what we will do. We will hide their divinity deep in the center of their own being, for humans will never think to look there." All the gods agreed that this was the perfect hiding place, and the deed was done. And since that time, humans have been going up and down the earth, digging, climbing, diving, and exploring— searching for something already within themselves.*

This book is a guide to human potential. In the pages to follow, we will explore levels of health you never knew existed or, worse yet, convinced yourself were unavailable and unachievable. It's about walking in the shoes of your highest Self and optimizing your health on all dimensions of existence: physical, emotional, relational, mental, and spiritual (referred to as PERMS throughout the remainder of this book). On our journey, we'll try to understand exactly what it means to live—rather than just be alive. It's a journey to uncover who we are and unlearn who we are not.

"Who we are" is often equated with the biblical reference contained in two powerful words, *I am.* It is a reference to the "God within," our divine birthright, higher Self, true Self, heroic Self, authentic Self, and the famous quote by Pierre Teilhard de Chardin: "We are spiritual beings having a human experience." It equates to endless potential and what some call the seat of witness consciousness.

"Who we are not" is everything that comes after *I am.* It equates to an endless array of descriptors, limitations, and attachments such as, "I'm depressed, sick, too busy, stuck, not worthy." Or "I'm my job, my role," and so on. Simplicity lies in recognizing the difference between the I am and all the descriptors that follow.

Over a lifetime, we accumulate layers of complexity that distracts us from the valuable and attuning us to the valueless. This makes it nearly impossible to "find" and reconnect to our unified and unfragmented higher Self.

These complex secondary elements also distract us from primal elements, our body's innate wisdom. These primal elements are defined as the body's most fundamental operating systems that carry our motivations and desires to satiate and fulfill universal human needs such as safety, security, love, and contribution.

In essence, all healing is self-healing that involves a process of returning, connecting, or uncovering the power of our authentic Self (primal elements) amongst a sea of confusion (complex secondary elements).

The Alignment Continuum and Quantum Leaps

The Alignment Continuum

Soul's Awareness

Mind's Attention

Heart's Intentions / Feelings

Habits, Behaviors, and Actions

For the first time in history, humanity has the tools, resources, and capacity to satiate the basic deficiency needs (food, water, shelter, safety, security, and a general sense of community or belongingness) of every man, woman, and child on planet earth. Once satisfied, human beings are then free to pursue higher soul-based meta needs for growth, transformation, and contribution.

If you're reading these words, chances are you're blessed to be living in a modern progressive country where all your basic needs have and continue to be met with relative ease. Unfortunately, this also means that you may be one of many individuals unaware of this evolutionary luxury. Rather than pursuing higher levels of fulfillment, you spend your days frantically putting out fires, crossing out items on your never-ending to-do list, and engaging in activities that are mundane, uninspiring, unmotivating, and obligatory.

It's unfortunate that so many of us choose to spend an enormous amount of mental real estate on decisions pertaining to our next coffee latte or on time pursuing valueless activities (e.g., phone and TV surfing) and addictive non-nurturing behaviors (e.g., binge eating and tobacco usage).

Imagine how you could transform your life, your health, and your relationships if all your energies were directed toward nurturing those things that were valuable, transcendent, transformative, and growth-producing? Imagine how amazing your life could be if you rejected self-betrayal and lived a life by design? Imagine how life would unfold if you followed your heart and soul's most intimate desires?

People engaged in the self-actualizing life, consciously or unconsciously, are following a very specific formula that can be traced back, in various iterations, to our ancient wisdom traditions, modern-day psychology (e.g., CBT or cognitive behavioral therapy), and new-age metaphysics. I call it The Alignment Continuum—the alignment of our soul's awareness, our mind's attention, our heart's intentions/feelings, and our habits, behaviors, and actions. In short, it's about aligning all aspects of yourself to that everlasting and deepest part that remains untouched by personal history and in direct connection to life itself.

This book is about the achievement of such alignment. It is about a decision to take a miraculous and quantum leap on all dimensions of health—physical, emotional, relational, mental, and spiritual while never abandoning, rejecting, or isolating any one part at the expense of another. This new way of being entices us to throw out societal conformities, such as climbing the proverbial ladder of enlightenment, rung by rung, in favor of quantum leaps. This is accomplished by becoming greater than our circumstances and environment, reprogramming our mental models, elevating our emotions and feelings, and aligning with our divine inheritance.

Lemons and Lemonade

Most likely, you have heard the adage, "When life gives you lemons, make lemonade." But have you ever really contemplated its profound implications? It's not telling us to push harder and harder or grin and bear it. It's not telling us to muster up more resilience or live according to the dictum, "Whatever doesn't kill us makes us stronger." Rather, it asks us to redefine "change" as the transcendence over our current reality.

It's important to distinguish change from transcendence. Change, as a metaphor, involves the hypnotic activity of rearranging the furniture on the deck of the sinking Titanic. Transcendence, on the other hand, involves embracing new, energic, and vibrational states.

Imagine, as its metaphor, the life cycle of H_2O. Place a bowl of ice on a table outside in the sun. Come back a few hours later, and you will see a new transcendent energy state—water. As the months pass, the sunlight warms the water's surface, causing the molecules to move faster and faster until they escape into the air as water vapor— another transcendent energy state.

Our journey begins with the understanding that our destination is not returning to a time prior to illness. Rather, we are talking about jumping to a completely new transcendent destination—the embodiment of your highest, healthiest, and most heroic Self. As famous mythologist Joseph Campbell says, "We must let go of the life we have planned, so as to accept the one that is waiting for us." You are the hero and author of your life.

Die Empty

Bronnie Ware, an Australian nurse, during a highlighted time in her career, had the soulful opportunity to care for a host of terminally ill patients as they approached the last few weeks of their lives. During this time, she routinely spoke to her patients about their regrets.

Paraphrasing, she asked, "If given a 'genie in the bottle' wish, granting you the power to rewind your life and start anew, would you have done things differently?" In her book *The Top Five Regrets of the Dying,* she chronicles the top five answers:

> - I wish I'd had the courage to live a life true to myself, not the life others expected of me.
> - I wish I hadn't worked so hard.
> - I wish I'd had the courage to express my feelings.
> - I wish I had stayed in touch with my friends.
> - I wish that I had let myself be happier.

What she didn't hear was:

> - I wish I'd spent more time binge-watching Netflix.
> - I wish I'd have worked a few more overtime shifts and stayed away from my family.
> - I wish I could have traded in my experiences for more things.

Reflecting on one's potential future regrets, a spinoff on the classic ancient Stoic technique of negative visualization, can be a welcoming practice, inviting courage, presence, and inspired action to enter our chaotic, unsatiated, unfulfilled, and frustrated lives. Someday in the distant future, we will, inevitably, find ourselves sitting quietly, musing, and judging the totality of our life—by what we said, what we did not say, how we acted, how we sat timidly on the sidelines, how we showed up, how we retreated, and whether or not we stood in the shoes of our heroic Self.

As author Todd Henry in *Die Empty* states, "Don't go to your grave with your best work inside you. Choose to die empty."

The regrets of the dying have more to do about what we did not do (our trapped unactualized potential) and less to do about what we did do. It's as if the universe is beckoning us—*please leave no song unsung, no page unturned, no dream undreamt, and no wine untasted.* All of us contain a divine spark waiting to be conceived and birthed. Unfortunately, we are held back from stepping into our highest Self by life's adversities, traumas, limiting beliefs, and our overall concept of who we think we are. All these so-called limitations we will, collectively, call "our past."

There is no denying that our past experiences have molded and contributed to our current self-identity. However, a hidden, nonintuitive truth about the past exists—it can and does change. The past is, in fact, more subjective than objective. It exists only in the present moment as recollections of thoughts, memories, and beliefs. Each time we recall the past, we assign and attach meaning. For example, a past adversity recalled at two different intervals in your life could evolve from the worst experience to the most life-altering positive experience. Thus, as we grow and evolve, our past must grow and evolve. If our life is stagnant, we have most likely allowed our past to keep us victims and prisoners to a non-nurturing past self-identity. In this respect, we can say the past (a belief) is controlling who we are in the present moment.

Stepping into the person you wish to become involves rejecting the idea that the past causes our current reality. In other words, we can break the chains of our past by evolving our past and attaching constructive rather than destructive meanings. This is not a fanciful idea of rewriting our history, past factual events, or experiences. Rather we are talking about taking the content of the past and evolving the container (the present moment context) it's held within. As we uncover our true Self, we will begin to identify with an evolving future Self rather than a fixed, constricted, and limited one.

Be, Do, and Have

Here is a true story of two friends contemplating life's struggles one day over dinner. One was an attractive tall blond, former FBI agent, successful entrepreneur millionaire in Silicon Valley, consistently emanating positivity, joy, and happiness. The other, a man, was struggling financially, emotionally, and relationally. He was unable to find his way, so to speak, in the great game of life. After years of conversing, the man mustered up the courage to ask, "Is there a secret to your accumulated success?" She leaned over and whispered, "What if THIS is heaven?"

Noticing the look of bewilderment, she described the details of a heart attack she had at age twenty-four where she was medically pronounced dead for a total of seven minutes, reemerging for a brief stint before being thrown into a one-month coma. When she awoke, she mused silently, "Am I in heaven?" She continued to speak to her now captivated friend, "You see, there was no

"What if I lived as if I could be, do, and have everything I ever wanted?"

real way for me to prove the contrary. So, from that moment forward, I decided to live each day as if I was in heaven." The question that guided her actions, and the very same question that can guide ours, is:

What if I lived as if I could do, be, and have everything I wanted?

I-llness to We-llness or I to We

I to We is at the core of this book's thesis and represents a monumental shift away from our current finite reality to a transcendent and infinite one. It is synonymous with the idea of awakening as found within all the Eastern traditions. We begin to wake up and recognize the prisons, ceilings, and boundaries that held us back were self-imposed, made of glass, and built of unlimited potential.

This quantum shift can be broken down into three distinct perspectives: spiritual (Heaven), physical (Earth), and heart-centered (merging of Heaven and Earth). I will introduce these perspectives briefly and expand on them in the pages to follow.

Spiritual

From a spiritual perspective (absolute truth, Heaven), there is only *one problem* (the fragmented and separate I) and *one solution* (the unified and connected We). The *We to I* orientation is the leading story embedded in our culture today. It is a belief in separation from ourselves (good parts, bad parts, wounded parts), our actions and behaviors, our highest Self, others, Mother Nature, and all her children (human and nonhuman). This belief is the cause. Its effects include ecological degradation like climate change, poverty, and hunger. The idea of separateness is our greatest moral and spiritual obstacle today. We have fragmented the world and ourselves into parts and abandoned life's interconnection.

The drive to an *I to We* orientation is referred to as the spiritual imperative and serves as the anecdote for society's predicaments. The *I to We* orientation is about connectedness and helps to uncover and reconnect us with the wisdom and guidance of our higher Self. It moves us from being a victim to a cocreator self-authoring consciousness. It is manifested through miracles. A miracle, as we will discuss, is not some fanciful and unobtainable ideal. Rather, it is easily accessible, replicable, and available to everyone in every moment. As Jesus says in the Gospel of Luke, "The kingdom of God is within you." A miracle exists in the present moment. In fact, just one new decision has the power to change your life forever.

We to I is the story of humanity's separation from *who and what is most important*. Millions of people caught in the story live an unexamined life preoccupied with the busyness of the mundane, trivial, and valueless. From this perspective, our highest Self is made a servant to the ego's desires, attention, and automations. *I to We*, on the other hand, helps reinforce The Alignment Continuum. It is here where our awareness, attention, intention, thoughts, emotions, desires, values, needs, and actions are in alignment with our higher Self. Our ego, in this scenario, becomes the rightful servant to our higher Self.

When we identify with an isolated aspect of ourselves (e.g., limiting beliefs, different personalities, emotions), we starve our potential, live in scarcity, look outside ourselves for peace and happiness, and remain prisoner to life's circumstances. When we identify with spirit, our potential is awakened, we live in a world of abundance, look inside for peace and happiness, and break free from our self-imposed prisons.

Marianne Williamson, American author, spiritual leader, and political activist, in her book *The Law of Divine Compensation,* states this sentiment succinctly, "We are heir to the laws that rule the world we identify with. If you identify only with the material plane, you place yourself at the effect of pretty severe economic realities of scarcity and lack. If you identify with the spiritual plane, you are under no laws but God's." In other words, if we identify with the body, we place ourselves at the effect of the body's limitations. If, however, we identify with the part of us that is transcendent to the body, we are at the effect of spiritual laws that are miraculous, limitless, abundant, and full of unlimited potential.

Paradoxically, our ego holds to a belief system, *We to I,* which is a literal impossibility. To understand the magnitude of the ego's deception, we can reflect on the wisdom of Marianne Williamson once again, "Just like a sunbeam can't separate itself from the sun, and a wave can't separate itself from the ocean, we can't separate ourselves from one another. We are all part of a vast sea of love, one indivisible divine mind."

Physical

Back down on Earth in the nonspiritual plane of existence, life, as it often does, exists as a myriad of paradoxes. In direct opposition to the spiritual plane, its motto is "Many problems and many solutions." In other words, it asks us to embrace the idea that everything affects everything and to abandon the idea of one simple cause and effect in favor of multiple causes and effects.

Furthermore, illness (I) and wellness (We) represent two diametrically opposed health care systems. Pathogenesis, the illness and mechanistic model, believes we are isolated islands with no influence or connection to the ocean that surrounds and holds us. Using this metaphor, the illness model believes our organs exist as independent islands. Therefore, treatment relies on finding the best physical prescription (e.g., drugs and surgical interventions) and medical specialty (e.g., cardiologist or endocrinologist) to treat the corresponding isolated organ or disease.

Salutogenesis, the wellness model, expands past the mechanistic model and ascribes the power of connection. Its motto is summed up as causes and effects. Our organs, psyche, emotions, and spirit exist in a symphonic relationship. Humans are multidimensional organisms and, therefore, require a holistic and multi-dimensional treatment plan. As we layer and stack various dimensional practices (e.g., diet, exercise, emotional intelligence), the effects have the potential to transcend addition and move into the realm of multiplicative or exponential healing.

Heart-Centered Perspective

The heart is the rainbow bridge, connecting the spiritual and the physical. This heart-centered perspective embraces another of Jesus's teachings found in the Gospel of John, paraphrased, "We must live in the world but not of the world." In this light, we transcend dichotomies and integrate all the PERMS without contradiction.

This holistic approach is not about achieving perfection or balance in all the areas of our life. Rather, it asks only that we become integrally informed and include, rather than neglect or abandon our strengths, weaknesses, and shadows. It asks that we find coherence (not balance) and fulfillment (not happiness). In doing so, we can hold a loving and compassionate container for all aspects of our Self. From this new center of equanimity, we invite our higher Self to work in and through us. *A Course in Miracles* states, "The Holy Spirit cannot do for you, what he cannot do through you."

History has taught us that when we leave "the heart" out of life's equations, no path exists to hold heart-centered perspectives and make heart-centered decisions. We can see how this experiment is playing out in various sectors of our economy. Big Pharma, Wall Street, and large corporations are, in part, running their day-to-day business practices with little to no heart-centered accountability. In turn, the poor become poorer, the marginalized become more marginalized, and Mother Nature suffers disastrous consequences as her oceans and lands are neglected, polluted, and stripped. Solving for effect (climate change, restrictive governmental policies, etc.) rather than the cause (the underpinning separation narrative) is not an either/or but rather a both/and imperative.

The shift from *I to We* brings the heart to the center of the health and wellness equation. Although most of us identify who we are as more than just a physical body, our choices and behaviors don't reflect this intuition. For example, food can be eaten through an egocentric lens, relying strictly on the physical body's desires, wants, and taste preferences. However, a higher and more integrated level of consciousness (e.g., mind, body, heart, and soul) allows us to add satiation of needs, connection with others, concerns over environmental degradation, and animal treatment into heart-centered perspectives and decision-making.

Dr. Will Tuttle, author of *The World Peace Diet,* states, "Choosing to be blind to what we are actually doing when we shop for, prepare, and eat food, we blind ourselves not only to the horror and suffering we are instigating and eating, but also to the beauty of the world around us…Becoming insensitive to the pain we cause daily to defenseless animals, we also become insensitive to the beauty and luminosity of the creation that we oppress and from which we disconnect at every meal."

This shift in consciousness is a movement from egocentric (I, me, mine) to Kosmocentric (We). This higher level of consciousness as we will discuss, expands the concepts of power, love, and peace. The evolution of power, for example, moves from "things happening to me" (victim consciousness or reacting) to "things happening by me and through me" (cocreator consciousness, intentional action, and responsibility).

The evolution of love moves from conditional (my family, my religion, my race) to unconditional love (all of humanity, Mother Nature, and all her animals and plants). Finally, the evolution of peace shifts from trying to find peace outside oneself to an understanding that peace is found within. In this manner, happiness is about finding the seat of our higher Self that is unaffected by inner and outer weather patterns.

Imagine making decisions from this higher level of consciousness where all brain centers (reptilian, mammalian, neocortex, and higher Self or angel lobes) become embodied and integrated. The effects on our personal health and the collective are magnified.

As we attune to higher levels of consciousness, our love and compassion expand. As we begin to act through this new center, we are rewarded through various spiritual laws such as "giving is receiving" and "doing good is good for you." For example, when we choose to omit factory-farmed animal products from our diet, we protect our body (from antibiotics and GMOs) and help stop the barbaric animal practices that cause needless abuse and suffering.

Everyday Miracles

This book is about the miraculous life that awaits you. It's about becoming a miracle worker and manifesting daily miracles. Thus, I ask you to abandon the idea that miracles are the auspices of the extraordinary. Miracles, as defined here, are everyday occurrences.

Inspired by the metaphysical text *A Course in Miracles,* I equate miracles with courage and willingness. I define them as any shift in consciousness, perception, emotion, feeling, thought, or behavior that moves us, metaphorically, from an embodiment of fear to love. Therefore, a miracle occurs every time we create an alignment, regardless of duration, with our higher Self—a movement we will refer to, synonymously, as *I to We.*

Every time throughout the day we become aware of non-nurturing reactions, thoughts, and behaviors and muster the willingness to consciously realign ourselves to *who we are* and *what's most important*—a miracle is performed. Examples include:

- Comfort to courage
- Self-betrayal to values-driven life
- Automation to a life by design
- Present moment awareness
- Surviving to thriving
- Taking a deep breath
- Choosing a better narrative
- Saying, "I love and forgive myself"

How Is this Book Organized?

This book is about closing and bridging the gap between who you are and who you wish to become. It's about living a life by design rather than self-betrayal. Each section of this book will provide you with the necessary tools to go back "home" to the place you never left. This book is broken down into three sections: The Compass, The Map, and The Territory.

Before we start our journey, we must be aware that these three sections contain another of life's great paradoxes—that between *the why, the what, and the how.*

Without a map and trusty compass, our awareness can be likened to getting in a car and driving aimlessly, with no understanding or visualization of our destination. Without these tools, one will never be able to drive to the destination of their dreams. Although we may find it helpful to be navigated by a compass and trusty map, we must always remember that the map is not the territory.

Thus, life is a paradox for most of us. Though we need a sense of direction to move forward, where we are is enough. We are complete right now, though we may not sense it. Showing up fully in the present moment allows us to experience the intersection of divine eternity and our earthly physical plane.

The compass, map, and territory help guide your success. The compass and map offer a 10,000-foot view (the what and why), and the territory teaches you about the present (the how).

Section 1: Compass

This first section will deal with our compass, North Star, lighthouse, and the ultimate direction guiding our lives. This will include an exploration of our vision, goals, and values. In addition, we will explore the primal elements or operating systems that run our lives, including, in part, universal needs and emotions. Our ultimate destination is best represented by the psychological, spiritual, and mythological concepts of self-actualization, self-transcendence, and the hero's journey. Through these concepts, we will understand what it means to live a life of fulfillment on all dimensions, PERMS.

Section 2: Maps

The second part will provide us with two maps. The first and most common is referred to as *pathogenesis* or the origin and study of disease. The second, less known, is called *salutogenesis,* which explores the origin of health and focuses on factors that support human health and well-being rather than on factors that cause disease. Both maps are needed. For far too long, humans have neglected and abandoned the latter for the former. This section will bring light into new fields of genetics, give us a new health equation to solve all our health-related challenges and explore how trauma and wounds become embedded into the mind-body complex.

Section 3: Territory

The third and final part of the book will discuss the territory or the dirt and ground you're standing on. We move from the theoretical to the practical. I will provide you with eleven specific practices to create everyday miracles, optimize your health, increase longevity, slow down the aging process, self-actualize, and self-transcend:

- Awareness
- Diet
- Movement
- Detoxification and hermetic practices
- Coherence exercises
- The Sandwich Method
- The Elemental Diet
- Emotional-relational practices
- The Manifestation Method
- Spiritual and self-realization practices
- The Miracle Method

PART 1

The Compass

Live your life by a compass, not a clock.

-Stephen Covey

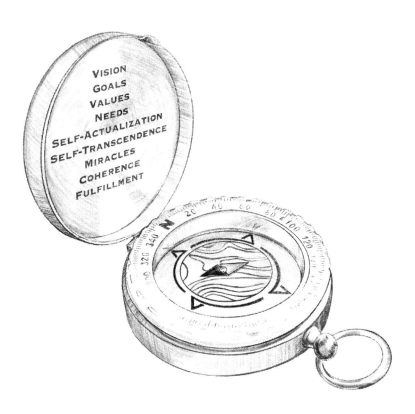

In the book *The War of Art,* Steven Pressfield tells us we have two lives, "the lives we live and the lives we are capable of living." The life we are about to create requires a compass. Most people live a life built around past programs running on autopilot. This pattern teaches us to climb the proverbial ladder of success, and often when we reach the top, we realize we were climbing the wrong wall and chasing other people's dreams and visions rather than our own. Paradoxically, we can't live without the brain's autopilot and default systems. Be forewarned, however, as these systems can run us into the side of a mountain or to the destination of our dreams.

The compass is our North Star. It acts as a beacon. No matter how off course we become, it guides us back time and time again to a place of refuge and solace within. It is the eye of the hurricane amongst the internal and external chaos. From this place of serenity, we send our roots deep into the earth for grounding. This solid foundation, in turn, gives us the ability to soar to higher and higher levels of growth and potential.

Maps are only good in known worlds that have been charted. Compasses, on the other hand, are perfect for the journey to the unknown. Your compass will be your guide as you explore and travel uncharted human potentials and find out just exactly who you are capable of becoming. Your compass will help elevate you to the 10,000-foot perspective, allowing you to see the inner and outer landscape laid before you.

Our compass is our unwavering center allowing us to actualize our potentials and bear witness to the sage advice given to us by the thirteenth-century Persian poet Rumi: "What you seek is seeking you."

In the pages to follow, we will explore the following concepts that make up your compass:

- Vision and goals: a compelling future and targeted milestones
- Values: core qualities and principles that give our lives direction and flavor
- The characteristics and ingredients that define Spirit, innate intelligence, and the hands of evolution
- Primordial elements: the true motives and desires underpinning everything we think, say, and do with particular attention to the gratification, satiation, and expression of universal human needs
- Complex secondary elements: the layers of complexity added to the primordial elements that cloud and distract us from our true desires, motivations, and needs
- Self-actualization, self-transcendence, and Kosmic consciousness: psychological and spiritual concepts that describe the pinnacle of human progress and our potential as human beings
- Coherence and fulfillment: the true measures of success and happiness
- Hero's journey: the more pragmatic understanding and encapsulation of self-actualization and self-transcendence
- Miracles: the true purpose of our lives and how to manifest them

CHAPTER 1

Vision to Values

In any situation in which you are uncertain, the first thing to consider, very simply, is "What do I want to come of this? What is it for?" The clarification of the goal belongs in the beginning, for it is this which will determine the outcome. In the ego's procedure this is reversed. The situation becomes the determiner of the outcome, which can be anything…The value of deciding in advance what you want to happen is simply that you will perceive the situation as a means to make it happen.

-A Course In Miracles

Most of us wake up each morning without a clear focus or inspired vision on how we want our lives to manifest or, more simply, what actions and behaviors, if taken, would make today a success. This lack of direction leaves us chasing low priority values and engaging in day-to-day activities that are out of alignment with who and what's most important to us. This, of course, is a grave mistake. Without a compass, other internal and external forces will compete and redirect our time, energies, priorities, and conscious intentions.

External forces come at us from all sides—phone calls, emails, friends, family, social media, obligations, to-do lists, errands, things we think we need to do, and more. Our internal forces are dominated by our subconscious mind, which holds a staggering 95 percent or more influence on our behaviors, decisions, reactions, responses, emotions, feelings, and thoughts. In other words, our subconscious shapes, controls, and influences nearly every aspect of our life.

Imagine all past experiences held and recorded as time capsules in the subconscious. The more an experience repeats, the larger the capsule. Now, imagine something or someone coming into your awareness. Like a computer, the subconscious compares this data to its capsule library until it finds a match. Once the right time capsule is found, our subconscious mind bursts the capsule and releases the stored content. We quickly become embodied with a past reality—a cornucopia of beliefs, thoughts, emotions, feelings, and primal responses. All of this happens without consultation, overriding any conscious desires. It works simply and impartially through an equation such as, *when I see this, I am commanded to do that...*

The internal and external forces keep us living a life on autopilot as they have predetermined our limitations, fears, comfort levels, and boundaries. The path to health, happiness, and peace starts with coauthoring and cocreation. This process has many facets, but one critical step is answering the "what, where, why, who, and how" questions. Don't be fooled into skipping this step, as your subconscious mind and life circumstances are all too happy to jump in and run your life for you.

Visioning, goal setting, and taking action (e.g., seeing things through to fruition or the art of manifestation) are rather simple processes. Common sense, however, is not common practice. Consider just one example–each year, a staggering percentage of New Year's resolutions fail. Reflect for a moment and try and grasp what this really means. You make a conscious decision to do something and are incapable of completing it. Who exactly is running who?

Becoming clear on your long-term vision, creating quarterly goals (in alignment with your vision), identifying obstacles, identifying daily tactics and actions (in alignment with your goal), and blocking out the time each week or day to complete these tactics and actions will usually help to ensure, more times than not, you succeed. These concepts are not new. What is new, however, is whether you will decide to change the course of your life today by using and committing to the tools laid forth.

This concept is also true for individuals suffering from chronic lifestyle diseases such as diabetes, heart disease, certain cancers, osteoporosis, depression, and more. Living on autopilot and doing the same things that created the disease or psychological state of suffering will continue unless we consciously decide to change the trajectory and commit to change, for example, to a more nourishing diet and lifestyle.

Vision

Our vision should give us an emotional charge. It is the picture we paint of a compelling future that's greater than our current reality. It gives us direction and guides all facets of our lives (personally, socially, professionally) around a meaningful purpose. It provides us with the necessary energies and fuel to wake up every morning and face the day with courage, love, conviction, and passion.

One way of understanding our vision is to differentiate it from fantasy. While our vision is a must, a fantasy remains something we just think about. Our fantasies, undoubtedly, will follow us to our grave as starved potentials—dying and vanishing into the ether from which they came.

Our vision is our North Star giving us the big picture of what we want, why we want it, and who we need to become. Our vision helps fuel us with the courage to push through the discomfort of change, fear, and uncertainty. Our vision provides muscle and keeps you pushing forward regardless of the challenges or obstacles thrown on your path.

One of the most important pieces to making your vision a reality is aligning your vision with your thoughts, emotions, feelings, and behaviors. This is the step that almost everyone leaves out and is the key ingredient to quantum leaps. Visioning is not a stand-alone mental imaginative process. Rather, it is defined as any mechanism that reinforces the embodiment of your future Self and moves you away from your conditioned past.

Put simply, nothing changes if nothing changes. In other words, we must recondition our thoughts, emotions, feelings, and behaviors alongside the reinvention of the environment we are accustomed to living in. If you wake up and do the same things, don't expect the visioning process to manifest.

Your vision can also be thought of as something you want to feel (peace, happiness, love, equanimity) rather than what you want to accomplish. If done correctly, visioning will transcend and integrate the polarities of dreaming and feeling. Your vision provides hope and faith to oppose the forces of conformity such as hopelessness and existential anxiety.

In conclusion, your vision should be crafted as your highest priority describing a distant future that ignites your soul. It is a declarative statement and commitment that we are leaving behind a past reality that is no longer compelling or serving our needs. Most importantly, your vision can be grand or simple. So, if nothing comes to mind immediately, consider committing to be better than you were yesterday and stepping into the shoes of your higher Self. In fact, the idea of self-actualization is a continuous process. No one ever becomes self-actualized. We can only ever be self-actualizing.

Goals

Goals are specific targets or concrete milestones along our path that lead us back to our greater vision. Goals provide us with clear end results and a success criterion to measure against.

The authors of the book *The 12-Week Year*, suggest changing your mindset around what constitutes a year. Most people and companies set annual goals and work plans. Of course, this is arbitrary. Using a smaller window such as the twelve-week year, as opposed to a twelve-month year, has proven to increase effectiveness and productivity in one's personal and business life. When the deadline is closer, it creates a sense of urgency. We tend to be less complacent, showing up each day with greater focus and engagement. We also become acutely aware of past tasks, actions, and behaviors that were needless, valueless, wasteful, and non-nurturing.

Regardless of the process, your goals should help prioritize your tasks, actions, and behaviors, guiding you, without effort, towards your greater vision.

Strategy and Tactics

Strategy and tactics represent our daily or weekly grind. Once we have created our long-term vision and goals, the next step is to identify the specific actions, tactics, or daily habits needed. Once this is completed, we schedule blocks of focused time in our weekly or daily calendar and commit to working on previously identified tactics or actions.

It is important to remember that we will always have more control over our tactics and actions than our results or goals. Thus, reviewing your vision and goals each day is important. Translating these concepts into actionable laser-focused tactics is where the rubber meets the road. It ripens the conditions to transform potentiality (our vision) into actuality. However, this is a step very few people take.

Values and Measurement

Values are not the same as goals. Values are qualities, ongoing actions, and directions we forever keep moving towards. For example, love, as a value, represents a verb rather than a noun. It is a quality of character we forever practice. It embodies empathizing, caring, sharing, giving, accepting, and forgiving. It is not something we achieve as an end result and say, "I have achieved love and can now move on to my next goal." Values represent the qualities we will embody in our daily practice, in the present moment, again and again as we move towards our vision and goals.

Values represent individual interpretations of universal needs such as safety, security, love, and self-esteem. They can also be considered core principles, beliefs, and convictions. They represent who and what's most important, desirable, useful, and meaningful alongside what we want to experience and how we want to experience it. Taken together, all this creates a moral compass guiding our decision-making and establishes a standard to measure our daily actions. Values let us know when we steer off course.

Values often, but not always, influence the direction of our thoughts, feelings, emotions, choices, and behaviors. A misconception pertaining to values is that they predict, with certainty and reliability, our results, behaviors, and actions. Some self-improvement gurus believe we need only look at one's behaviors (what they spend money on, how they spend their time, and so on) to uncover one's values. In other words, they equate behaviors with values. This, however, is not always true and can lead to unnecessary and harmful states of shame and blame. For example, one can value health but still smoke. One can value family but lash out against the people they love. These actions and behaviors are obviously not one's values.

The reason for the discrepancy lies in the dualistic nature of our conscious and subconscious minds. For example, the conscious, analytical, problem-solving, and rational mind says, "I value health." In contrast, the habituated subconscious mind says, "Tonight you will indulge in your favorite unhealthy foods, lie on the couch, and skip your workout." We must not forget that our conscious and subconscious minds have different needs.

Despite your conscious efforts, the reactive subconscious mind continues to run the programs that are familiar, comfortable, and safe—even though they may no longer serve you. These patterns are often the value programs of your parents, teachers, family, society, religious, and political leaders.

We all have two sets of values: conscious and subconscious. The key is to align the two. Sometimes, we must uncover the motives of our past wounds and shadows. Other times, we need only step back and reconnect with our highest and most heroic Self—a process I call The Miracle Method.

Becoming Our Values

One of the keys to manifestation, fulfilment, and the achievement of our dreams is to understand the deep metaphysical connection between goals and values. A goal has no inherent value. It only possesses the value we project on it. For example, one person can find value in purchasing a Ferrari or starring as the leading role in a movie. Others may find no value in such pursuits. Rather, they find immense value in reading a book, watching a sunrise, or shopping. Goals act as vehicles of presupposition when we believe their attainment will create an experience we value.

When we truly understand what goals represent, our lives will change forever. Why? We realize that for us to project values on a goal, the values must be coming from within. Without this realization, we will forever chase externals for value, happiness, and fulfillment. However, with this realization, we can turn inward to cultivate and uncover these inherent values (e.g., love, peace, and freedom). We begin to live from or with these values rather than states of emptiness, lack, and scarcity. These values, as we will soon discover, are the characteristics of our true Self and available at all times.

It is more effective to live in a state of fulfillment before the pursuit of any goal or dream. You may be thinking, *easier said than done.* The Manifestation Method and the self-realization practices, which we will discuss in the chapters of the same name, are some of the best ways to uncover these inherent values. Deep within us exists the very thing we are seeking. These practices, like exercise, will strengthen our spiritual muscles, allowing greater and greater levels of connection. *A Course in Miracles* reminds us that these values "wait on welcome, not time."

Values and Resistance

Part of a successful values elucidation process is to include, not fight, neglect, or abandon, any resistance to our vision or goal pursuits. We can ask, "What is holding me back?" or "What blocks or resistance are coming up?" Oftentimes, the answers to these questions are contextualized in a negative light as something we must get rid of. However, a more novel approach is to turn this resistance into a positive value. For example, if my resistance is anxiety or procrastination, I can ask myself, "What do I need to cultivate instead?" First, I may trace anxiety and procrastination to fear. Next, I realize I must cultivate courage as its anecdote. Now that resistance is contextualized in a positive light, I can add courage to my list of values.

CHAPTER 2

Spirit and Evolution

Where the spirit does not work with the hand there is no art.

-Leonardo da Vinci

To further understand the components that breathe life and make up our compass, no discussion would be complete without an exploration into its most important contribution—Spirit. Even though this concept is elusive and intangible, it remains, for most, the most trusted source of guidance and direction in our lives.

Is it possible to define Spirit? Is it possible to identify Spirit's primordial elements, drives, or the operating systems that are running our lives? Can we speak to the differences between being alive or dead? When we hear people say things like, "Follow your intuition," or "Trust your body's innate wisdom," is this something that can be uncovered, described, and concretized?

To start our discussion into this lofty investigation, we will attempt, ever so humbly, to define Spirit's life force energy by equating it with four compelling and universal evolutionary drives. From here, we will proceed cautiously to explore how these drives make their grand entrance into the human body and are translated from subtle energies into more concrete, understandable, and tangible energies (primal elements). Lastly, we will explore how these primordial or primal elements become distorted and hidden from us (called secondary complex elements) in a sea of endless effects—a condition at the core of humanity's suffering.

Since this section pertains to the first or primal elements driving and influencing what we think, do, and say, I have brought together an amalgam of theories and research that fit into a specific universal criterion. In other words, the research and theories chosen in the fields of integral meta-theory, evolutionary science, psychology, and behaviorism are universal and cross-culturally accepted—applying to all humans at any age and time in history.

The Perennial Philosophy

At the core of all the great religions and wisdom traditions is a belief in a single and shared mystical experience of ultimate reality. Although different names, languages, or pointers describe that which lies beyond our rational understanding, they all point to one universal truth.

This belief in the connectedness that goes beyond dogma or religion is often referred to as the perennial philosophy, and it is found in the esoteric and mystical branches of all the great religions—such as Gnosticism in Christianity, Kabbalah in the Jewish tradition, Sufism in Islam (think the great poet Rumi), and Vedanta in Hindu philosophy. The perennial philosophy has historic roots in the Renaissance but reached prominence through Aldous Huxley's 1954 book *The Perennial Philosophy*. Its core tenets are as follows:

- Spirit is not separate from its creation.
- We were born connected to Spirit (metaphorically symbolized as love).
- Culture, parents, leaders, and our environment have taught us separateness and disconnection (metaphorically symbolized as fear).
- Our journey is to unlearn separateness and rediscover or uncover our interconnectedness.
- Once this truth is embodied, the great burdens of time, fear, and existential anxiety will be relieved.
- The path of transcendence follows the great chain of being (see below).

The Great Chain of Being

As we look out over the sea of infinite existence, we begin to see the universal language in literally every corner of the universe. In Chinese medicine, it's the elements fire, earth, water, metal, and wood. In Indian Ayurvedic philosophy, it is fire, earth, water, air, and ether. In medieval Christianity, it was the great hierarchical chain of being starting with God and descending through angels, humans, plants, and minerals.

Regardless of the classification, a common universal story can be extrapolated. On one side of the spectrum is the door to the tangible (the grossest or most dense aspects of reality), and on the other side, the intangible (the least gross or least dense aspects of reality), the ultimate, ineffable, groundless ground of all being or what some refer to as the ether, universe, God, or Spirit. Here is a summation of the great chain of being as seen through the eyes of our ancient wisdom traditions:

- Matter (most gross and dense)
- Body
- Mind
- Soul
- Spirit (least gross and dense)

Each dimension or slice of reality is an organizing unit that receives, assimilates, expresses, and organizes potentiality and actuality. For the constructive purpose, presentation, and discussion throughout the remainder of this book, I have chosen to organize human existence into the following dimensions: physical, emotional, relational, mental, and spiritual, along with the environmental and epigenetic (genetic) contributions (PERMS). Within each dimension are specific subgroups or life categories such as health, fitness, finance, diet, and intrapersonal relationships (intimate, family, friends, children):

P	Physical
E	Environmental, Emotional, Epigenetic
R	Relational
M	Mental
S	Spiritual

Defining Spirit

Spirit has been defined as having the following characteristics: omnipotence (all-powerful), omniscience (all-knowing), and omnipresence (exists everywhere at the same time). Unlike Spirit, words have limitations and are, therefore, only pointers. Spirit is ineffable. Language, therefore, is incapable of capturing Spirit's true essence. We have no words for the rapture some experience when Spirit reaches down and touches our ordinary lives. The best we can do is try. Lao Tzu, a semi-legendary Taoist Chinese figure, wrote these words in the Tao-Te-Ching, which captures this sentiment beautifully:

> *The Tao that can be spoken is not the eternal Tao.*
> *The name that can be named is not the eternal name.*
> *The nameless is the origin of Heaven and Earth.*
> *The named is the mother of myriad things.*
> *The name that can be named is not the enduring and unchanging name.*

Spirit as Evolutionary Drives

To define the most primitive drives running our universe, our definition must be universal, shared, and inclusive to cover everything in existence—not just humans. Even though evolutionary theorists, philosophers, and scientists don't always agree, there is a consensus as to evolution's directionality. This is not an attempt to answer the great existential "why" questions. Rather, this is a summary of forces that appear to answer the more direct "what" questions that have brought us here today—all the way from the Big Bang to the twenty-first century.

Looking through the lens of one interpretation, American philosopher Ken Wilber's Integral Theory, this agreed-upon directionality from quarks to atoms to molecules and human beings includes the following characteristics captured by the words: Eros, Agape, agency, and communion.

Eros and Agape

Eros represents the "hands" and upward movement found within the universe that moves things along a continuum from simple to more complex. Eros is accomplished through the addition of a transcendent emergent property or novelty. In other words, something new is brought into existence that was not there before. Examples include insentient to sentient matter, single to multicellular organisms, and the emergence of the neocortex (new brain) in humans.

Agape, from ancient Greek, translates into English as unconditional love. It is a beautiful descriptive metaphor to explain the inclusive, embodying, and embracing forces of Spirit. As new emergent and more complex properties are added (Eros), the hands of Agape reach down to include the older, more primitive structures. In turn, the Agape forces do not repress or abandon but lovingly integrate and include all which came before.

All new structures of creation rely on their junior stages for existence. For example, atoms transcend and include quarks, molecules transcend and include atoms, cells transcend and include molecules, and sentient organisms (animals and humans) transcend and include them all—quarks, atoms, molecules, and cells.

Eros and Agape work in tandem. Agape provides the scaffolding and roots as Eros tends to creativity and growth. Collectively, they represent the most important forces in all of existence, transcend and include. They also possess two distinct upward and downward qualities directly related to the great chain of being. These forces represent the never-ending cycles or movements from the intangible to the tangible and the tangible to the intangible. Examples include:

- The Big Bang (something out of nothing)
- Death (form into Spirit) and birth (Spirit into form)
- Thoughts, dreams, goals (the intangible) into worldly manifestations (the tangible)

Communion and Agency

In addition to Agape and Eros, the evolutionary impulses hold two other paradoxical drives, one for agency and the other for communion. Anthropomorphically speaking, agency is the drive for self-autonomy or the need to stand apart, while communion is the drive for interconnectedness, holism, or the need to come together.

As we look around, we can see unique and individual structures of creation (agency), including distinct planets, trees, animals, humans, nations, and states. Underpinning these structures, however, is a magnificent and incomprehensible interconnectedness (communion) of all the parts—each relying on the other for survival. For example, individual structures such as atoms, cells, molecules, and tissues work holistically to make organs. Organ systems, in turn, work together to give life to a holistically functioning human being.

To give name to this paradox, science refers to everything in the universe as a holon (a term coined by Arthur Koestler in the book *The Ghost in the Machine*). It is defined as something that is simultaneous a whole (in and of itself), as well as a part of a larger whole. The entire universe is built upon these nested growth holons. Its metaphor would be the Russian nesting dolls—a set of decreasing-sized wooden dolls placed inside another.

Consider just one grand example found in nature located in south-central Utah called Pando. In Latin, Pando means "I spread" and is the scientific name given to the largest organism on earth. Pando appears to be a grove of individual trees occupying more than one hundred acres. Underground, however, everything is connected by a single and vast root system—a literal one tree forest.

The Four Drives

In conclusion, the culmination of the four evolutionary drives moves our world and the things in it from simple to complex and least to most inclusive. We can literally look at any aspect of the universe to see the signs of increased complexity, transcendence, inclusion, and emergence (novelty). The greatest show on earth started with the miracle of insentient matter (quarks and atoms) emerging from nothing and then life or sentience emerging from that same matter. The structures, in order of appearance, were physics (atoms), chemistry (molecules), and then biology (life).

Old school Darwinian and Neo-Darwinian theories see the universe as mechanical, purposeless, lifeless, and nonintelligent. They see common descent and change over time as a series of random events marked by natural selection. In their view, random changes (mutations) occur in the DNA, and natural selection comes in and selects the offspring that are best adapted to the environment and the ones that can best survive and reproduce.

In contrast, the four evolutionary drives give Spirit or the universe directionality—Eros, Agape, agency, and communion. The "what" of the universe is clearly self-organizing and self-correcting. Its primal drive is energetic reorganization and the creation of order out of chaos. According to complexity theory, the hand of Spirit moves creation to higher and higher levels of complexity. Although more complex, the new system is, in fact, more unified, inclusive, and encompassing. We will revisit this topic later and show its unfolding in the development of human consciousness.

There are two leading-edge evolutionary belief systems. The first, contingent evolution, supposes everything develops by random unpredictability. The other, known as convergent evolution, holds that evolution is purposeful and converges toward a certain outcome (e.g., Eros, Agape, agency, and communion), as we have just discussed.

Stephen Gould, the late evolutionary biologist, proposed a thought experiment that captures the heart of this debate. Paraphrasing, he asked, if you could rewind the tape of evolution, would it turn out the same? Take, for example, the creation of an eye. If evolution was random, how are we to explain the complex mechanisms of the eye (lens, pupil, neurological connections, and interpretations of voltage to the visual cortex of the brain) evolving at different times and in separate lineages such as squids, snails, spiders, and, of course, vertebrates?

The answer is both, eliminating the need for debate. Of course, some things happen by chance (e.g., an asteroid colliding with Earth), but evolution is also drawn to certain outcomes—more complexity, self-organizing, self-correcting, and more inclusive.

We need to abandon the old idea that life is about separation and the survival of the fittest at the hands of natural selection, *We to I*. Common sense dictates that if survival to reproduce was the only game in town, bacteria had this mastered three billion years ago. In fact, bacteria still survive better than just about any other life form on the planet. Thus, if it was all about survival and reproduction—greater complexity, connectedness, and increased novelty, *I to We*, would hold no evolutionary value. The universe has direction–Eros, Agape, communion, and agency.

CHAPTER 3
The Primal Struggle and Elements

Just as there are primary colors from which all of the others come forth when they're combined, so there are primary vibratory qualities of energy and light within us.

-Frederick Lenz

The Primal Struggle

All humans, regardless of age, gender, and culture, have the same core needs. We are all motivated toward a desire for needs fulfillment. The primal struggle is the name I give to the tension (without negative or positive connotations) that arises as we navigate life, attempting to satiate our needs and express our emotions. Thus, the story of our lives revolves around how our needs are met, unmet, or frustrated. Understanding this concept will be one of the most important keys to unlocking humanity's unlimited potential. I believe there is no greater tool to sharpen than this:

- Understanding our needs (both conscious and subconscious)
- Self-fulfilling our needs (sometimes referred to as self-parenting)
- Communicating and expressing our needs
- Receiving needs from others and understanding the universal spiritual principle, *giving is receiving*
- Understanding the needs of others
- Creating a growth environment for others to understand, self-fulfill, communicate, receive, and nourish their own needs

Our earliest needs were formed with the dance of our genetic makeup, our primary family of origin (our caretakers, parents, and our early childhood environment), and transgenerational factors (the struggles of our primary caretakers with their own unique familial and environmental influences).

In human development, the first universal human needs to emerge were survival, safety, physiological, and love. As a defenseless and codependent infant, we relied exclusively on our primary family of origin to satiate our needs. Psychologists characterize healthy satiation of needs through a caregiver's ability to provide nourishing physical touch along with responding, attuning, mirroring, and attending to a child's primitive nonverbal emotional communication. Simply put, caregivers have the means to provide too much, too little, or appropriate, inappropriate needs fulfillment.

In addition to needs, our caregivers taught and mirrored to us which emotions were acceptable and which ones should be made blacklisted. The cliché here is parents teaching boys to man up and avoid feelings of sadness, while instructing girls not to speak up or show excessive excitement levels in various social settings.

In healthy human development, we begin to move from the codependency of childhood to the independence of early adolescence. During this evolution, other needs become dominant and develop sequentially, such as the need to fit in (communion), followed by the need for personal power, autonomy, or the need to stand out (agency).

In short, how initial needs were met, unmet, or frustrated determines the trajectory of a child's overall psychological development. We learn simple to complex strategies, from our caregivers, on acceptable and nonacceptable ways to meet our needs and express our emotions. These strategies, in turn, become etched in the subconscious as they are reinforced day in and day out by our primary caregivers and our repetitive habits.

Although research is devoted almost exclusively to a child's formative years (e.g., attachment theory), the need dynamic never ends and extends to our very last breath. In other words, as we continue to mature, our needs exist in constant flux, moving from safety and security to higher, more complex needs (meaning, purpose, creativity, growth, and contribution) and back again.

To help understand the complexity of various psychological theories, the primary family of origin can be equated with various environmental weather patterns. As you read the following descriptions, imagine how an infant or child growing up in such an environment would have been influenced and molded:

- Sunny and warm–caregivers that were emotionally open, loving, responsible, safe, secure, and mirrored appropriate reactions and responses to environmental cues
- Hot–caregivers that were overbearing and smothering
- Icy and cold–caregivers that were constricted, distant, and participated in neglect or abandonment
- Stormy–caregivers that were physically, mentally, emotionally, or sexually abusive
- Mixed weather patterns–caregivers that were unpredictable or disorganized leading to high anxiety states

Spirit Translation

Throughout history, various traditions (both Eastern and Western) have conjured up a multitude of philosophies, religions, and theories to describe how Spirit enters and gives life to the human body. Ancient Indian and Chinese seers postulated that Spirit enters through subtle energy fields surrounding the body. Metaphysically speaking, they have been referred to with familiar names such as astral bodies and auras.

These subtle energies then travel into portals. Again, from a metaphysical perspective, the ancient seers viewed these portals as running rivers of energy (meridians), wheels (chakras), and mystical doors (marma points). These portals direct, disperse, feed, and give life to every one of the fifty to one hundred trillion cells that make up our gross human body.

Regardless of one's belief structures, the ideas laid forth are simple attempts to explain a real phenomenon (the living versus the dead) with the inadequacies of words and modern scientific methods. We mustn't, however, disregard empirical phenomenology. So, for now, the auras, astral bodies, chakras, and meridians will serve as metaphors pointing to some unknown mechanism that the heart knows all too well, but our intellect finds all too easy to reject. We will refer to these theoretical concepts collectively and simply as subtle bodies and energies and make no distinction as to kind.

The Primal Elements

The elements that keep us alive, run, direct, and govern our physiology, motives, desires, thoughts, and behaviors will be collectively referred to as the *primal or primordial elements*. They are universally shared by all human beings and can be thought of as our body's most primitive operating system, often running behind the scenes and outside our conscious awareness. The primal elements are the effects of the Spirit's impulses (Eros, Agape, agency, and communion) as they are miraculously translated into our body.

The most well-known and researched primordial elements are:

- Universal human needs, instincts, drives, and motivations as initially proposed by Dr. Abraham Maslow
- Universal fears as proposed by Dr. Karl Albrecht in his hierarchy of fears model ("feararchy")
- The primary emotions identified in contemporary psychology by researchers, including American psychologist Paul Ekman, in his landmark study and findings on universal facial expressions
- Universal physiological processes or responses as uncovered through the work of various pioneers, including endocrinologist Dr. Hans Selye (who coined the word stress), scientist Stephen Porges (polyvagal theory), and John Bowlby (attachment theory)

> - The emotions of love and fear (as found in the perennial philosophy and wisdom traditions) that serve as all-encompassing poles and metaphors for the expression (love) or lack thereof (fear) of our true Self or *I am.*
> - The universal laws of nature or how we share relational space with the great Kosmos

I have expanded (transcended and included) on the initial works listed above and humbly attempted to amalgamize their most salient points into a universal theory of primal elements. My purpose is to understand the most basic and fundamental drives of human beings so we can use this information to maximize human potential in all areas of life.

CHAPTER 4

Universal Needs and Fears

There is nothing, absolutely nothing, more important
than meeting our basic human needs.
-Simon Cohen

Psychologist Abraham Maslow's famous theory of motivation states
that all humans share a set of universal needs which stem from the
physical, nonphysical, and metaphysical realms. At the pyramid's
base are some of our most basic biological and physiological needs,
such as air, water, food, security, survival, and safety. Maslow states,
"It is quite true that man lives by bread alone—when there is no
bread. But what happens to man's desires when there is plenty of
bread, and his belly is chronically filled?"

According to Maslow, once the lower deficiency needs are met, or
a firm foundation is achieved, a human being can jump to new and
greater levels of desires, motivations, and needs.

At first, it's the need to fit in (love and belongingness), the need for
autonomy (personal power), and the need to stand out (self-esteem
and self-expression).

This evolution is a movement from deficiency (ego) to growth-based (soul) needs. Deficiency needs arise and are motivated by deprivation or lack (no food, living in an unsafe environment, no money). The desire to fulfill these needs becomes stronger and stronger the longer the needs are deprived. For example, human beings living through the aftermath of a hurricane, without food or shelter, can become contracted in thought and vision, having very little, if any, motivation for higher growth or soul-based needs. Their focus is understandably on deficiency needs and survival.

In contrast, growth needs do not stem from a lack of something or someone. Their motivations and desires stem from the need to grow past the confines of known boundaries toward their highest and most heroic Self.

Self-actualization and self-transcendence make up the top two layers of the pyramid and represent the pinnacle of our soul-based needs. Collectively, they refer to the fullest expression of our human potential—namely, to be all that we can be. In self-help and self-development circles, they are simply summarized as the growth and contribution needs. These descriptors, although helpful, fall short of conveying the depths and promises of these profound universal human needs.

Self-actualization, as the name implies, is about the Self and can be thought of as a type of personal fulfillment. It is the drive, duty, and journey of being, becoming, expressing, growing, evolving, and actualizing the greatest version of oneself in the physical, emotional, relational, and mental dimensions.

Self-transcendence, on the other hand, is about transcending past our known ego-centered identity and self-interest. It is about finding meaning, fulfillment, and purpose in something greater than ourselves. It focuses on the spiritual dimension with a type of "transcend and include" integration of all the dimensions. Some of its most salient characteristics include peak mystical states, plateau experiences, traditional enlightenment, contribution, communion, and the concept of self-realization.

It's as if a time comes in life when the pain of staying focused on deficiency needs exceeds the pain of moving forward. At this moment, we begin our ascent towards self-actualization and self-transcendence. Maslow asserts, "In any given moment, we have two options: to step forward into growth or to step back into safety."

All needs, if unmet or frustrated, just like vitamin deficiencies, will produce not only physiological pathologies but psycho-emotional pathologies, as well. Maslow states, "If the essential core of the person is denied or suppressed, he gets sick, sometimes in obvious ways, sometimes in subtle ways, sometimes immediately, sometimes later."

For example, deficiencies in the love and belonging or self-esteem needs can create limiting beliefs such as "I am not loved" and "I am not enough." As we grow and develop, these psycho-emotional deficiencies become shadow elements that play out in complex ways through our interpersonal relationships, work lives, and finances.

Maslow believed the needs for self-actualization and self-transcendence, although considered higher soul-based needs, were, paradoxically, characteristic of all other basic needs. Self-actualization and self-transcendence, just like food and water, Maslow asserts, is a basic human need, for without them, maximal happiness and fulfillment are unachievable. He emphatically states, "If you deliberately plan on being less than you are capable of being, then I warn you that you'll be unhappy for the rest of your life."

Universal Human Needs

We will now look specifically at the universal human needs. They are broken down into ego (basic), and soul (meta) needs. Recall, basic needs are drives to satisfy deficiencies, whereas soul-based needs stand at the pinnacle of human potential.

I have included all the needs as originally proposed by Maslow but have added many additional layers. For example, I have included pain as a universal human need simply because the denial, suppression, resistance, and avoidance of pain and its corresponding emotional and feeling states will, ultimately, lead to physical disease and psychological suffering.

As our expectation for comfort in today's world increases (the speed of your phone, convenience in obtaining food), our tolerance for discomfort decreases. Many of us try to insulate ourselves from all emotional discomfort at all costs. In doing so, we not only disassociate with the emotion but the underlying message or gift it is there to reveal.

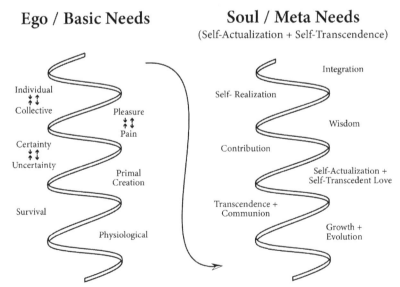

Ego / Basic Needs

Individual
Collective
Pleasure
Pain
Certainty
Uncertainty
Primal
Creation
Survival
Physiological

Soul / Meta Needs
(Self-Actualization + Self-Transcendence)

Integration
Self- Realization
Wisdom
Contribution
Self-Actualization +
Self-Transcedent Love
Transcendence +
Communion
Growth +
Evolution

In addition, I have teased out the more tangible characteristics of self-actualization and self-transcendence, including growth and evolution, transcendence and communion, contribution, self-actualizing and self-transcendent love, wisdom, self-realization, and integration.

Ego or Basic Needs

- Physiological: food (hunger), water (thirst), air, movement
- Survival: protection from harm and threat
- Sexuality, sensuality, and the primal creation or creative energies
- Polarities between certainty and uncertainty
  - o Certainty: safety, security, order, comfort, clarity, structure, predictability, and clear boundaries
  - o Uncertainty: variety, unpredictability, risk, adventure, novelty, mystery, and wonder
- Polarities between pleasure and pain (emotional needs)
  - o Pleasure: the experience and expression of the so-called positive states, feelings, and emotions such as joy, happiness, and play (Play is defined in the psychological literature as a physical or mental leisure activity that is undertaken purely for enjoyment or amusement and has no other objective meaning—an activity where means are more valued than ends.)
  - o Pain: the experience and expression of so-called negative states, feelings, and emotions such as discomfort, anger, and sadness

- Polarities between the individual and collective
  - o Individual: consists of the needs for personal power (control, agency, freedom, autonomy, and linked with the need for certainty), self-esteem (need to stand out and to be valued or accepted by others, to feel significant, to achieve mastery or competency, to creatively express oneself, to speak one's truth, to communicate for recognition, status, and prestige), and cognitive (need for knowledge, learning, and understanding)
  - o Collective: love and belongingness or the need to fit in

Soul or Meta Needs (Self-Actualization and Self-Transcendence)

- *Growth and evolution* is the need to express, grow, evolve, and actualize our potential on all dimensions (PERMS).
- *Transcendence and communion* is the need for union, unity, to transcend past our self-identity, and to connect with something greater than oneself, with nature (biophilia), animals, other humans, art, and beauty. These needs also includes the peak mystical states of consciousness that arise when the subject (you) and object (everything else) merge to become one.
- *Contribution* is the need to serve and give oneself to something greater than oneself. This selfless service often arises as a natural epiphenomenon of transcendence, communion, and higher cognitive development stages that shift our center of gravity to the I to

We consciousness. As this need is fulfilled, there is an inherent understanding and embodiment of the universal laws; giving is receiving, and doing good is good for you.

- **Self-actualizing and self-transcendent love** is the need for unconditional love, inner peace, and the transcendence and transmutation of fear.

- **Wisdom** is the need to transform knowledge, emotions, thoughts, feelings, past experiences, the future, and the present moment into greater levels of meaning, purpose, and understanding. This need includes living a values-driven life, following one's individual calling, and moving in the direction of who and what's most important. Wisdom can be summarized as self-awareness for self-management.

- **Self-realization** is the need for authenticity, the need to dismantle our persona, attachments, identifications, shadows, masks, roles, jobs, societal conformities to reveal the essence of who we really are—the I am, the higher Self.

- **Integration** (transcend and include) is the need to merge Heaven (physical, emotional, relational, and mental) and Earth (spiritual), allowing our eyes to see the sacred in the ordinary. It's learning to live in and through all the dimensions—a full chakra experience. Integration resolves and holds dichotomies and polarities with acceptance and awareness (past and future, communion and personal power, being and doing, equality and freedom, and transcendent peak mystical experiences with the daily tasks of living).

Understanding Needs More Fully

The following nine tenets attempt to clarify ideas falsely attributed to the acquisition of needs. For example, many would be surprised to know Abraham Maslow never used a hierarchical pyramid and never stated that needs had to be met sequentially. In addition, self-actualization and self-transcendence have never been about quantity or magnitude of scope. Quality rules. In other words, a stay-at-home mom or dad can be self-actualizing in much the same way as the economist trying to solve world hunger.

1. Needs are universal and shared by all humans regardless of age, gender, time, history, or culture.
2. Needs are never in conflict. However, the strategies we use to obtain them often are. According to the theory and practice of Nonviolent Communication (NVC), interpersonal conflict arises when needs aren't understood, communicated, or fulfilled. All human conflict, therefore, will continue indefinitely if we remain blind to each other's needs and pathologically focus on the strategies to obtain our needs (e.g., the complex secondary elements).
    o   Imagine two people arguing over a particular political position. One person strategizes the use of opinions and low arousal emotions (e.g., sadness), while the other uses hyper-arousal emotions (e.g., anger), facts, and belittling. Unbeknownst to both of them, the true purpose of their encounter is to satisfy their needs for connection, love, safety, and autonomy.
    o   As they focus on the strategies (arguments, facts, and beliefs) rather than their shared humanity (universal

needs), they will remain forever disconnected and stuck in a *We to I* consciousness.

3. We have conscious and subconscious needs that are sometimes in alignment but, most often, remain in conflict. In the depths of the subconscious lies a pathological strategy for comfort, safety, and security. The attempt to keep the status quo is often in direct opposition to one's conscious needs, desires, and goals. Examples include:
   o The use of unhealthy strategies (e.g., addictions) to satisfy a deficiency or void in the love and belongingness needs.
   o The use of self-defeating and self-sabotaging strategies every time one tries to move past their comfort zone and take a leap of faith (starting a new business or changing careers).

4. Values are unique interpretations of universal needs. Our individual strategies to live, express, and satisfy our needs gives color and flavor to our lives. Each person has a set of shared universal needs and, at the same time, a set of unique and prioritized values.

5. Deficiencies and frustrations in universal needs bring varying degrees of pathological changes or effects in any or all the following dimensions: physical, emotional, relational, mental, and spiritual.

6. The more deficiency needs are satiated, their motivations decrease (e.g., the more we eat, the less hungry we are). The more our soul or meta needs are satiated, their motivations increase and we expand our capacities for greater and greater levels of growth, peaks, and plateaus. Along with these new motivations there may arise ever-increasing existential

frustrations or anxieties which, if used constructively, will forever act as catalysts or fuel for further growth.

7. Needs and values evolve and regress as life circumstances change. For example, adults living in war-torn countries may regress to prioritizing safety, security, food, and shelter over self-esteem and self-actualizing needs. On the opposite spectrum, as consciousness grows and evolves, we can revisit and reimagine any past lower need and evolve, transform, and transcend it from a deficiency to a growth or soul-based need.

   o We can use food for pure sustenance (e.g., eat to live) or we can evolve and use food as a spiritual rite of passage, for physical and spiritual cleansing, ecological harmony (cultivating food with respect for the earth), and connection (sharing culture, stories, love, and friendship).

   o We can transform deficiency love (simple gratification and conditional love) into self-actualizing and self-transcendent unconditional love, communion, and contribution.

   o We can modify ego and externally-based self-esteem needs (obtaining the respect of others through building status, recognition, fame, attention, and approval) to internal soul-based self-esteem needs that are contingent on oneself rather than others.

   o We can shift polarity needs (e.g., certainty and uncertainty) to evolve into an integrated whole as dichotomies and polarities are transcended.

   o We can transcend cognitive (knowledge) and emotional needs (pleasure and pain) and evolve to wisdom (self-awareness, self-mastery, greater levels of meaning, understanding, purpose, and emotional intelligence).

8. Although needs are often satisfied hierarchically (e.g., safety and security before growth and contribution), this is not always the case. There is no standard progression, formula, or pyramid that each person must follow. Consider the following examples:

    o A peak mystical experience can occur at any age.

    o While experiencing the horrid conditions of hopelessness and misery in a Nazi concentration camp, Victor Frankl, an Austrian psychiatrist, managed to go past the need for survival and safety to find existential meaning within the suffering. He later published *Man's Search for Meaning*, which is best summarized by the following quote: "We who lived in concentration camps can remember the men who walked through the huts, comforting others, giving away their last piece of bread. They may have been few in number, but they offer sufficient proof that everything can be taken from man but one thing: the last of the human freedoms—to choose one's attitude in any given set of circumstances, to choose one's own way."

9. Each need or experience is filtered through our stage of development, localisms, culture, and level of consciousness. For example, peak mystical states, as we will discuss, are shared universal experiences but interpreted through one's culture and psychological level of development. So, one can have a universally shared peak mystical experience or

ecstatic state described in many tongues and traditions—Jesus, Mohammad, Ganesh, or the Virgin Mary.

Primal Beliefs

A primal belief is tied directly to a need. Complex limiting beliefs, stories, mental constructs, and emotions add clouds of disorientation and confusion. At their core, however, the complexity of the various stories we tell ourselves can almost always be traced back to primal beliefs:

- I do not have enough to survive. I live in a jungle of scarcity. I'm just trying to make it through another day.
- I do not feel safe, grounded, or secure. I live in a constant state of fear and vulnerability from real or imaginary threats (thoughts or emotions).
- I am undeserving and incapable of experiencing happiness, joy, and the pleasures of life.
- I let negative emotions, thoughts, feelings, and sensations run my life.
- I deny and try to avoid or suppress all negative emotions, thoughts, urges, and sensations. I numb the hurt and pain by engaging in distraction.
- I am undeserving and incapable of experiencing sexuality and sensuality from another.
- I feel shame and guilt.
- I cannot experience or pursue pleasure and play.
- I need to control everything. I am constantly trying to create order and structure.

- I have too much order and structure. I need more spontaneity, fewer boundaries (physical and mental), and more variety.
- I am powerless. I self-sabotage. I am a victim of life's circumstances. I have no willpower.
- I have no boundaries, or I cannot create healthy boundaries with myself and others.
- I am not loved. I do not feel accepted. I do not belong. I do not fit in. I fear rejection.
- I am not enough. I am unworthy. I will never love.
- I cannot express myself. I will never achieve anything. I will never be recognized or significant. I cannot stand out.
- I feel trapped. I feel stuck.
- I am not pursuing my destiny. I am not living a life by design.
- I feel as if life has no meaning.
- I have nothing to contribute.
- I am unable to connect beyond myself to something greater.
- I cannot resolve contradictions, polarities, the past, the future. I am unable to live in the present moment.
- I am unauthentic. I do not know who I am. I live in self-betrayal to the greatness that lies within.

Universal Fears

Universal needs and fears are two sides of the same coin. Understanding which needs are unmet or frustrated will lead you to discover your conscious or subconscious fears.

The list of universal fears includes death or extinction (both the fear of physical death and the fear of ego death or loss of self-identity or self-worth), loss of freedom, separation (loneliness, loss of connection, abandonment, and rejection), threat, attack, unsafety (loss or violated boundaries), and meaninglessness.

Chapter 5

Emotions and Responses

No matter who we are, no matter what our circumstances, our feelings and emotions are universal.

-Josh Groban

Universal Emotions

For an emotion to be considered primary, it must be shared universally by all people regardless of geography, language, time, race, or ethnicity. Research from American psychologist Paul Ekman points to the following seven emotions as primary: enjoyment or happiness, anger, surprise, disgust, fear, sadness, and contempt.

Another researcher and psychologist Silvan Tomkins categorizes emotions as positive, neutral, and negative. His research shows emotional pairs of low-to high-intensity energies, including enjoyment-joy, interest-excitement, surprise-startle, anger-rage, distress-anguish, fear-terror, shame-humiliation, and disgust-dissmell (e.g., reactions to bad tastes and smells along with impulses to avoid or discard).

Although not all researchers agree on the full spectrum of emotions as universal or primordial, there appears a consensus. The universal emotions, defined here, are feelings, sensations, and reactions, originally without context, history, narrative, culture, interpretations, mental constructs, or experience. They come hardwired and simply express a binary system of intensity (high or low) and valence (positive or negative). In fact, all emotions (primordial and complex) can be classified this way. For example, passion and joy are high-intensity energies with positive valances. In contrast, apathy and depression are low-intensity energies with negative valences.

Another universal characteristic pertains to their evolutionary role. Primal emotions act as signposts giving us information about our internal states—pleasant, unpleasant, arousal, neutral, calm, and chaotic. In addition, they signal our relationship with the primal struggle letting us know if we are

- moving towards or away from a need,
- moving towards or away from who and what's most important to us, or
- moving towards or away from threat, pain, or pleasure.

Lastly, all the great religions, as well as new-age psychological, metaphysical, and self-development schools of thought, tend to categorize emotions with even greater simplicity. They use two emotions—fear and love.

Love, in this context, represents all the associated emotions such as joy, happiness, enthusiasm, and internal states that evoke pleasant, calm, and positive arousal energies. On the other side, fear represents emotions such as hatred, anger, pain, and internal states that evoke unpleasant, chaotic, and negative arousal energies.

Fulfillment of universal needs fuels us with the emotion of love, whereas deficiencies, frustrations, or unfulfillment emotes fear or "a call for love." This concept will be helpful in our later discussion on miracles.

Universal Physiological Responses

At first glance, the array of reactions and responses a human being can choose from may seem endless. The truth, however, is there are only a few primordial or evolutionary preprogrammed physiological responses that are intimately linked to emotional states. Emotions and responses, just like needs and fears, can be thought of as two sides of the same coin.

At every moment, our nervous system's tentacles are picking up information and cues, subconsciously and consciously, from inside our body (emotions and sensations), outside our body (the environment), and in-between (e.g., two people engaging, connecting, or fighting). When all this data is computed, it responds. Let's look at a few theories:

- Motivational triad theory: Our responses are limited to seeking pleasure, avoiding pain, and conserving energy.
- Autonomic nervous system: Reactions are broken down into two categories, sympathetic (fight/flight) and parasympathetic (rest/digest). The sympathetic nervous system is responsible for mobilizing energies that help us, for example, respond to danger and threats. This is accomplished through a series of complex physiological bodily changes that include increased heart rate, blood pressure, and respiration. In contrast, the parasympathetic nervous system, dominated by the vagus nerve, is involved in calming, conserving, and slowing down-type energies. This is accomplished by another set

of complex processes that slow down or decrease our heart rate, blood pressure, and respiration.

- Polyvagal theory: The theory that adds a third branch to the parasympathetic nervous system is called the social engagement system. This newest addition is located on the front (ventral) side of the vagus nerve. Evolutionarily, it was the last branch to develop. It helps us detect environmental cues for safety and security, allowing activation of physiological pathways and emotions that allow us to engage and connect with others.

- Attachment theory: Offers a more complex view that includes psycho-emotional-behavioral patterns called "attachment styles" that develop as a response to our primary caregivers and the environment we grew up in (see the previously listed weather patterns in the primal struggle section). These attachment styles fit into one of two categories, secure or insecure. The insecure attachment style is broken down further into anxious, avoidant, and disorganized.

A New Theory: Combining Emotions and Responses

What all these and other theories have in common are emotions and responses that

- are on a continuum of mobilizing or immobilizing type energies
- are on a continuum of high to low intensity/arousal type energies
- have a positive or negative valence (nourishing or nonnourishing)

- are associated with a need and are on a continuum of moving us towards or away from their attainment (e.g., connecting with others).

An amalgam of these different theories asks us to throw out the old and outdated model of the nervous system as binary—sympathetic (bad) and parasympathetic (good). Unfortunately, this thinking has become so prevalent in today's health care arena that we often hear doctors, health advocates, and gurus tell us the only way to healing and peace of mind is to move from the monkey-mind sympathetic activities to the meditative and mindfulness practices of the parasympathetic nervous system. This is misleading and inaccurate.

Healing and nonhealing energies, activities, and responses exist on a continuum and can be found equally in both the sympathetic and parasympathetic branches of the nervous system. For example, depression and apathy are parasympathetic, while engaging in passionate activities is sympathetic. Other examples include the fighting or fleeing sympathetic energies and the immobilizing freezing parasympathetic energies. Depending on the context, they can be negative or positive, nourishing or nonnourishing. We can fight to defend or harm, flee to protect or avoid.

Here is a simplified quadrant model to help better understand the various postures we can take:

- High intensity and positive valence
  - fight, flight, and avoidant energies that help one to defend or protect
  - befriending, safe, and social responses that are passionate and highly charged
  - emotions that are joyous, passionate, and motivating

- o states of flow
- o awakened, beta, brain states that are nourishing
- High intensity, negative valence
  - o fight, flight, and avoidant energies that are non-nurturing or destructive
  - o emotions such as rage
  - o brain states that produce attention deficits
- Low intensity, positive valence
  - o befriending, safe, and social responses that are calm and peaceful
  - o immobilization (without fear) such as cuddling, breastfeeding, rest, sleep, and recovery
  - o emotions that are calm and peaceful
  - o meditative, theta brain states
- Low intensity, negative valence
  - o immobilization (with fear) that leads to inappropriate shutdown and collapse
  - o emotions such as apathy and severe depression
- Mixed
  - o various combinations of the above
  - o detached, disassociated, fusion (e.g., codependency)

The Gift

Emotions are gifts that act as lessons, questions, and signposts to self-awareness. Consider the following list of emotions and the gifts they provide:

Anger asks us to look at boundaries that were crossed, threatened, or harmed by Self or others. Examples include commitments we promised ourselves, the voice of the inner critic, physical harm, and infidelity.

Sadness and grief asks us to reflect on our attachments and resistance to life (what is). Are we unable to let go of someone or something? Are we avoiding the present moment? Are we grieving over something we received but didn't deserve, or didn't receive but deserved?

Fear asks us to differentiate real from imaginary threats and to cultivate courage.

Joy and happiness reminds us of the love present within and around us.

Guilt and shame is linked to prosocial issues and violations of our code of conduct or values. These emotions ask us to evaluate our behaviors and internal dialogue. Are we hurting someone? Are we hurting ourselves? How can I be the best version of myself? Who do I have to become? How can I be more authentic?

Anxiety asks us to consider our accountability to act or respond and our existential aloneness in doing so. The Danish theologian Soren Kierkegaard describes anxiety as the "dizziness of freedom." In other words, it is the dizzying effect of looking into the boundlessness of one's own possibilities.

Hope is the counterforce to anxiety. It is yearning for something you deem valuable and feel you lack. Hope compromises a view of the future, agency you can accomplish it, and an emerging pathway or strategy to get there. Closely linked with hope is faith or the deep internal voice that you can obtain this most important thing.

A Note on Emotions and Feelings

Emotions are the collection of raw physiological data streams or "energies in motion" interplaying in the body, such as pressure waves, the rumbling of our stomach, sugar spikes, and sound waves. Emotions arise as effects in or on the human body and can manifest at any moment—after eating a meal, the anticipation of an event, riding a roller coaster or getting ready for a presentation.

Emotions highlight needs that want to be met and help mobilize or immobilize behavior (e.g., to act or not act). As we layer mental constructs on top of primal emotions, we create very sophisticated emotional-feeling-thought complexes (e.g., shame and guilt). For our purposes, we will only distinguish primal emotions and emotional-feeling-thought complexes (complex secondary elements).

It may also be helpful to think of emotions as public and feelings as private. In other words, we wear our emotions but internally experience our feelings. Imagine mixed feelings-emotions when speaking to a friend. Have you ever emoted a sense of agreeableness but felt betrayed and hurt internally?

CHAPTER 6

Nature's Laws

If you want to find the secrets of the universe, think in terms of
energy, frequency, and vibration.
-Nikola Tesla

Dissecting our definition of Spirit (Eros, Agape, communion,
agency), the primal elements, quantum physics, and biology, we see
clearly that life is relational. As we enter this ever-present, intersubjective *We* space with all of manifestation, it's helpful to understand
the laws of nature acting upon us. We have two choices, to resist or
ride alongside the laws governing our lives. I believe we can summarize the natural, spiritual, and metaphysical laws of nature as follows:

- We are all energy.
- We are all connected.
- We are all cocreators.
- With cocreation comes responsibility.
- Resisting *what is* causes devolution and suffering.

Law of Vibration, Repulsion, and Magnetism

The universe is made up of energy vibrating at various frequencies. Slowly moving energies and frequencies are more dense, more physical, and can be seen with the naked eye. Fast-moving energies and frequencies are less dense, less physical, and cannot be seen by the naked eye.

Depending on our vibration, we are, consciously or unconsciously, either magnetizing or repulsing other energy fields. Thus, all fields (e.g., other people in our vicinity) are interacting, dancing, and influencing each other at every moment. The Alignment Continuum is an example of how to best use this law—energy flows where our awareness, attention, and intention is directed.

Law of Creation (I Am; Therefore, I Create)

At every moment and because we exist, we are always cocreating. *A Course in Miracles* states, "There are no idle thoughts." Only when we become aware of this truth can we decide to participate consciously. All creation has a rhythm, a gestation period, and a cycle of birth and death. Respecting the season of our life—being or doing, winter or summer—is an important part of our hero's journey.

Law of Relative and Absolute Truth (the Law of Polarities)

There are two worlds, metaphorically symbolized as Heaven and Earth. Scientists refer to these as relative (Earth) and absolute (Heaven) truth. Relative truth is fractured, separate, incoherent, and exists as polarities like up and down and light and dark. Our relative mind wrestles with life's duality paradox by using various strategies such as either/or and binary thinking. Absolute truth (Heaven) is whole, coherent, and connects everything in existence. The universal or absolute mind holds polarities and dichotomies without conflict and uses both/and thinking.

The Law of Reciprocity

Because we are energy, connected to all that is, and cocreating at every moment, we must recognize an already intuitive truth, giving is receiving. This realization leads to many spiritual insights, such as what you do to another you do to yourself, and abundance, rather than scarcity, rules the world. We will discuss this law at length when we talk about the pinnacle of human evolution (Kosmic consciousness), summarized as *doing good is good for you.*

Law of Resistance

Resisting what is (the aforementioned laws) causes devolution, suffering, and pain.

CHAPTER 7

Complex Secondary Elements: Our Thousands of Problems

You will be lost, and unlost, over and over again, relax love. You
were meant to be this glorious. Epic. Story.
-Nayyirah Waheed

The primal elements can be thought of as analogous to the primary
colors (red, yellow, and blue), whereby all other colors (secondary
elements) can be obtained by mixing. As the universal needs, fears,
emotions, and physiological responses danced with our "experiences,"
more complex emotions, feelings, mental constructs, and behavioral
responses emerged. These complexes formed in direct response to
whether our needs were met, unmet, or frustrated. All the seemingly
endless array of combinations and colors produced are collectively
referred to as secondary elements. In turn, the original primordial
meaning, need, or response became hidden and lost to complex
layers of stories, beliefs, and cultural indoctrinations.

The primordial elements serve as the bedrock and foundation of
cause, origin, meaning, and truth. Secondary elements are effects,

relative, and acculturated. They can be considered primordial elements "lost in translation," clouding and distracting us from our true desires, motivations, and needs. Everything that is not a primordial element will be referred to as a secondary element.

If we understand and embrace these concepts, secondary elements have the potential to serve as faithful beacons, pointing us back to origin and cause—the primordial elements. However, if they are not used in this manner, they will continue to keep us spiraling in a never-ending loop of discontentment, hypnosis, and symptom-based solutions.

As we take the journey to trace secondary elements (the thousands of ways we act, speak, and behave) back to their primordial causes, we are pulled out of the darkness, revealing the true nature of our suffering. This process can become one of our greatest sources of self-discovery as it allows us to see that there are not thousands of problems but rather universals of which there are few. This idea is further elucidated and embodied in The Miracle Method described in the chapter of the same name.

In short, *primordial or primal elements are universal needs, fears, emotions, and responses. And complex secondary elements are everything else.*

Although the complex elements are the source of our greatest suffering, they are, paradoxically, the very thing that makes us who we are. They are the textured

nuances of our personality that have been molded by nature (our genes) and nurture (the environment). Through the creative process of secondary complexes, we have developed, consciously and unconsciously, our very own hierarchy of values. In turn, these values are one of the major contributing factors running our life.

All the secondary signifiers, mechanisms, and strategies can be broken down into two major areas—those that are conscious and those that are unconscious. In other words, some of the complexes are known and explicit, while others are covert and remain hidden from our conscious awareness.

In the conscious world, our costumes, armor, masks, and shells are some of our strongest influencers. They are worn and used to protect our identity, to hide behind, to inhabit an alter ego, to present the version of who we think we are to others, and to conform to how culture and society dictates or thinks we should behave. They are the most comfortable aspects of ourselves that we are most able and willing to expose.

In the subconscious world, our shadows, like the iceberg below the water's surface, are the largest, most powerful, and most hidden aspects of ourselves. They consist of unconscious physiological facilitated neural patterns, drives, habits, behaviors, thoughts, emotions, and feelings. These complex strategies include parts of ourselves that often play out childhood roles and aspects of ourselves we do not love or have disowned.

Moving from a general (conscious and subconscious) to a more nuanced classification of secondary signifiers, we return once again to the dimensions—physical, emotional, relational, mental, and spiritual. Within each dimension, there are thousands upon thousands of mechanisms and strategies. We will not be able to cover all of them. I will, however, highlight some of the most important ones. What follows are complex strategies and mechanisms that keep the universal needs hidden from our conscious awareness and stepping into our greatest actualized potentials.

The Triune Brain

We will start this discussion on secondary elements by exploring the brain and how, initially, its primal structures were helpful and protective but evolved, paradoxically, to become one of our greatest sources of suffering.

The triune model of the brain was formulated in the 1960s and detailed in the book *The Triune Brain in Evolution* by neuroscientist Paul MacLean. This theory is best viewed as a metaphor rather than strict quantifiable neurological divisions. The three brains were the reptilian (brain stem and cerebellum), paleomammalian (limbic system), and neomammalian (neocortex or rational brain) systems.

Since that time, a fourth evolutionary center—aptly referred to as the angel lobes—has been evolving, in real-time, alongside humanity's highest growth stages and levels of consciousness. It includes our highest needs and values and represents the pinnacle of who and what we can achieve and become.

Let's look at each component of the brain from this basic model to see how automations, reactions, fusion, disconnection from our higher Self, time and cognitive distortions, complex emotional-feeling elements, and the inhibition of our greatness (e.g., the Jonah's complex) are birthed out of each area.

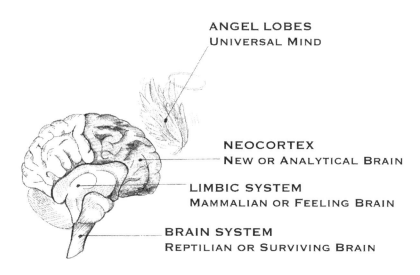

ANGEL LOBES
UNIVERSAL MIND

NEOCORTEX
NEW OR ANALYTICAL BRAIN

LIMBIC SYSTEM
MAMMALIAN OR FEELING BRAIN

BRAIN SYSTEM
REPTILIAN OR SURVIVING BRAIN

The Reptilian Brain

The reptilian part of our brain is the part that is reactive, unconscious, and automated. It helps our hearts to beat and lungs to breathe, performing, day and night, without any conscious effort. In addition, it keeps us safe, allowing us to react at lightning speed to threats and harm.

On the opposite side of the spectrum, it can also become the wellspring for many pathological mental and emotional complex secondary elements. For example, one of its primary functions is running automated unconscious programs. This process, when turned upside down, can incarcerate us to a life of unhealthy habits, behaviors, and decisions, despite our conscious values, hopes, goals, and dreams. The reactive part of the reptilian brain can also cause us to inappropriately react, rather than respond, to loved ones, circumstances, and events.

Mammalian Brain

The mammalian part of our brain can be thought of as the seat of our emotions—the right brain. It helps us see, experience, and feel life in all her glory, colors, and textures. It provides us with an embodiment of feelings and emotions, allowing us to experience a fusion-like state with joy, ecstasy, love, and happiness. The mammalian brain includes social engagement networks, allowing us to connect deeply with loved ones, friends, family, fur children, and nature.

The complex secondary elements that have arisen from this part of the brain are responsible for some of the most substantial blocks to self-actualization. Although it is sometimes desirable to become lost or fused with an emotive state (making love, gratitude, or happiness), it can, unfortunately, backfire, turning us towards the darker side of fusion.

For example, anger and sadness can be used as gifts for the recognition of attachments and crossed boundaries. If, however, we pathological fuse with anger and sadness, we may find ourselves engaging in behaviors that are harmful and destructive, entering states of severe depression, rage, apathy, and hopelessness. In this manner, we no longer have anger and sadness; we are anger and sadness. Fusion can inhibit discernment, and right action, cause an identity crisis (e.g., equating who we are with an emotive or feeling state), and keep us disconnected from our higher Self.

Neocortex

The neocortex is the seat of our intellect, rationality (left-brain thinking), and cognition. When we make decisions and solve complex problems, we use this modern-day structure. If we use this part of our brain constructively, we make decisions based on our values, needs, and highest Self. Our ego, in this respect, becomes a servant to our higher Self.

The secondary elements that grow out of this region are by far the most sophisticated, nuanced, and complicated. Let's explore some of the most important strategies:

- Examples of stories, theories, narratives, equations, limiting beliefs, and mental constructs that range from simple to complex and restrain our potentiality by imposing imaginary constraints, blocks, and ceilings about ourselves, others, and the world include:

   o I am…not worthy, unloved, bad (shame), in a state of hopelessness, driven by my desires/addictions.

   o People are…evil, unreliable.

   o You are…untrustworthy, my enemy.

   o My relationship is…failing, unsupportive, holding me back.

   o The world is a…nightmare, fairytale, battlefield, playground, classroom, obstacle course, magical (reality distorter), jungle, meaningless (nihilism).

   o The "I have to" and "I need to" mentality are statements of "fact" that often keep us lost in the mundane and valueless as opposed to energies spent on the things that matter most and the pursuit of our dreams. Examples include *I have to clean the house* and *I have to run this errand.*

   o The "if-then" mentality" sounds like *If I get the raise, then I will be happy,* or *When the kids go to college, then I will pursue my career.*

   o Catastrophizing, overgeneralizing, fortune-telling, expectations, perfectionism, judging, over-rationalization, minimizing, magnifying, exaggerating, denying, disqualifying the positive, repression, sublimation, displacement, comparisons, blaming, tunnel vision, polarization, cognitive dissonance are common strategies.

- Complex emotional-feeling-mental constructs are primary emotions mixed with stories, beliefs, experiences, reactions, and more. Examples include shame, guilt, and jealousy.

- Time distortion is a pathological focus on the past and future where our fears, insecurities, and anxieties are born and fed. A particular type of time distortion, time poverty, is the most prevalent and pervasive. It represents an existence of reality whereby we live moment to moment everywhere but in the present moment. It can be equated to sitting on a train looking out the window and watching our life (experience) pass us by as we hyperfocus on the valueless. This distortion can show up in various ways, such as the pathological concentration on outcomes (goals) rather than processes (our actual experience).

- Final examples include the inability to reconcile doing (will power, courage, strength, and action) and being (humility, vulnerability, trust, surrender, and inaction), Heaven and Earth, dichotomies, masculine and feminine, yin and yang.

Angel Lobes

The angel lobes are postulated as the next jump in brain evolution. It is the origin and location that houses our deepest connection to our higher Self. Although the angel lobes, for now, represent a metaphor, one of the most interesting secondary complex elements to emerge from this area is what Dr. Maslow calls the Jonah's complex. It occurs when we stand face to face with our potential and greatness.

The Jonah's complex is an inner thermostat, often set by others, representing our limits on love, finances, happiness, and success. When we try to exceed or go beyond this ceiling, a trigger or upper limit is activated, pulling us back to safety, security, and comfort. In short, we feel guilty when they try to embody our heroic Self. We are told, "You can't," and we consequently self-sabotage.

The Jonah's complex is fear, anxiety, resistance, and evasion of self-actualization. We are unable to fathom our God-given potentials and instead succumb to fear. We erroneously equate higher pursuits with arrogance and delusions of grandeur. It's as if we simultaneously fear our best as well as our worse. Psychological projection grows stronger as we are kept in despair and stripped of our self-worth. Complex emotion-feeling-mental complexes such as humility and pride must be reconciled. *Who, me?* needs to be answered with an emphatic, *If not me, then who?*

Parts

One of the largest categories of complex secondary elements is the mind-body's creation of parts or subpersonalities. Each part comes with its own set of needs, desires, and functions. These parts are distinct ways of being. At the time of their creation, their original roles and strategies served a vital protective function.

These parts were born out of the primal struggle, trying to figure out what to do, how to act, and what to say as needs were met, unmet, and frustrated. They are, to a degree, the internalized voices of our primary caregivers, friends, family, leaders, cultural influences, and more. Therefore, our personality is not a reflection of our authentic Self. Rather, it is an amalgam of the parts that kept us safe.

Our ego keeps each part in isolation. Some parts, exiles, are locked away and their voices forever silenced. One of the greatest spiritual practices is connecting with our true Self and healing our severed and fragmented personalities. We must integrate, love, give gratitude, befriend, and understand the needs, wants, and desires of each part. As the entire internal family is connected, a new center of gravity is created. The true Self, from this new center, shines brightly and makes decisions as a unified whole without allowing any internal part to push or pull us down into pathological conformity and safety.

Here is just a small list of parts you may be familiar with: the critic, the saboteur, the wounded self, the inner child, the protector, the codependent adult, and the victim. Awareness of each part is critical. For example, if you listen very closely, the saboteur speaks every time you try to experience happiness, love, recognition, and success. The inner critic speaks when you make lists of grievances and comparisons. And the wounded child is summoned when you look at your traumas.

According to Internal Family Systems (IFS), developed by Dr. Richard Schwartz, parts can be broken down into the following three categories:

- Exiles: These are often the youngest parts of ourselves that hold vulnerabilities, shame, blame, guilt, memories, emotions, and needs that were ignored or unresolved. During our childhood, we did not have space or time to process the unmet or frustrated needs or trauma. These parts were asked to hold the burden and condemned to a life of exile.
- Managers: These are protector parts that are preemptive and manage our day-to-day activities. They help protect exiles so

the functioning part of ourselves can carry on with the daily grind.

- Firefighters: These are the reactive and impulsive parts of ourselves. They are extreme versions of protectors or managers. They have a critical job—make all pain, sadness, and hurt go away. These parts often force us to shut down, self-destruct, and engage in addictions. Their role is simple—put out the fire (symptoms) and avoid the cause. They keep exiles protected, fearing what could arise if their voices were heard.

Our true Self, on the other hand, is the agent of psychological healing, having the ability to love and integrate all parts. According to IFS, you can recognize your true Self by identifying and connecting with the following qualities: calmness, compassion, courage, clarity, creativity, curiosity, connectedness, presence, persistence, perspective, patience, and playfulness. When we identify with a part, we become fused, blended, and clouded to their qualities. In turn, less Self-energy is available. As we unblend and unfuse, our Self-energy increases.

Shadow

The shadow is any material we are unaware of within our makeup or personality. Our exile parts dominate the shadow. The shadow consists of four characteristics: addictions, boxing, dancing, and digging. Our shadow elements originated in our formative years as highly functioning protective, survival, and defensive strategies to solve a real or imagined threat. However, over the years they have evolved into hundreds and thousands of iterations. Today, they are so layered, abandoned, and exiled that their true cause, meaning, and purpose have become difficult to access, uncover, and understand.

Shadow elements always move from first to second to third person. The process involves disowning a part of ourselves (first person) and projecting it onto someone or something else (second and third). For example, *I am bad* morphs to *You are bad* and, finally, into *The entire world is bad*. The shadow material aims to separate, exile, and sequester parts of yourself from your true integrated spiritual Self.

The 3-2-1 shadow process, developed by Ken Wilber, is one of the best methods to help bring the shadow into the light. The reclaiming of exiled and separated parts involves a reversal of shadow formation (first to second to third person). In other words, we integrate lost parts or shadows by, first, identifying the shadow (awareness), talking about it (third person), talking to it (second person), and then talking as if you were the part (first person).

In general, shadows lead to the loss of present-moment awareness as our psyche attaches, boxes, digs, and dances, pathologically to the past and future. They keep us separated from our true nature as childhood narratives continue to play out—in and through our adult life. Shadow energies make it impossible to say "yes" (e.g., making room for the new) or to say "no" (e.g., letting go of the things which no longer serve us). In addition, shadow elements make it difficult to transcend (e.g., addictions), include (e.g., boxing), and integrate (e.g., dancing).

In psychology, the mind uses many strategies in the formation of shadows. Here are two important processes:

• Psychological projection occurs when we take aspects of our internal world (our deepest desires and dreams as well as abandoned and disowned parts, feelings, emotions, and characteristics we don't like) and project them onto the screen of the external world (e.g., other people).

- Psychological introjection is the opposite of projection. With introjection, we identify with externals (people, objects, religions, a sports team, a political affiliation, and our roles) so deeply and strongly that our identity fuses with it.

How to Spot Shadows

The easiest and most reliable way to spot your shadow consists of the following:

- Look at your life for things or people that negatively charge you (anger, judgments, irritations). Psychologist Carl Jung states, "Everything that irritates us about others can lead us to an understanding of ourselves." This idea is best understood by the adage, "When you spot it, you got it!" or the idea of holding a fist and pointing your index finger at another person. Looking closely, you will notice three of your fingers pointing right back at you.
- Look at your life for things or people that positively charge you. For example, imagine putting a guru, celebrity, or religious figure on a pedestal of infallibility. This may signify who you want to be, but a deeper part of you thinks you cannot achieve greatness. These ideas can become projected onto others.
- Look at your out-of-alignment actions, behaviors, and habits that directly conflict with your goals, dreams, and values.
- Look at the "things not going right" in your life.

Shadow Addictions

Addictions are attachments that keep us from transcending, growing, and evolving. They are direct blocks to Eros. They can be physical, such as addictions to drugs, food, and cigarettes. They can be emotional, such as attachments to an emotive state of depression or hyperarousal. In the mental dimension, they may be limiting beliefs, pathological identifications, or obsessions with certain parts of our body, masks, costumes, or personalities. Addictions can even be spiritual. Imagine an individual searching for a quick fix enlightenment scheme using psychedelics.

Shadowboxing

Boxing represents mechanisms and patterns consistent with resistance, suppression, denial, disassociation, or avoidance. Boxing oftentimes manifests in our life as psychological projections where things we dislike in others are really areas that we dislike and fail to see in ourselves.

Shadow Dancing

Shadow dancing represents repeating experiences cloaked in different externals as we struggle to learn the lesson that would allow for personal evolution, transformation, and wisdom. Shadow dancing is seen in the movie *Groundhog's Day*, where actor Bill Murray's character wakes up repeating the same day. However, the spell is broken the moment he learns the lesson of unconditional love. Shadow dancing keeps us stuck in a perpetual loop that goes around and around and around. The energies of dancing often accompany habitual distractions and stunted growth.

Shadow Burying

The mechanisms arising from the shadow element are used to bury, rather than confront, our exiles, past wounds, and yet to be future anxieties.

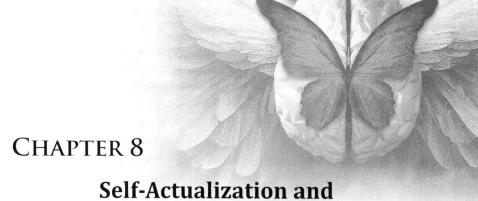

CHAPTER 8

Self-Actualization and Self-Transcendence

Musicians must make music, artists must paint, poets must write
if they are to be ultimately at peace with themselves. What human
beings can be, they must be. They must be true to their own nature.
This need we may call self-actualization... It refers to man's desire
for self-fulfillment, namely to the tendency for him to become actually in what he is potentially: to become everything one is capable
of becoming.

-Abraham Maslow

Self-actualization and self-transcendence represent humanity's shared
universal purpose. They are internal, biological, and innate forces
attracting, pushing, pulling, and beckoning us towards a life by design
and away from a mundane life of self-betrayal. Self-actualization and
self-transcendence embody growth, evolution, and transcendence
for their own inherent value as opposed to an intrinsic or extrinsic
assigned value, meaning, accolade, or goal. As a reminder:

- Self-actualization, as the name implies, is about the "Self." It is the drive, duty, and journey of being, becoming, and actualizing the greatest version of oneself in the physical, emotional, relational, and mental dimensions. It can be thought of as a type of personal fulfillment. In psychological circles, it is synonymous with growth and evolution.
- Self-transcendence is about transcending beyond our self-interests and ego-centered identity. It is about finding meaning, fulfillment, and purpose in something greater than ourselves. It focuses on the spiritual dimension with a type of "transcend and include" integration of all the dimensions. Some of its most salient characteristics include peak mystical states, plateau experiences, traditional enlightenment, and the concept of self-realization. Dumbing down these esoteric concepts, self-transcendence is often synonymous with contribution.

Self-actualization and self-transcendence include the ideas of potentiality and actuality. Potentiality can be considered the "stuff" that lives within the acorn—waiting patiently to awaken. Actuality, on the other hand, is the fulfillment of this potential or sacred contract from the ether to the manifest. We are called to carry out this sacred contract. However, as *A Course in Miracles* reminds us, "All are called, but few choose to listen." Thus, every human being (and all of manifestation) contains a desire to realize or actualize full potential.

The ancient Greek philosopher Aristotle calls this actuality our entelechy. It refers to the essence of ourselves, which becomes fully realized. It is the wisdom of our innate intelligence guiding and directing an organism towards self-actualization. For example, the entelechy of the acorn is the oak. The entelechy of the egg is the bird. And the entelechy of a human being is the dictum—*what we can be, we must be!*

To not self-actualize is to a degree akin to one of the seven deadly sins such as slothfulness, envy, or gluttony. Ancient theologians referred to this as accidie. It describes an individual who does not live up to his or her potential. St. Thomas Aquinas, the famous Italian Dominican friar and philosopher, likens it to a mortal sin whereby the flesh utterly prevails over the spirit.

Taken together, self-actualization and self-transcendence become the evolutionary drives of both being and becoming your heroic Self. It is the metaphoric merging of Heaven (the spiritual dimension) and Earth (the physical, emotional, relational, and mental dimensions). It is not self-transcendence or self-actualization. Rather, it is self-actualization and self-transcendence. For example, a self-transcendence experience (e.g., traditional enlightenment) does not entitle us to pathologically abandon the other dimensions (self-actualization). These drives are not mutually exclusive. The pinnacle, in other words, is captured by Jesus's teaching of living in the world but not of the world.

Self-actualization and self-transcendence are accomplished by the embodiment and qualities of fulfillment, coherence, and purposeful imbalance as opposed to classically held notions of enlightenment, traditional happiness, and living the so-called "balanced" life—which I call the self-actualizing pathologies. We will discuss these pairs of opposites in the next chapter. For now, let's explore a few important aspects of these higher human needs.

Peak Experiences

Peak experiences are flashes of ecstatic, transcendent, physical, mental, and emotional states. They are like walking through a door to another dimension gifting us with insights, a hyper-focus on the "now" moment, and a profound feeling of interconnectedness.

The classically accepted states of consciousness include the following: waking, dreaming, deep sleep, flow, unnatural or altered (via psychedelics), and everyday emotions such as being in love, anger, fear, and joy. During an intense emotional state, for example, the emotion engulfs our very being as we cannot separate who we are from the emotion we are experiencing. Thus, we are not just experiencing that emotion, but, rather, we are that emotion—a kind of state experience.

Peak experiences share common features with these everyday state experiences; however, they differ in that they are a great big exclamation mark within the waking state that helps lift us from the ordinary to the mystical. Maslow describes them as *"rare, exciting, oceanic, deeply moving, exhilarating, elevating experiences that generate an advanced form of perceiving reality and that are even mystic and magical in their effect upon the experimenter."*

When our attention is focused on satisfying our lower deficiency needs (safety and security), we are caught up in the world of the human condition. With self-transcendence, peak, and plateau experiences, we jump to another level of experience as the human condition is pushed to new limits, boundaries, frontiers, and abilities.

There are various types of peak experiences ranging from the ordinary, the transient, the ineffable (an experience that defies our ability to explain or put into words), to the noetic (seeing something beyond or hidden from our day-to-day sense experience).

Although peak states are universal doors to deep mystical experiences, their interpretations are not. The Wilber-Combs Lattice, an idea that was arrived upon independently by Ken Wilber and Allan Combs, describes the fact that a person, at virtually any stage of development (baby, teenager, adult, sage, mystic, racist), can have a state experience (waking, dream, deep sleep, flow states, mystical peak experiences, nirvana, or enlightenment). These state experiences, however, will always be interpreted according to the person's stage of development, culture, and localisms.

For example, if a traditional Christian or Hindu, or even a five-year-old child has a peak mystical experience—the Christian may report contact with Jesus, the Hindu may report contact with Ganesh, and the child's interpretation would probably be no different from their usual stream of magical and imaginary thinking. So, we must be very careful to equate the experience and the interpretation of the experience as synonymous. The equating of gods, goddesses, supernatural beings, Jesus, Moses, and Mohammed to the mystical peak experience are all examples of what developmental psychologists refer to as mythic-literal consciousness. German theologian and mystic Meister Eckhart wisely observed, "Theologians may quarrel, but the mystics of the world speak the same language."

To get a small glimpse of these peak experiences, it may be helpful to recall a time when you were totally immersed and absorbed in an activity, and your perception of time became distorted; time stood still and a second seemed like an eternity. Psychologists refer to this experience as a flow state, a term coined by Hungarian psychologist Mihaly Csikszentmihalyi in 1975. It can be likened to the experience of being "in the zone," as reported by athletes. It is, in fact, during these specific flow states where athletes are elevated to the realm of superheroes as they display superhuman levels of focus, attention, and capabilities.

The peak experiences, as described by Maslow, are quite similar in description to spiritual or mystical experiences—ideas of nirvana, enlightenment, and to a lesser degree, the flow states. In essence, they all point to another dimension or state of consciousness that is often hidden from our awareness.

Plateau Experiences

Even though peak experiences are transitory, they can change a person forever if, for example, the insights gained are profound enough to tear apart previously held beliefs, self-concepts, and paradigms. One's entire focus, purpose, and pursuit of happiness can shift from an immature lens for extrinsic things (accolades, cars, fancy clothes) to a more mature lens for intrinsic rewards (peace, equanimity). This more permanent, evolving level of consciousness is what Maslow refers to as a plateau rather than a peak experience.

Plateau experiences share similar characteristics to peak states but are more lasting, serene cognitive states and can be thought of as analogous to human development. For example, once a person learns a language, how to communicate, or how to write, it tends to stay with them throughout the entire life cycle—albeit no physical or psychological ailments or disease.

Imagine, for a moment, an individual so enraged, hurt, full of anger that he lashes out both physically and emotionally at the love of his life. In the chaos of darkness, an "aha" moment is birthed. He sits, if just for a fleeting moment, as a witness to how the emotion of anger engulfed his very being and how he transformed and became anger. This level of understanding and profundity, previously hidden, now becomes more permanent as he reflects, muses, and begins to separate his divine nature from his actions. He realizes his responsibility and can now sit as the seer of his emotions. He no longer pathologically reacts with behaviors incongruent with his divine essence. He is now able, quite simply, to respond.

Pulling It Together

Peak and plateau experiences transcend the personal self and make room for states of consciousness that are difficult to describe in words and can only be appreciated experientially. It is like trying to describe the experience of a rose's fragrance. As we do so, we discover our limits, not the roses. We may know the fragrance, but how does one speak of the fragrance. As Lao Tso is quoted as saying:

Those who know do not speak
Those who speak do not know

If we try to put language to these experiences, we begin to see how they open the door to the mystical and aesthetic, help transmute fear, and provide emotional states of intense joy, peace, and feelings of unity consciousness. In addition, scientists have identified brain regions that become activated during these state experiences. These regions are responsible for igniting super-human capacities for concentration, effortless action, creativity, and pattern recognition. It is no wonder why many have traveled to distant shores to meet with saints, sages, and mystics, as well as experimented with various psychedelics to achieve the promises of peak experience. Our society is hyperfocused on various state-altering experiences from the common, uncommon, harmful, and harmless: smoke breaks, happy hour, coffee breaks, illicit drugs, licit drugs, and virtual reality.

Each tradition uses different words, pointers, and practices. If, however, we ignore the semantic lenses and siphon out the most salient aspects and core realizations of all these state-like experiences, a confluence of shared characteristics is discovered. Pulling from and expanding on research from Abraham Maslow these state-like experiences include some or all of the following:

- You sense a loss of time and space with a hyper focus on the ever-present "now" moment.
- Unity consciousness with a loss of the sense of self, loss of body awareness, and a merging of you (subject) with the environment (object). You feel complete interconnectedness and unity. The surfer becomes one with the wave; you become one with the task you are performing.
- Witness consciousness: You stand as a witness to all that is arising, your thoughts, emotions, feelings, and behaviors.
- You experience effortless action, behavior, creativity, and expressiveness that is not confined by conformity, strain, or struggle.
- You feel increased emotions of love, joy, peace, freedom, and liberation.
- You sense a freedom from attachments.
- A transcendent level of clarity, or what is referred to as psychological freedom prevails. You become becomes less dependent and beholden to the environment for happiness and fulfillment.
- A sense of ultimate reality is experienced past the world of our so-called physical senses.
- Lower deficiency needs become irrelevant. Personality development frees the person from the neurotic, infantile, and

"unreal" problems of life to what Maslow refers to as the "real" problems of life "…the intrinsically and ultimately human problems, the unavoidable, the 'existential' problems for which there is no perfect solution." As deficiency needs are satisfied, we are free to pursue higher or more purposeful needs. Thus, growth is maximized, and safety is minimized.

- Fear, scarcity, inhibition, doubt, and self-criticism decrease.
- Capacities for pattern recognition, data accumulation, and concentration increase.
- Intuition and intelligence increase.
- Awareness increases.
- Dichotomies, polarities, and conflicts are fused, transcended, or resolved. Mutual exclusiveness, opposites, and zero-sum game notions are transcended. We hold, without conflict in our mind's eye, both the sense of surrender to the present moment as well as the pursuit of our dreams and deepest desires. The concepts of being and doing merge.
- Sacred is seen in the mundane.
- All the dimensions become integrated rather than mutually exclusive. Lower needs are transformed. For example, the act of eating goes from simply satisfying pleasures to a deeper understanding of our interconnectedness and the ripple effects directly related to our food choices.
- We understand the dictum, "giving is receiving."
- Research has identified the following words to encapsulate this experience: wholeness, perfection, completion, justice, aliveness, richness, simplicity, beauty, goodness, uniqueness, wonder, awe, abundance, and humility.

CHAPTER 9

Coherence and Fulfillment

Enlightenment is but a recognition, not a change at all.
-A Course in Miracles

Enlightenment, Peak, and Plateau Experiences

Traditional and new age descriptions of enlightenment often confine attainment to peak ecstatic state experiences (e.g., pure bliss) found in the spiritual dimension of existence. The mythos around enlightenment tries to convince us that this mystical state will free us of all our earthly chains (the physical, emotional, relational, and mental dimensions of reality) and immediately elevate a person to a plateau level of perfection and infallibility.

Traditional enlightenment tends to conjure up pictures of gurus sitting in a cave atop a mountain, in deep meditative contemplation, patiently waiting for their divine insight or aha moment. Enlightenment is believed to be a goal or destination reserved for the elite few. Once achieved, the guru can sit with confidence, knowing he or she has reached their ultimate destination. The guru now has the freedom and luxury to live by faith alone.

In this childish interpretation, the guru has a profound meta-physical realization or state experience and is then entitled to abandon the world. No need to worry about relationships, sharing gifts, where and how to find food and shelter. This is best summarized by the adage describing the twenty-first-century spiritual zealot, "awoke and broke."

More mature interpretations from the great wisdom traditions define enlightenment as a type of remembering or awakening. They speak of an uncovering process that allows us to realize an ever-present transcendent truth. This new reality encompasses a state of being, a state of clarity, and a continuous state of clear awareness which allows us to see, with spiritual eyes, life's interconnected threads.

Of all the enlightenment descriptors, it is best equated with the concept of self-realization or the unlearning of who we are not (our roles, jobs, or shadows) and the immediate recognition of who we really are (our divine essence or higher Self). English philosopher, Anthony Flew, defines it as the "…direct or unmediated experience of the divine, in which the soul momentarily approaches union with God." It is in this moment we uncover our divinity, the divinity of everything around us, and come to the metaphysical realization that they are one and the same.

One of the most important realizations from Abraham Maslow is that not all actualizers (think self-actualization) are transcenders (think self-transcendence) and not all transcenders are actualizers. In other words, one can have an enlightenment or peak experience and be undeveloped in almost all other areas of life. On the opposite spectrum, one can devote a lifetime on actualizing their potentials, self-development, and the like while never experiencing an enlightenment or peak experience.

Happiness

Unfortunately, the traditional ideas of happiness have confined, and reduced attainment to the positive emotions and feeling states as found within the emotional dimension. We have been falsely taught that happiness equals success; it's an achievement or goal. It should be sustained, not fleeting, and we should strive to abandon or avoid the so-called negative emotions.

The traditional teachings, unfortunately, have it all wrong. Happiness, by definition, is a state experience that comes and goes, ebbs and flows. As we go about our lives holding onto these more traditional ideas, we, inevitably, are less happy, less fulfilled, and more depressed.

Why?

Life is a polarity consisting of ups and downs, darkness and light, good and bad, life and death, happiness and sadness. Thus, hyperfocusing our attention, time, and energies on resisting one side of the pole will lead to endless suffering.

Self-Actualizing Pathologies

The Happiness and Enlightenment Trap

Whenever we engage in non-nurturing behaviors, experiences, or pursuits, we stunt self-actualization. One of the most pervasive illustrations of this is the happiness and enlightenment trap. It occurs when we

- limit happiness to fanciful and elaborate things (car, money, house) in the physical dimension.
- live our lives constantly trying to suppress or get rid of pain, suffering, and negative emotional states.
- limit happiness to a perfect lifetime relationship in the relational dimension.
- limit happiness to accolades, goals, and achievements in the mental dimension.
- pursue Eastern concepts of enlightenment as the great pinnacle of achievement.
- postpone the present moment and limit happiness to specific outcomes, expectations, or circumstances.
- fail to understand that not all actualizers are transcenders and not all transcenders are actualizers.

Mutual Exclusiveness

Mutual exclusiveness is defined as the self-actualizing in one dimension (physical, emotional, relational, mental, and spiritual) at the expense, mutual exclusiveness, or pathology of another dimension. Consider the following examples:

- An individual putting all their efforts and attention into their work (the physical dimension) at the expense of their marriage (the relational dimension).
- An individual putting all their attention on lofty spiritual goals and dreams for humanity (the spiritual dimension) at the expense of their loved ones (relational dimension).

- An individual who is highly intellectual (mental dimension) at the expense of being in touch with emotions (emotional dimension).

- An individual who loves family and country but considers everyone else an outsider, an enemy, or an infidel. This conditional-based love (my religion, my creed, my race) leads to various forms of discrimination, including racism, sexism, and xenophobia (an extreme pathology of the relational dimension).

The Antidote: Coherence (Not Balance) and Fulfillment (Not Happiness or Enlightenment)

The antidote to self-actualizing pathologies is, of course, self-actualization and self-transcendence. To achieve actualization from a practical standpoint, we will now explore the concepts of coherence and fulfillment, which are diametrically in opposition to traditional ideas of happiness, enlightenment, and living a clichéd balanced life.

The concepts of coherence and fulfillment are much more nuanced and go beyond the idea of finding balance or happiness within the PERMS. For example, balance is defined as equal and opposite forces. On the other hand, coherence is defined as a synergistic harmony or unity between all the parts in a system. It can be likened to the beautiful music manifested by individual musicians in an orchestra playing in sync and complementing one another. In doing so, they create a kind of wholeness, unity, or blending of their individual talents that can't be achieved by one alone. Thus, the whole is greater than the sum of its parts.

When the parts of the human body (electrical energies, breathing cycles, brain waves, heart rhythm) work together in a coherent and orderly fashion (rather than in a chaotic, imbalanced, and disease-oriented manner), our health leaps to a new level of healing. For example, when someone eats healthy, they obtain a certain level of health. When they compound it with exercise and sleep hygiene, an even higher level of health can be obtained. Coherence offers a kind of exponential growth that of which cannot be obtained through single focus activities such as concentrating on diet alone.

From a practical standpoint, embracing coherence and fulfill-ment means we mustn't let one area of our life overtake, override, or become overburdened at the pathological expense or mutual exclu-siveness to one or more areas of our life. To further appreciate the dif-ference between balance and coherence, consider the classic "work/life balance" cliché.

With balance, an individual working eight hours a day would, hypothetically, upon arriving home, need to conjure up an additional eight hours of time to spend with family. Unfortunately, this equa-tion relies solely on quantity.

Coherence and a state of inner peace, on the other hand, could be achieved, in the same example, by working the same eight-hour shift and engaging the rest of the evening in time spent through the following activities: one hour of self-care (exercising) followed by only one to two hours of conscious, focused attention, and presence (without distractions), to cherished loved ones—the greatest gift we can give to another human being.

All of this, of course, is highly individual. One of the key ele-ments to remember is that *if everything is important, then nothing is important.* The overriding principle is quality rules over quantity.

With coherence and fulfillment, factors such as quality, quantity, effectiveness, and efficiency are considered. Therefore, coherence and a sense of fulfillment can be achieved instantaneously (a deep breath, a moment of gratitude, a kind word) anytime we find ourselves engaged in activities, flow experiences, or moments that touch our soul and heart. States of inner peace, tranquility, and equanimity can be achieved regardless of the time spent. One of coherence and fulfillment's qualities can be likened to the forever practice of non-resistance to the glory of the present moment. And as this occurs our angel lobes, brain, heart, and respiratory patterns align moving from chaos and incoherence to a state of coherence.

Coherence

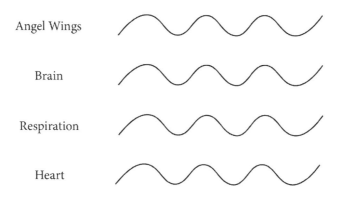

Incoherence

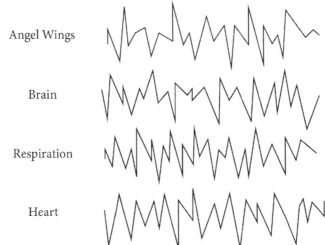

CHAPTER 10

The Levels of Consciousness

The level of consciousness you choose to tune in to each moment of each day will determine the quality of your experience of the world.

-Debbie Ford

Consciousness can be defined in many ways. From a scientific and psychological perspective, it is the state of being awake and aware of one's surroundings. It is an effect originating and produced by the brain's hardware.

From the perspective of the perennial philosophies, consciousness is much more profound. It signifies existence and life itself. The brain, in this narrative, is not producing consciousness, but rather consciousness is using the brain as a conduit or container. In the discussion to follow, we will embrace both concepts as well as include the qualities of Eros, Agape, communion, and agency as previously discussed.

According to Integral Theory, consciousness has two essential aspects. The first includes the states of consciousness such as peak experiences, witness, unity, wake, dream, and deep sleep. The second—the topic of this discussion—includes structures or stages of consciousness.

Throughout human existence, each stage of consciousness co-evolved alongside a specific economic, political, and social system such as agriculture, industry, and information technology. Although each stage dominated at certain times in history (the collective) and development (the individual), all stages (old and new) are present and available in our mind-body complex. Ignoring this fact is one of the greatest causes of disease. Lastly, each stage has nurturing (positive) aspects that transcend and include the prior stage as well as pathological (negative) and shadow aspects.

Structures of consciousness evolved in many ways. One of the most important to our discussion is the stage conception model embraced by nearly every psychological and evolutionary theorist. Combining the works of philosophers Ken Wilber (founder of Integral Theory) and Jean Gebser (author of *The Ever-Present Origin*), individual and collective consciousness can fit neatly into the following categories: egocentric, ethnocentric, humanocentric, worldcentric, and Kosmocentric. These structures are the most important of all the operating systems and software running our mind-body-spirit complex.

The easiest way to define the word Kosmic is to understand both its placement and context on this continuum. Before we do, let's see where we are going, the 10,000-foot view. To get a feel for this stage conception model, it's easiest to look at three of their most defining features: power, love, and peace.

Power, Love, and Peace

As stated previously in the introduction, the evolution of power moves from things happening to me (victim consciousness or reacting) to things happening by me and through me (cocreator consciousness, intentional action, and responsibility). The evolution of love moves from conditional (my family, my religion, my race) to unconditional love (all of humanity, Mother Nature, and all her animals and plants). Finally, the evolution of peace shifts from trying to find peace outside oneself to an understanding that peace is found within.

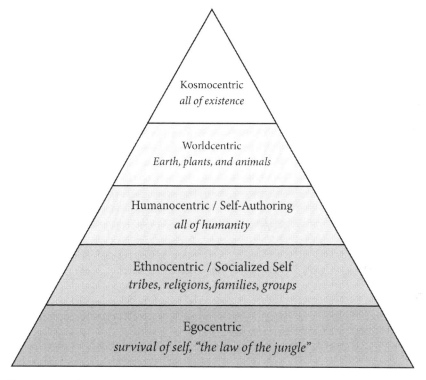

Egocentric

Egocentric can be thought of as a world view or level of consciousness that begins with and revolves around "me, mine, and I." It is here where one believes he or she is the literal center of the universe. It can easily be seen and appreciated in the formative years of childhood development and our early ancestors. It is driven by biological and physiological needs and the desires for safety, security, power, sex, food, and water.

Infants, embodied by egocentric consciousness, are without a sense of a separate self. They are unable to tell where their body, emotions, and feelings end and the environment begins. They are one with the environment, undifferentiated, and in a state of pure fusion. For example, they think, *If I'm sad, everyone is sad*, or *If I'm happy, everyone must be happy*. According to Swiss psychologist Jean Piaget, the egocentric child assumes that other people see, hear, and feel exactly as they do.

In addition to the individual, egocentric consciousness was also ripe in the ancient structures of our primitive ancestors, where survival of the self and the law of the jungle were the only games in town. Thinking was magical and power-driven (mimicking early childhood development) and coevolved alongside the economic, political, and social structures of foraging, hunter-gathering, and, later, horticulture (digging stick and handheld hoe).

Our early ancestors and children today often practice animism, where human characteristics and motives are ascribed to external objects, phenomena, and events. Examples of magical thinking include, *The volcano erupts because it's mad at me*, *The storm rolled in because the sky is crying*, and *Mom can manifest my meals from thin air*.

In summary, this egocentric structure is undifferentiated and dominated by power, biological drives, and magical thinking. It can be seen today dominating early childhood development, street gangs, superstitions, voodoo, and various illnesses such as severe depression and Alzheimer's. We encounter these drives as adults when our purely biological needs and desires for food, water, sex, safety, and security surface within.

Ethnocentric or the Socialized Self

Evolving consciousness moved from egocentric to ethnocentric or a type of "conditional love" whereby care, compassion, and concern were extended past ourselves to those in our immediate clan, tribe, religion, nation, and family. This level of consciousness can be seen in early childhood in what Piaget calls concrete operational ages, from seven to eleven. A milestone in child development, for example, occurs when the child begins to understand that Mom and Dad have different thoughts, emotions, and feelings that are unique and unlike their own. This is the birth of psychological perspective-taking.

In addition to child development, ethnocentric consciousness evolved in our early ancestors as we came together in distinct groups based on race, sex, color, and creed. It co-evolved alongside the agrarian (agriculture revolution) economic, political, and social system (e.g., the animal-drawn plow). It came online around 4000 BCE and dominated until the Renaissance and Enlightenment. It was during this time all the world's great religions emerged. Magical and superstitious thinking was replaced by myth, specifically of the religious kind.

Joseph Campbell, the legendary mythologist, has noted that people mistakenly misinterpret myths in one of two ways. They either say they aren't true or accept them as a literal fact. Consider the two phrases: Johnny runs like a tiger, and Johnny is a tiger. The former phrase is a simile, and the latter is a metaphor. The description of Johnny as a tiger (the myth) conjures up emotion, feeling, and an understanding of how Johnny runs. To say that the phrase isn't true or to accept it as a fact would both be considered mistakes of myth.

Myths are simple attempts to explain the ineffable or that which simply cannot be explained. They point to higher truths that can only be experienced. If myths were understood from this context, we would read scriptures as poetry rather than prose and allow it to uncover the reference to which it is pointing. Myths represent attempts at explaining the depths of our soul and the workings of the universe.

In its healthy forms, myths are seen in childhood beliefs surrounding the mythos of the Easter Bunny, Santa Claus, and the like. It is alive in the world's greatest stories, Adam and Eve, Noah and the Ark, Hindu's lineage of supernatural, mythical beings, and Ayurveda's five-element theory (air, ether, water, fire, and earth). Mythology is a vital part of human development and acts as the foundation for rationality as we try to make sense of the world, first through metaphors and, later, through science.

This ethnocentric level of consciousness is embodied by what we call the traditional worldview. Today it can be summed up succinctly as "saints and sinners," "the good and the bad," and "God-country-family." Healthy versions of traditionalism include family values, law, and order. Underpinning this assumption, however, breeds a pathological, conscious, or unconscious belief in the superiority of one's clan, tribe, family, or nation. Its mandate is, "we are the chosen one." This, unfortunately, led to the emergence and birth of society's isms—racism, sexism, speciesism, and so on.

All religions, being ethnocentric, have some type of struggle, from mild to extreme. In the healthy version, we can preach to you, try to convert you, and try to convince you of our view. In its more pathological representation, we try to coerce you, and if we can't convince you, then we will kick you out or kill you. Every human conflict, past and present, is a form of ethnocentric confrontation.

Humanocentric or Self-Authoring

As the hands of evolution continued, a more humanocentric consciousness began to emerge. This is the first stage of consciousness that embraces all of humanity as a brother and sisterhood. Care, compassion, and concern were extended to those outside one's clan, tribe, or nation regardless of race, sex, creed, or color.

In our individual development, this consciousness comes online as we move from childhood to adulthood, at the beginning of our teenage years. It includes the emergence of the self, the need for recognition, thinking over feeling, and a focus on self-esteem needs. In the collective, it first appeared, albeit in a primitive form, during the Enlightenment and Scientific Revolution, coevolving alongside the Age of the Machine (the Industrial Revolution).

Humanocentric can be equated with modernity and summed up succinctly as "winners and losers." Modernity birthed science and the ideas of business success, merit, accomplishment, excellence, wealth, achievement, freedom, intrinsic power, and individual responsibility.

During this stage of development, rationality and facts overtake mythical thinking. Children question the truth of Santa Claus and the Easter Bunny, while our ancestors questioned the reality of the great mythical stories of long ago. For example, in 1543, Copernicus asserted that the earth revolved around the sun. The Church and other mythos, with evidence at hand, began to concede their old narrative. During this period in history, the earth was no longer the center of the universe.

Modernity brought about capitalism and democracy. In its healthy form, means of production are owned by the individual rather than the government. Thus, a level playing field emerged alongside healthy competition. Unfortunately, pathological forms, such as predatory capitalism, have arisen. In this narrative, means of production are owned by a few individuals or corporations who, in turn, own and control the government. An uneven playing field is created and begins the great divide between the rich and the underserved.

Worldcentric

Worldcentric or ecocentric is a recent phenomenon occurring in the past one hundred years, culminating with its strongest presence during the revolutions of the 1960s. It embraces the earth and all of humanity as one nation. During this time in history, a strong critique of capitalism (in its current predatory form), materialism, racism, fundamentalism, sexism, ageism, patriarchism, and speciesism emerged. Large masses of people began to embrace the marginalized and underserved groups in society, including animals, minorities, the disabled, women's rights, and protection for Mother Earth. As a consequence, we saw the emergence of the animal rights movement, the civil rights movement, ecological movements, and more.

Worldcentric is equated with post-modernity or multiculturalism and coevolved alongside the Informational Age and the Love Generation. It can be summed up as "love and equality." It changed the focus away from thinking (rationality) to feeling (intuition) and from freedom to equality. This sentiment, treating all of humanity as equal, was instrumental in helping to create laws for the underserved.

Paradoxically, fighting for equality became a direct threat to the traditional and modern world views on liberty, responsibility, and freedom. Are all children really equal? Do we throw away recognition and individual achievements to ensure everyone feels equal? In other words, a pathology arose that could not reconcile the truth that our divine natures are equal while our surface structures are clearly not.

An infant, for example, cannot play in the NBA, yet an infant and an NBA player both contain a divine essence.

The divide in our political affiliations grew deeper as traditionalists valued equal opportunity and post-modernity valued equal outcomes. These ideas, of course, are not mutually exclusive. Traditionalism began to view post-modernity as Pollyanna (throwing out the idea of equality altogether), and post-modernity viewed traditionalism as a threat to evolution (throwing out the ideas of law, order, and family values).

Kosmocentric

Kosmocentric consciousness is the leading edge of consciousness. It is an all-inclusive perspective of care, compassion, and concern for humanity (regardless of race, sex, creed, or color), the cosmos, all sentient beings (regardless of species, embracing the six-legged speck to our canine counterparts), and all of manifestation (all that can be seen and that which cannot).

The word *Kosmo* is distinguished from the word cosmo in that the former includes consciousness, spirituality, the material and non-material subjective and objective realities of the individual and collective. The latter only includes the physical dimensions of reality, such as the stuff that comprises the earth, stars, other planets, and other celestial bodies.

Another way of simplifying all of this is to say that humanity's consciousness and evolution moved from an egocentric to a conditional love to one's "tribe," to an extended conditional love to all of humanity, to a truly embracing unconditional love—or oneness with all the Kosmos.

Kosmocentric consciousness is equated with an integral mindset that blends the dichotomies of freedom versus equality. We move away from either-or to both-and thinking. It embraces the transcend-and-include model of evolution. All junior levels have truths. The goal is to include, integrate, and transcend the unhealthy parts.

CHAPTER 11

Kosmic Health–Doing Good Is Good for You

It has been said something as small as the flutter of a butterfly's wing can ultimately cause a typhoon halfway around the world.

-Chaos Theory, The Butterfly Effect

By expanding our sphere of compassion and influence, we become acutely aware of a metaphysical universal law that states, "Doing good for the Kosmos is, in essence, indistinguishable from doing good for us as individuals." Thus, the golden rule becomes reinterpreted from "Do unto others as you would have them do unto you" to "You and the other (all of manifestation) are one, so whatever you do to another, you do unto yourself."

In essence, giving and receiving are interpreted as synonyms. Varying disciplines, from philosophy, quantum physics, to metaphysics, suggest that we do not only live in the universe, but the universe lives in us. We begin to see that we are not islands onto ourselves and, therefore, can no longer behave with this pathological autonomy.

As we increase more and more of our consciousness from egocentric to Kosmocentric, our health, in turn, expands. Simply put, Kosmocentric consciousness leads to Kosmocentric health. As we attune to these new realities, we are rewarded with the fruits from the great Tree of Life—vitality, wellness, amelioration of lifestyle diseases, finding our true north or individual calling, along with fulfilled and joyous relationships with all sentient beings or earthlings.

As we dismantle our egocentric persona, our new identity ensures us that we can no longer be seen as our greatest mistakes, we are no longer our emotions, we are no longer separate entities, and we are no longer subject to the illusions of a finite reality. As we take this journey inward, we extend these notions to all we meet, and they, too, are no longer seen through the prism of their mistakes, false self, species, race, color, or creed.

Thus, we must expand our definition of health to include this Kosmocentric perspective simply because we can no longer be blinded by another treatise on health and wellness that focuses solely on egocentric concerns that do not consider life's interdependence simply because *doing good is good for us.*

We all know that we are much, much more than our physical bodies. We have a body, we have emotions, we have a mind, we engage in relationships, and we possess a spirit—we are spiritual beings inhabiting a physical body. Even though we can acknowledge this intuition, we still tend to make decisions about our health and act as if we were only a body made of flesh. For example, we can choose to eat food from an egocentric lens of reality—eating to satisfy or to quench only our emotional pleasures, tastes, and needs while ignoring the food's impact on our body, the environment (e.g., the packaging the food comes in), and our fellow sentient creatures on planet earth (e.g., factory farming). This exclusionary type of thinking can, quite literally, be applied to every dimension of life: physical, emotional, relational, mental, and spiritual.

The greatest discovery, I believe, is that the game of life is set up exactly as it should be—as you do the right thing, you are rewarded. Period. It is our duty to include a broader lens of reality (Kosmocentric consciousness) as we move forward on this health and wellness journey. As Gandhi said, "Be the change you wish to see in the world."

In other words:

- When we practice self-care, we increase our capacity to heal. As we heal, those around us heal. We are literally influencing everyone and everything we come in contact with. This is the theory of emotional contagion, the butterfly effect, and three degrees of separation.
- When we choose organic foods, we protect both the environment and our bodies from pesticides, herbicides, and the like.
- When we take a stance against factory farming, we protect our bodies from the harmful effects of antibiotics and cholesterol-laden foods, and we undermine needless animal abuse and suffering.
- When we treat our fellow sentient inhabitants with kindness and compassion, we feed our spiritual Selves.

- When we give to others, we are rewarded with a hit of the neurotransmitter dopamine.
- When we connect with others, we are rewarded with the hormone oxytocin.
- When we stand up for the environment, the environment gifts us with clean air, water, and so on.

Dr. Will Tuttle author of The World Peace Diet explains this beautifully:

> *Simply stated [referring to the Golden Rule], we can never expect to be happy if we cause suffering to others, to be free if we confine others, to be healthy if we cause sickness in others, to be prosperous if we steal from others, or to have peace if we are violent to others and cause them to be afraid. As the Buddhists say, whatever seeds we plant and nurture through the actions of our body, speech, and mind will grow, and we will experience their fruits in our lives as abundance, joy, love, and inner peace, or anger, misery, pain, and lack.*

Morphic Fields, Archetypes, and the Collective Unconscious

The question put forth by Charles Eisenstein in his book *The More Beautiful World Our Heart Knows Is Possible* is, "Can changing a woman's bedpan change the world?" His answer is, "If you do it to change the world, it will not; if you do it because she needs her bedpan changed, it can."

If we assume the classical contributory modes of transmission influencing evolution and inheritance to be physical only (e.g.,

DNA), we may struggle with this answer. As we will explore in later chapters, the fields of epigenetics, metagenetics, and transgenetics open the door for newly discovered nonphysical vectors. Small acts of kindness without notoriety do influence personal and collective inheritance and evolution.

Our brain is both local (physical) and nonlocal (nonphysical). It connects the physical structures of the triune brain with the non-physical energies that make up humanity's unified One Mind. This includes, in part, the collective unconscious and archetypes as pro-posed by psychologist Carl Jung and the morphic fields as theorized by scientist Rupert Sheldrake.

The thread that connects these and other similar theories is that certain energetic organizing fields contain "memories" and "instruc-tions" that are not stored in the physical body. Rather, they exist outside in the unified One Mind.

Morphic resonance picks up where Jung's collective conscious-ness leaves off. Namely, transcending the human shared collective mind and expanding it to all of life. Thus, each species shares a col-lective memory, contributes, and draws upon it.

The theory of morphogenetic fields, the collective unconscious, and archetypes are held implicitly by billions of people who hold to ideas of reincarnation, the someday future ability to see loved ones who have passed (in that foreign land we call "Heaven"), beliefs sur-rounding transmigration, faith in mystics of long ago, and the new age mediums of today. In short, the explicit universal belief shared is that someone's essence does not die with the individual and does not lie dormant within the physical brain. Rather, the essence continues to live on.

The wisdom traditions go even further through their descrip-tions of this phenomenon in the sacred texts. Consider just one, the

Akashic records, which represents a compendium and warehouse of all human events and memories ever to have occurred in the past, present, or future stored in a nonphysical plane of existence.

More modern names to describe this field can be found in a host of disciplines, such as the study or field of electrodynamics (zero point field), quantum physics (universal quantum field), particle physics (grand unified field), and the implicate order of the great theoretical physicist David Bohm.

All energetic information and memories have, as their foundation, a primal blueprint or universal patterns of organization called archetypes. Archetypes are thought to be the original patterns from which all other similar objects, life, ideas, concepts, and themes are derived, copied, modeled, and emulated. Through eons of evolution, more intricate energetic information has been added.

The theory of morphogenic fields supposes that our brains act more like a TV receiver than a tape recorder. Memory storage and retrieval exist in the unified One Mind internet rather than in the dusty halls of a library, which is limited by the physicality of the brain's inert matter. In this model, the hardware of the brain would tune into (referred to as morphic resonance) memory rather than store it as a physical trace. This is analogous to how a smartphone or computer contacts the cloud or how a radio receiver tunes into a radio station. This universal One Mind, therefore, is where memories are stored and can be downloaded as a kind of energetic blueprint, app, or instructional booklet.

To help place the home of these universal energetic fields and memories, we will use the metaphor of an iceberg alongside Jung's elaboration and various distinctions of "mind":

- Conscious: The part of our mind that we are conscious of. This can be thought of as the tip of the iceberg.
- Unconscious: The part of our mind running most of our behaviors and actions, albeit unconsciously. This represents the entire iceberg below the water's surface. If we wanted to expose this hidden dimension somehow, one would need to dive down to the depths of the water to unearth and bring these unconscious elements to the light. There are two basic types:
  - o Personal unconscious: the storehouse of our personal experiences
  - o Collective unconscious: the storehouse of archetypes
- Superconscious: The mind of God. This is where potentiality exists, awaiting manifestation from the intangible to the tangible. It is a kind of quantum superposition. This is represented by the water and air surrounding and holding the iceberg.

The morphogenic fields, serving as a collective warehouse of sorts, offer us a model for understanding how each one of us plays a contributing role in humanity's evolution—from the person who dynamically influences millions working in the nonprofit sector to the life of a mother who chooses to stay at home and raise her children on a bedrock of virtues. It also extends genetics, for example, to those engaged in same-sex marriages whereby they each contribute their "genetic" equivalents to the Kosmic bedrock without ever passing their so-called physical genes, in the traditional sense, to an offspring.

In 1954, Sir Roger Bannister, a British middle-distance athlete, shocked the world when he became the first man to run a mile in under four minutes. Before this achievement, the four-minute mile was thought to be a mystical barrier deemed impossible and as dangerous and deadly as climbing Mt. Everest. However, forty-six days after history was made, the record was broken again. In the decades to follow, Roger Banister's record-setting feat would be surpassed again and again as athletic training benefited from advances in sports sciences and, maybe more important, beliefs changed from *it is impossible* to *it can be achieved*. Breaking the four-minute mile shows us that the limits and barriers we impose on ourselves may be more mental, psychic, and energetic than physical.

Additional evidence and experiments done on rats, long-term crystallization experiments (e.g., drugs), and the global rise in IQ (the Flynn Effect) help give credence to a new paradigm of morphic resonance. The effects of these phenomena show an increased ease of learning when others (contributing to the collective nonlocal mind) have already achieved a certain degree of proficiency. For example, suppose a certain species (e.g., rats) learns a specific behavior or adaptation in London. Looking at subsequent generations of similar species in North America, with no physical contact, these new offspring find it easier to learn that specific behavior or adaptation.

Isn't that what the Buddha and Jesus Christ did? These self-actualized individuals lived their lives as a testament to that which could be actualized. In other words, they contributed to the collective One Mind making it easier for all of us to access.

Any change, therefore, that happens anywhere creates a field of change that makes that same change easier somewhere else. An act of love, compassion, and grace will strengthen the primordial archetypes or fields of love and compassion so that a person across the globe, when faced with choosing between love or fear, becomes compelled or ever so slightly pushed to playing the love card. This is all the direct result or effect of a single individual contribution. Our mantra again reverberates, *doing good is good for you* and, of course, the mantra, stated differently, *doing good is good for us* is exactly the same. Another way of summarizing all of this is to extend and understand the concept of karma (cause and effect) in that it works in, on, and through not only the individual but also the collective.

This thesis directly argues against spiritual bypassing or the tendency to use spiritual ideas and practices to sidestep or avoid facing unresolved emotional issues, psychological wounds, and unfinished developmental tasks. This term, spiritual bypassing, was introduced by John Welwood, a Buddhist teacher and psychotherapist, in the early 1980s. In short, it represents inaction in the social and political arenas in favor of pathological pacifism.

Finding the Sacred in the Mundane

Joseph Campbell tells a mythical story in the book *The Hero with a Thousand Faces* about an elderly Hindu man who comes to rest near the Ganges River. He lies down and places his feet on a sacred statue near the bank's end. A Sikh gentleman passes by and is offended by the Hindu man's act of un-holiness and asks him, with both determination and hostility, to move his feet from the sacred statue. The Hindu man is agreeable but asks the Sikh if he would kindly come over and move his feet from the statue to a location that would not offend him. As the Sikh moves the Hindu man's feet to the right, a sacred statue materializes out of nowhere. He then proceeds to move his feet to the left, but once again, a sacred statue materializes out of nowhere. No matter where he tries to move the Hindu man's feet, he encounters a miraculous materialization of a sacred statue.

This story reminds us that sacredness is all around us, within us, encompassing, and permeating. It is as if it is hidden from plain sight, simply awaiting recognition. There is no place or time where we end and the sacred begins. The sacred, therefore, is found in the secular, the profane, the ordinary, the earth, and the mundane.

The running thesis behind the concept of Kosmic Health is that there is a divine wisdom of interconnectedness and sacredness that runs the galaxies, the planets, the rocks, our bodies, and on and on. As we become intimately connected and uncover this truth, we will begin to embrace our inherent, God-given cocreative powers while, at the same time, and with humility, begin to acknowledge and use our spiritual vision to see that it exists within everyone and everything we encounter, as well. We soon discover that we need only get out of our way, remove the blocks, and allow the treasures within the kingdom of God to express in and through us.

With this understanding, the journey we are about to take will help resonate and uncover a paradoxically simple yet deep universal truth that can be summarized by the following tagline:

Doing Good Is Good For You=Us

It is here where health turns from I-lness to We-llness or from a focus on I, me, and mine to the interconnectedness of we. The power of this understanding is one of the greatest secrets ever unearthed in humanity's short history on this planet.

We do not have to go to a far-away monastery, seek an enlightened guru, or learn some new meditative technique to achieve what was deemed the auspice of an elite few or the esoteric. We simply need to look every day for the sacred in the mundane, strengthen our deficiency needs, allow more time to be spent in leisurely pursuit, and use the concepts and ideas as presented in the following chapters to help ourselves self-actualize. In doing so, the transcendent becomes a stretch goal—just out of our reach but there for the grasping.

Three Big Bangs

Holmes Rolston III, professor of philosophy emeritus at Colorado State University, divides the creation of matter, energy, life, and mind into three great big bands. First, 13.8 billion years ago, brought online the "universe," the space/time continuum, matter, energy, and the billions of galaxies we call our universe. This is referred to, collectively, as the physiosphere. Second, 3.8 billion years ago, life (prokaryotic cells) emerged from matter (the primordial soup)–there is simply no other way to describe this other than by calling it a miracle. This is referred to as the biosphere. Lastly, 1 million years ago, brought about the noosphere or the emergence of human consciousness.

How we integrate the pysiosphere (matter), biosphere (life), and noosphere (human consciousness) is humanity's greatest challenge. We will leave this pondering, for now, and simply reflect on the words, found in a letter to President Washington, attributed to Native American, Chief Seattle:

The President in Washington sends word that he wishes to buy our land. But how can you buy or sell the sky? The land? The idea is strange to us. If we do not own the freshness of the air and the sparkle of the water, how can you buy them?

Every part of the earth is sacred to my people. Every shining pine needle, every sandy shore, every mist in the dark woods, every meadow, every humming insect. All are holy in the memory and experience of my people.

We know the sap which courses through the trees as we know the blood that courses through our veins. We are part of the earth and it is part of us. The perfumed flowers are our sisters. The bear, the deer, the great eagle, these are our brothers. The rocky crests, the dew in the meadow, the body heat of the pony, and man all belong to the same family.

The shining water that moves in the streams and rivers is not just water, but the blood of our ancestors. If we sell you our land, you must remember that it is sacred. Each glossy reflection in the clear waters of the lakes tells of events and memories in the life of my people. The water's murmur is the voice of my father's father.

The rivers are our brothers. They quench our thirst. They carry our canoes and feed our children. So you must give the rivers the kindness that you would give any brother.

If we sell you our land, remember that the air is precious to us, that the air shares its spirit with all the life that it supports. The wind that gave our grandfather his first breath also received his last sigh. The wind also gives our children the spirit of life. So if we sell our land, you must keep it apart and sacred, as a place where man can go to taste the wind that is sweetened by the meadow flowers.

Will you teach your children what we have taught our children? That the earth is our mother?

What befalls the earth befalls all the sons of the earth.

This we know: the earth does not belong to man, man belongs to the earth. All things are connected like the blood that unites us all. Man did not weave the web of life, he is merely a strand in it. Whatever he does to the web, he does to himself.

One thing we know: our God is also your God. The earth is precious to him and to harm the earth is to heap contempt on its creator.

Your destiny is a mystery to us. What will happen when the buffalo are all slaughtered? The wild horses tamed? What will happen when the secret corners of the forest are heavy with the scent of many men and the view of the ripe hills is blotted with talking wires? Where will the thicket be? Gone! Where will the eagle be? Gone! And what is to say goodbye to the swift pony and then hunt? The end of living and the beginning of survival.

When the last red man has vanished with this wilderness, and his memory is only the shadow of a cloud moving across the prairie, will these shores and forests still be here? Will there be any of the spirit of my people left?

We love this earth as a newborn loves its mother's heartbeat. So, if we sell you our land, love it as we have loved it. Care for it, as we have cared for it. Hold in your mind the memory of the land as it is when you receive it. Preserve the land for all children, and love it, as God loves us.

As we are part of the land, you too are part of the land. This earth is precious to us. It is also precious to you.

One thing we know—there is only one God. No man, be he Red man or White man, can be apart. We ARE all brothers after all.

CHAPTER 12

The Hero's Journey

No mud, no lotus
No chrysalis, no butterfly
No acorn, no oak
No crucifixion, no resurrection
No death, no life
-A conglomerate of life's teachings

To end our discussion on human potential, I wanted to use the tale of the hero's journey to summarize and symbolize, from a 10,000-foot view, the ingredients of self-actualization and self-transcendence, so we don't lose sight of the ultimate aim and destination.

The hero's journey is one of the most potent metaphors and maps describing the universal story of humanity played out in and through our personal lives. As I explain the details, a curious observer might question why this concept is not included in the "map" section of the book? The answer has to do with the punchline—which, as you will see, is always the same. In other words, you travel the hero's path, over and over again, encountering trials, tribulations, births, deaths (emotional, psychological), and rebirths. You are, however, always brought back, in a circular narrative, to the same location—the sanctuary within, your compass.

Joseph Campbell, the great mythologist, formulated the hero's journey to serve as the great mono-myth or shared archetypal story of man and womankind's transcendence over adversity, their growth, and the universal threads that connect each one of us. He is probably best known for the mantra, "Follow your bliss," which serves as the doorway to our individual calling. As we follow our heart and soul's desires, we move away from the comfort and security of who we are and jump headfirst into the unknown.

His magnum opus is his book published in 1949, *The Hero with a Thousand Faces* which describes the archetypal hero, or the universal story found in worldwide mythologies. It is represented in all cultures and throughout all times. It takes on different masks, forms, and exteriors—but the content or interiors are universal. It is the story of Jesus, the Buddha, the mythologies of the great religions, awe-inspiring poetry, and, of course, the threads that make up the story of our lives.

Throughout the millennium, there has always been a predictable sequence of self-discovery. It all starts with the universe's metaphorical or literal call to adventure.

The Journey's First Steps

We are called out of a barren landscape where potentials are starved, lives are uneasy, and the weight of dissatisfaction hauls us backward again and again to life's predictable status quo. Each of us hears the call. Unfortunately, however, not all of us answer the call. This leaves most of us dying with our dreams starved deep within the caverns of our souls. If one is not actively engaged in the hero's journey, then he or she is most likely asleep and intoxicated by safety, security, and comfort.

However, as we start to answer the call, our adventure begins. We take our first steps by leaving home—a metaphor for all that is safe and secure in our life. We immediately encounter various demons and dragons, trials and tribulations in the outside world and deep within the recesses of the interior mind. We are given two choices: to be pulled back to the safety of the life we know or to ride alongside the evolutionary drives to higher transcendent realities. This journey is, paradoxically, both exciting and frightful. The pain of our mundane life gives us a gentle push, but the call and the *What if* questions beg us to ask ourselves what potential will help pull us out.

If we are honest and look deep enough, we will all be able to uncover a place within ourselves that has broken away from our true Selves—our masks, shadows, and self-personalities. This fragmented self, oftentimes, leads to self-betrayal. It catapults us towards self-destruction and a perpetual life where we remain stuck.

It is here we enter the metaphorical belly of the whale or the "dark night of the soul." In one interpretation, this space is a deep and disturbing state of confusion because we no longer can identify with the Self of the past yet, at the same time, are unable to identify with the new person we are becoming. We are thrown into a mayhem of disassociation with who we thought we were—our shadows, personalities, and masks. We are sensing the emergence of the new self—the chrysalis and the butterfly. This dark night allows us to face the toughest question of all—*Who am I?*

It is easiest to spot whether or not we are in a dark night or the metaphorical belly of the whale if we resonate with the declaration: *Where I am is not who I am.* As we say no to self-betrayal and follow our bliss, Joseph Campbell tells us, "…the universe will open doors where there were only walls." In this way, the obstacle becomes the way.

Once the internal and external battles are won, completed, resolved, transcended, and all the dragons are slain, we are gifted with our unique boon or elixir, which, in some ways, represents a new state of equanimity, a paradigm shift in thinking, and maybe even the gift of awareness to our true divine identity. Yet another quote from Campbell captures this, "…the privilege of a lifetime is being who you are." The journey, however, does not stop here. The hero has one more step to take.

The Journey's Last Steps

The hero does not stop to selfishly enjoy his spoils. Rather, the universe calls out again and beckons for a return home. If we heed this second calling, this is where we are transformed from the ordinary to the hero. The hero is one who returns home (the metaphoric place he or she has never left) to share this self-discovery with the world.

In other words, the true hero is not called a hero until he or she takes what was received, shares these gifts, their spoils, and lives a life in service to something greater than oneself. This is the state of self-transcendence or the notion of transcending past oneself. This can take on many forms and need not be any loftier than the simple act of opening our heart space, sharing who we are with others, and living true to ourselves. We begin to live in the world but not of the world, and the culmination of our hero's journey ends with a kind of aha moment as we awaken to the sacred in the secular, our Buddha nature, and the Christ within.

The last part of the journey reflects a higher purpose and a new model for humanity's survival and evolution. It is best encapsulated by the Buddhist teaching of the bodhisattva. The Buddha, or the

Enlightened One, proposed that there was a step more evolved than enlightenment, or the personal release from suffering. It was the ability to share, guide, and act as a loving beacon for others as they walk their path. This is compassion in action. The Buddha called those who had evolved to this stage of sharing the ultimate truth bodhisattvas. It should be no surprise that the word bodhisattva translates as "heroic-minded one" or, in common parlance, "superhero."

From yet another perspective, *The Course in Miracles* talks about the embodiment of the concepts of gospel and charity. In the Course's terminology, the word gospel becomes a beautiful metaphor synonymous with the word love. Thus, we teach by spreading the gospel (love) and becoming mirrors to one another. What we do to another is done to us. We embrace, once again, the idea of *giving is receiving*. Charity is defined as "…a way of perceiving the perfection of another even if they cannot perceive it in themselves." We pay charity by assuming a level of development in another beyond what they have achieved. We see the potentiality in others and are determined to help them regain their sight, as well.

Lastly, Dr. Maslow holds a unique view in that the hero's selfish and unselfish tendencies merge into one. He states, "The healthy person finds happiness in helping others." This form of unselfishness is selfish. He continues, "They get selfish pleasures from the pleasures of other people, which is a way of saying unselfish." The healthy person, in other words, is selfish in a healthy way, a way which is beneficial to him and society.

Jean Houston, the author of *The Wizard of Us: Transformational Lessons from Oz,* suggests that Glinda, the good witch from the classic story, *The Wizard of Oz*, represents Dorothy's entelechy or highest guidance towards her full potential. Recall the classical and beloved story—a tornado carries Dorothy far away from the safety and security of her hometown in Kansas. She suddenly finds herself thrown into a magical and foreign land where she begins her journey desperately seeking to return home to the land she had always known and trusted, Kansas. Unbeknownst to her, the very means of her transportation to get back home and to find peace were always there, sitting silently within her and in plain sight—metaphorically symbolized in and through her beautiful bright ruby red slippers. However, the problem was that recognizing the value of the ruby slippers was outside of her conscious awareness. Glinda, her guide, lovingly watches over her, nudging her to rediscover this truth and to bring it back into the light of her awareness.

Each one of us holds the power of Dorothy's ruby red slippers to transport us back to Kansas. We needn't go off to some mystical place or seek truth in esoteric philosophies or religions—we need simply to look within. We, therefore, begin our journey with the understanding and awareness of this sleeping entelechy that waits to be birthed into our highest self. We must not underestimate the dictum, *What we can be, we must be* as a basic human need. Let these words sink into your core, and use this story as a simple reminder of the greatest that lies dormant within. Follow the wisdom of your Glinda to find your way back home. The time is now. The place is here, and all the resources you will ever need are available and hidden within you and your ruby slippers, as this scene from *The Wizard of Oz* perfectly portrays:

> Dorothy asks Glinda, the Good Witch, "Oh, will you help me? Can you help me?"
>
> "You don't need to be helped any longer," a smiling Glinda answers. "You've always had the power to go back to Kansas."

"I have?"

"Then why didn't you tell her before?" Scarecrow demands.

"Because she would not have believed me. She had to learn it for herself."

The Tin Man leans forward and asks, "What have you learned, Dorothy?"

"Well, I… think that is… that it wasn't enough just to want to see Uncle Henry and Auntie Em… and that if I ever go looking for my heart's desire again, I won't look any further than my own backyard; because if it isn't there, I have never really lost it to begin with."

CHAPTER 13

Miracles

Where there is great love, there are always miracles.
-*Willa Cather*

A Course in Miracles suggests that we are all hypnotized or duped into thinking that we have thousands upon thousands of worldly problems. Imagine a never-ending to-do and grievance list. Most of us could easily write down a litany of problems and issues such as financial insecurities, job dissatisfaction, relational issues, overwhelm, increasing demands, and health-related challenges. Some people are even experts in the art of making problems out of the trivial (the luxury of living in a developed country) by stressing over the right pair of jeans or the best flooring or paint for their new home.

From a spiritual perspective, however, the reality is simpler, less catastrophizing, and less chaotic. It suggests that our shared human tragedy arises from only one problem or cause. This problem is referred to as "the tiny mad idea" and rests in our belief that we were somehow able to achieve a type of separation from our divine inheritance—a movement from "*We to I.*"

It's a form of victim consciousness that scripts us into surrendering our power and standing as an isolated island or wave in the vast power of the ocean. The answer, the spiritual imperative, rests in uncovering the truth of connectedness and realigning to our cocreative powers and self-authoring consciousness—a movement from *I to We.*

The idea of separation may sound abstract. It is, however, rooted in psychology and neurobiology. As we separate from who and what is most important to us (God, strength, peace, love), our masks, armor, shells, and shadows grow stronger, and our heart contracts. We create misidentifications with our true Self as we fuse with the conditioned images, emotions, and mental constructs of our small self. In doing so, the ever-present now moment is lost to our personas and the incessant chatter of the mind's preoccupation with the past and future.

This tiny mad idea teaches us, unconsciously, that the world "out there" is the cause, and we (our mind, body, and soul) are the effects. It's as if we've been duped by our parents, teachers, and culture as they handed us a backward cause and effect formula.

Yes, some things happen in life that are out of our control, such as accidents and severe weather. However, the truth is that much more of our life is under our control than previously imagined. If we begin to bring the light of awareness to our mostly automated life, the formula reverses, and we begin to embody the truth that "we" are the cause, and the effects are "out there."

In other words, our outside world can be viewed as a projection of our internal state of being. The great spiritual teacher and author

Wayne Dyer said it best: "If you change the way you look at things, the things you look at change."

As you will soon see, the miracle asks you to suspend the notion that the complex secondary elements, or the thousands of problems, are the real problems. It even asks you to suspend the idea of a hierarchy of problems. It asks you to accept the radical notion that *all problems are the same. The problem is not the problem.* The problem, paradoxically, is both simple and complex. It is a universal singularity. It is the disconnection from who we are, our highest Self.

From a spiritual perspective, all circumstances, injuries, or wounds can be overcome by miracles. A characteristic of the miracle perspective is that all the thousands of problems are seen without hierarchy or discrimination. No problem is too big or inconsequential. From this perspective, miracles are available to everyone in the forever present now moment.

Nightmares and Dreams

Bringing the light (e.g., our cocreative power) to the darkness (victimhood, lack of responsibility, our thousands of problems) is akin to stepping into a dream or a child's worst nightmare. As we do so, we get lost and caught up in the ensuing drama (the thousands of problems) and begin to participate in a never-ending spiral of illusions as we try to fix the nightmare's storyline. As we engage in the dream, we forget our true purpose—to awaken. As stated before, it's as if we are continually rearranging the furniture on the deck of the sinking Titanic.

Our motivations, gratifications, and satisfactions are transient. We continue to trade one problem for another, one desire for another, and one need for another. This cements an infinite hedonistic rat-race that inevitably produces endless cycles of suffering. Most of us can resonate with the feeling of achieving a long-term goal or reaching a new summit in our lives only to find out that we are, once again, unfulfilled and wanting more. This is akin to entering the pearly gates of Heaven, looking around, and noticing an internal desire to change or redecorate the clouds and the celestial artwork.

Our goal, according to *A Course in Miracles*, is to bring all our so-called problems (the darkness) to the light of pure awareness. In doing so, we "awaken the child" and free him or her of nightmares. As we awaken from the dream, our hypnotic trance is lifted, and, in the light, the darkness of the nightmare (our thousands of problems) vanishes instantaneously. Allowing the light of awareness to shine brightly in and through us, we begin to live as sculptors and painters and are summoned to create our masterpieces.

What Is a Miracle?

A Course in Miracles defines a miracle, metaphorically, as the transformation of fear or any of its associative emotions (anger, hatred, anxiety, jealousy) into states of inner peace, coherence, and love. A miracle, therefore, is an inner practice that removes the blocks to the awareness of love's presence. It can be likened to an internal prayer that dismantles all fears and worldly problems and redirects us back home to our one and only cause—the power of our awe-inspiring mind.

We can imagine two discrete entities residing in the mind. The first is our ego (misguided, misidentified, and wrong-mindedness), and the second is our highest or heroic Self (right-mindedness). One path leads us away from our rightful inheritance (peace, love, and equanimity) and traps us in a perpetual cloud of fear and chaos. The second path, in contrast, offers a divine life-altering reality.

This sentiment is best expressed by an old Cherokee parable that describes a grandfather talking to his grandson. The grandfather says, "In life, there are two wolves inside of us at battle. One is a good wolf which represents things like kindness, love, bravery, and compassion. The other is a bad wolf which represents things like hatred, greed, and fear." The grandson stops and thinks about it for a second and asks, "Grandfather, which one wins?" The grandfather replies, "The one you feed."

The parable speaks to the great power of aligning with our highest Self. We mustn't forget, however, feeding the good wolf leaves us with a very hungry "bad" wolf. As we feed the good wolf it's important to integrate, transcend, and include the ego (the hungry wolf).

The Course states, "The holiest of all the spots on earth is where an ancient hatred becomes a present love." We need to look no further than the sacred altar of our very own mind. It is here where we have the freedom to choose again, align with right-mindedness, and receive the bounty of instantaneous peace.

As we find the courage to break free from our egoic conditioning, we summon guidance from that part of us that has forever remained in direct communication with divine inspiration. Every time we choose the path of divine inspiration, regardless of how small or insignificant, a miracle is birthed. Our humanity ensures us that this will be a forever practice as life will challenge us every day with opportunities to practice the art of miracle making. This can be seen in the same light as exercise and meditation; we don't just do it one time and proclaim a forever completion.

Miracles, more specifically, are achieved when we engage in the process of transmuting, alchemizing, and transcending complex secondary elements (pathological, toxic, maladaptive, and non-nurturing patterns, mechanisms, and strategies) into ones that are constructive, adaptive, nurturing, and healing. Examples include transmuting toxic codependent relationships into nurturing relation-ships, destructive thoughts and emotions into constructive ones, and unhealthy food choices into healing ones. Thus, a miracle, as defined here, occurs anytime a shift towards growth, evolution, self-actual-ization, and self-transcendence is unearthed, realized, or manifested.

Miracles Are Instantaneous and Await Welcome, Not Time

Many philosophers, scholars, and spiritual and religious thinkers have talked about the power of this ancient practice, but none, in my opinion, have offered a more poetic definition than equating it with the emotive punch and power encapsulated in and through the word, miracle. The power of miracles, thereby, rests simply in our ability to choose right-mindedness. In this sense, miracles are always available.

The Course reminds us, "If you are tempted to be dispirited by thinking how long it would take to change your mind so completely, ask yourself, 'How long is an instant?'" In this light, miracles are brought to manifestation in the moments we find peace in conflict, say we are sorry, nurture gratitude, take courage, and offer ourselves self-compassion. We are called moment to moment to walk ourselves back, thought by thought, breath by breath, to divine inspiration. We are called, simply, to choose again.

We are always creating our reality. The moment of our power and inspiration is found in the ever-present now moment. Miracles reside here in eternity. Eternity is not everlasting time. Rather, eter-nity is a moment without time—the present now moment. Miracles, therefore, live in eternity and act as the "eye of the hurricane" and the place of solace amidst our outward and internal chaos. The spiri-tual truth is that love's presence never disappears, only our awareness does. Love waits on welcome, not on time. Our goal is to thread a continuity of miracles, one after another, again and again, regardless of how many times you falter or fall.

Willingness and Intention Are All That Are Needed

All that is ever required for miracle manifestation is a little willingness along with heart-centered intention. This approach only asks that we desire peace and miracles more than we desire illusion, pain, suffering, the need to be right, or the achievement of a specific outcome. In other words, we are willing to let go of wrong-mindedness more than we want to keep it.

A miracle is not some Pollyanna-like plea that asks you to perform impossibilities, such as stopping negative thoughts and walking on water. Rather, the goal is more realistic. It invites us to release any negative thoughts we keep, hoard, or remain attached to. In turn, willingness and intention allow us to hand over wrong-mindedness to a higher and more sophisticated part of our human nature—our internal therapist, heroic, and highest Self.

In short, if we have faith, a willingness to see things differently, and an honest desire for peace as our goal, we can sit back, breathe, and surrender in a state free of psychological anxiety, as we learn to trust the process. The Course states, "Those who are certain of the outcome can afford to wait—and wait without anxiety."

I to We

As previously stated, the miracle moves us to an *I to We* orientation. As we align with miracle-mindedness, we no longer find ourselves walking the path alone, as a separated ego-self. Rather, we walk together with our highest Self, allowing divine inspiration to guide our thoughts, emotions, feelings, actions, and behaviors. The Course states, "The Holy Spirit (our highest Self) cannot do for you what he cannot do through you." Our healing comes from trust in a collective "We" rather than an isolated "I." The African proverb sums this sentiment up perfectly, "If you want to go fast, go alone. If you want to go far, go together."

Miracles open our eyes to a unique type of spiritual confidence and humility. We are asked to be confident because the "kingdom of God" rests within us and, at the same time, show humility because it exists in everyone. This is best appreciated through the well-known Indian greeting, Namaste, which translates, "I bow to the divine in you." When we see the light of shared divinity in everything, our experiences blossom, and the nectar of life is sweetened. Miracles, in this sense, are bi-directional and embody the spiritual doctrine, *giving is receiving.*

To summarize, a miracle can be thought of as a shift from *I to We* consciousness. The "I" represents the fragmented, chaotic, and separated states of our inner (thoughts, emotions, feelings, and sensations) and outer worlds. The "We" represents reconnection to life's underlying unity and seeing through the illusion of isolation, fragmentation, and separateness.

PART 2

The Maps

It's not down in any map. True places never are.
-Herman Melville

Maps help to simplify complicated information, offer a bird's eye view of the territory, and provide us with the necessary vision to navigate already chartered lands. In this section, we will explore two maps or models of health.

The first model, pathogenesis, is the study of the origin of disease. It's the model that's most familiar to you and the one that dominates nearly every aspect of our conventional health care system today. It teaches us how things go wrong. Universities, medical schools, and libraries have been erected to integrate, synthesize, and educate this model to our doctors, scientists, social workers, and mental health care practitioners.

All the pathogenic-based books and degree programs teach different stories on the origin of disease from the silo and lens of their perspective specialty. For example, heart disease, for one cardiologist, is a genetic disorder. For the psychiatrist, a stress or brain disorder. Regardless of the specialty, the punchline is always the same—drugs and surgery. Lifestyle contributions, in most conventional settings, are, unfortunately, dismissed or thought of as noncontributory. If advice on dietary and lifestyle measures is given, it is usually an afterthought mimicking how it was taught in their university training.

The second map, salutogenesis, is the study of the origin of health. It focuses on those factors (e.g., diet and lifestyle) that support human health and well-being. In this model, we are told to forget the diagnoses and focus our time, energy, and attention on the fundamentals (health-promoting inputs) such as diet, exercise, and stress reduction practices. The punchline, in this model, is always the same—regardless of disease or diagnosis, start with the fundamentals and allow the body to repair, heal, and regenerate. This, of course, is in stark contrast to the pathogenic model, which studies only those factors that promote or cause disease.

Both maps have pathological versions. In their healthy versions, however, both are necessary and complementing. Far too much time and focus have been spent on disease diagnoses causing doctors and patients to turn a blind eye to the health-promoting inputs. Thus, patients are left waiting to make the necessary changes until confronted with a health crisis. The salutogenic map, presented in the following pages, becomes the starting point for all health-related challenges.

We will explore the following concepts:

- The healthy tenets of both maps, contrasting them with the unhealthy beliefs and practices of our current health care model
- The salutogenic and pathogenic health equations
- Causes of disease, stress, and their perspective anecdotes
- The Unifying Theory of Genetics (UTOG), which contains three unique fields of contributions: epigenetics, metagenetics, and transgenetics
- The origin of wound development

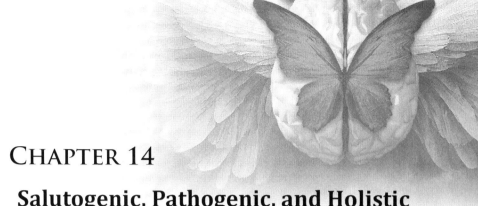

Chapter 14

Salutogenic, Pathogenic, and Holistic Principles

The preservation of health is easier than the cure of disease.
-B.J. Palmer, founder of Chiropractic

To start our discussion, our definition of health will embrace all the previously mentioned tenets, including the concepts of self-actualization and self-transcendence. In addition, I will add the healthy tenets from conventional, traditional, and allopathic medicine along with integrated, holistic, functional, and complementary models. Listed below are some of their most salient principles.

Individuality

Each human being is unique and multi-dimensional. All treatment, therefore, must reflect this biochemical uniqueness. Treatment should not be aimed at the "disease." Rather, it should be redirected to the "person with the disease." For example, the causative nature of one person's diagnosis of depression might be situational (e.g., death of a loved one), for another, a chemical imbalance (e.g., dopamine or serotonin insufficiency), and, for others, could include a myriad of complex factors such as self-worth, poor diet, and abuse (sexual, emotional, mental, physical).

Symptom and Causative Treatment

Treatment should include both symptoms and causes. Neither should be neglected. Symptoms should be reinterpreted as outward manifestations of "dis"ease, representing warning signals (smoke) rather than the inherent cause (fire). We can use symptoms as metaphors and pointers to uncover underlying physical and metaphysical causes which have been neglected, disregarded, or overlooked.

Another important aspect is the concept encapsulated by the phrase, "It was the final straw that broke the camel's back." Let me explain. Symptoms are often the last "straw" in a series of months to years of deleterious dietary and lifestyle abuses. At the time of symptom emergence, whatever behavior we were engaged in becomes erroneously associated or correlated with the said symptom. For example, imagine someone saying, "I bent over in the shower to pick up the soap, and my back just gave out!" In this scenario, the soap, of course, is not the culprit, nor is bending for it at that moment. More likely causes are weak core muscles, postural dysfunctions, or dehydration. Repetitive unhealthy dietary and lifestyle choices load the gun, and the activities in the days or week prior to symptom emergence pull the trigger.

One last way of envisioning this is to think of your body as an inflammatory bucket. Over the years, we have added to the bucket through poor, unhealthy choices. It is not, however, until the bucket overflows that we experience symptoms. This is why some people have a hard time differentiating cause and effect. For example, we can imagine someone helpless in trying to understand why some days a particular food aggravates them and on others it doesn't. We must be careful to distinguish symptoms (e.g., the last thing we ate) and true cause (e.g., the culmination of microaggressions that contribute to increasing the inflammatory bucket).

Prevention

Use of preventative strategies as it is always easier to prevent than treat. This is especially true when speaking about lifestyle diseases, including heart disease, cancer, diabetes, autoimmune, type-2 diabetes, depression, anxiety, osteoporosis, and more.

The Treatment Ladder

Use of noninvasive, nurturing treatments (e.g., diet and lifestyle) before consideration of more intrusive or invasive methodologies (e.g., surgery).

Partnerships, Not Dictatorships

The creation of a doctor/patient partnership is essential rather than establishing a dictatorship of the doctor over the patient. For example, the current "MDiety complex" holds tightly to a view that fosters both patient and doctor as victims rather than participants in the journey to healing. The new and enlightened goal is for doctors to act as teachers, facilitators, students, and coaches while aiding their patients to reestablish autonomy over their health, body, happiness, fulfillment, and life.

The Healing Continuum

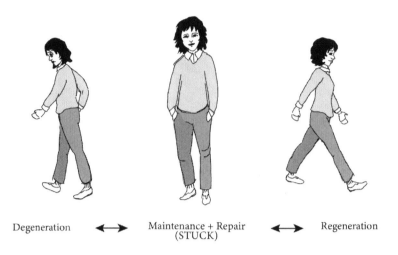

Degeneration ←→ Maintenance + Repair ←→ Regeneration
(STUCK)

The Healing Continuum

Our health is not static. For example, it is impossible to understand someone's health by asking "How are you?" and obtaining a simple "good or bad" response. Rather, health is in a constant state of dynamism and flux. True health is not a destination but rather a journey. We must move away from a binary "you either do or do not have a disease" to a more granulated continuum. This approach allows us to identify "dis"ease before more conventional ideas of pathology arise.

The pathological conventional health continuum is a simplified movement from sick to not sick. It tricks us into thinking that if we are not sick (e.g., no symptoms), then we must be well. However, we only need to look at the following example to understand the dangers of adhering to such a belief. Suppose two people are standing in front of you. One is bleeding, their skin is red, and in pain (a paper cut). The other presents without any symptoms (undiagnosed metastatic cancer). Who is "sick"?

A more nuanced healing continuum goes above and beyond ideas of "the average," "not sick," and "no symptoms." Rather, it includes the fulfillment and actualization of human potential on all dimensions. The new continuum adds the element of thriving as opposed to just surviving.

Physical Changes

For most individuals, our body's "repair and maintenance" button is always on. With a constant attack of harmful dietary and lifestyle choices, our bodies stay in a continuous energy deficit, scrambling to repair and maintain damaged tissues. Ultimately, if the body cannot keep up with the demands, our tissues, cells, and organs will degenerate. This process, called cellular entropy, can be defined as the body's loss of energy, time, and attention for order, reorganization, and healing in favor of cellular disorder, proliferation, inflammation, incoherence, and chaos.

However, if we commit to and remain consistent with dietary and lifestyle excellence practices, we can move from disease to transcendence and regeneration. This includes clean-up (called autophagy) of senescent, zombie-like, nonoptimally functioning cells, proteins, and mitochondria (mitophagy) to the quantum stage of self-organization and cellular regeneration. This is the stage where new healthier cells and tissues are produced at higher-than-expected numbers. Thus, the healing continuum can be summarized as degeneration (two steps back), maintenance and repair (one step forward, one step back), autophagy, clean-up, and recycling (one step forward), and regeneration (two, three, four steps forward).

In short, degeneration occurs when our window of tolerance or ability to adapt to stress is compromised or decreased. In turn, we become brittle and more fragile. Leon Megginson, management and marketing professor at Louisiana State University at Baton Rouge, states, "According to Darwin's Origin of Species, it is not the most intellectual of the species that survives; it is not the strongest that survives, but the species that survives is the one that is able best to adapt and adjust to the changing environment in which it finds itself."

During degeneration, aging accelerates the physiological processes of inflammation, sclerosis (hardening of arteries), oxidation (the process that causes metals to rust), cellular ex-differentiation, and cellular entropy.

The concept of cellular ex-differentiation, according to biologist and professor of genetics David Sinclair, is when "unhealthy" parts of the DNA "unspool" and begin to express or get turned on. Conversely, regeneration reverses inflammation, sclerotic and oxidative damage, activates cellular differentiation (the expression of healthy longevity and anti-aging genes), and increases cellular organization.

Emotional and Mental Change

Along with the physical changes, the healing continuum correlates in the mental and emotional dimensions, as well. In other words, we move from psychological defense, safety, and survival to growth, transcendence, and discovery.

The growth versus safety choice relies on the virtue of courage. Fear is not the obstacle. Our relationship with fear is the problem. We need to move from holding fear in pain, paralysis, hopelessness, and depression to holding fear in tandem with the energies of empowerment, responsibility, and excitement.

We need to feel fear, along with its associative unpleasant emotions, and do the things we are scared of, uncertain of, don't want to do, or don't know how to do. When the gap between where you are and where you want to be is illuminated, and you commit to a definitive yes, courage visits and fuels your journey from surviving to thriving.

Our universal blind spot is that we convince ourselves to wait. Our tomorrows, however, begin to add up to a lifetime. It's as if we all live within the safety and defense of a self-inflicted prison—our limited glass ceiling of potentiality. We must find the courage to allow our fear of regret to be stronger than our fear of failure and mediocrity. As we shatter the defenses and move past what we know is safe, the boundaries of our self-identity expand. In turn, a new and higher glass ceiling replaces the old, and the dance continues as we climb higher and higher to increasing levels of infinite potential. Ultimately, the healing continuum reminds us that our purpose is to grow, learn, and evolve (e.g., transcending and including). Our suffering, in this light, can be used as fuel for growth as we begin to make meaning out of what we thought was meaningless.

In summary, moving from psychological defense and safety to growth, healing, evolution, discovery, and wisdom is bridged by courage.

Above-Down and Inside-Out

Consider our body's intelligence: we have fifty to one-hundred trillion cells in the human body, with something like 100,000 to 200,000 reactions occurring each second in every cell. The number of simultaneous reactions is quite literally breathtaking and mind-boggling. So, are we really that arrogant to believe that healing comes from a spoonful of medicine? That we can coordinate this power? As we begin our healing journey and look to expand our current understanding of health, we must begin to trust in the God-given faculties that instruct and guide our innate wisdom to do what it does best—healing from "above-down and inside-out."

Instead of believing we can micromanage the fifty to one-hundred trillion cells from the outside, we should be striving to allow this innate, inborn intelligence to micromanage from inside of us with the faith and trust in its connection to an eternal reservoir of potentiality. In other words, healing goes from "above-down and inside-out" or from the spiritual to the physical. In doing so, we are called to embody the affirmation, "The power that made the body heals the body." So, you may ask, what exactly is this "power" we are striving to unleash?

It is the very power or mystery that sparked our first breath into life. The power that can direct a simple acorn to actualize into a mighty oak tree, as well as the awe-inspiring power that transforms the caterpillar into the butterfly. It is the power that brings together the sperm and ovum, allows the earth to revolve around the sun, fuels the galaxies, and that which is found in the fifty to one-hundred trillion cells in the human body. Therefore, health becomes a practice of true humility through partnering with and uncovering our divine inheritance and our body's untapped potentialities.

Holism

Holism is the concept of treating the body as a symphony of interactions rather than a reductionist, "organo-centric" medical specialist approach that believes that organs exist in isolation and are in no relation to each other.

CHAPTER 15

The Health Equation

Shallow men believe in luck. Strong men believe in cause and effect.
-Ralph Waldo Emerson

There is a predictable and reliable framework that can be used methodically in the treatment and amelioration of all disease. This framework can be seen dramatically when applied to degenerative and lifestyle diseases such as heart disease, cancer, diabetes, autoimmunity, and osteoporosis. In this section, we will explore and propose a new salutogenic and pathogenic theoretical model. For now, we start with its simplest iteration as represented through the following equation:

The Health Equation

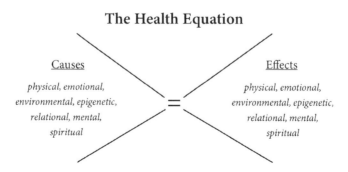

Causes — physical, emotional, environmental, epigenetic, relational, mental, spiritual = Effects — physical, emotional, environmental, epigenetic, relational, mental, spiritual

Using the lens of systems theory, as applied to our health, there is no such thing as a cause-and-effect relationship. Rather, we should begin to view our health as causes and effects. Furthermore, using the lens of quantum mechanics, we move away from victim consciousness. As its substitute, we can embody a participatory cocreator consciousness that asks us to *be the cause to create the effect* and to understand that *you are in charge of your reality, and the moment of power is always found in the forever now moment.*

Everything affects everything. Looking for one single causative agent for every effect will, inevitably, lead you down the proverbial rabbit hole. Consider, as an example, your current diet, your relationship to food, and your habits surrounding food consumption. Can you say with any level of certainty what caused you to eat the way you did today? Of course not. Decisions are driven by factors such as personal taste, addictions, marketing, culture, familial influences, food availability, environment (such as friends and social settings), school education, and so much more. Seeing things as interrelated rather than independent is the key to this new holistic and integrated model. Holism postulates that human beings are multidimensional, diseases are multidimensional, and treatment, therefore, should be multidimensional.

It is naïve to think we can find one simple cause and one magic bullet to heal all our ills. A holistic mindset tells us that all manifestations, phenomena, and experiences have multiple layers, realities, and dimensions in both the subjective and objective domains. For example, in the realm of healthcare, we must take into account the subjective realities of the patient (beliefs, feelings, emotions), their intersubjective realities (culture, relationships, family dynamics), their objective realities (the physical body and all its correlates such as exercise, nutrition, sleep ergonomics), as well as all of the interobjective structures (socioeconomic status, insurance, and so on) that are in place and influencing the patient—albeit consciously or unconsciously.

The Conveyor Belt Metaphor

The health equation, metaphorically, represents the conveyor belt of life. It starts with our birth, ends with our death, and represents our human potential. What determines how fast or slow we walk or are carried along by the conveyor belt are the "causes."

What are the causes?

In short, everything as found within the dimensions of existence—physical, emotional, relational, mental, spiritual, environmental, genetic. They include the most important of all the contributing factors—our choices and the stories we tell ourselves.

If we eat healthy, exercise, love, and forgive, the conveyor belt may slow down. On the flip side, if we engage in unhealthy eating habits, smoking, and other addictions, the conveyor belt may speed up. In the former, the person's biological age (age of their cells) is lower than their chronological age (the number we tell someone when they ask us our age). In the latter, the person's biological age is greater than their chronological age and can, inevitably, lead to decreased quality of life and premature death.

Stressors or Causes

We will define and attribute stressors to be the sole cause of disease and health promotion. From this perspective, stress can be used as a synonym for the causes as found within the dimensions (PERMS) categorized as physical (P) and non-physical (ERMS).

Stress can generally be acute or chronic and intermittent or constant. Stressors can be thought of as inputs that cause the body to adapt. This adaptation, in turn, initiates a stress response (the effect), categorized as good (eustress), bad (distress), and extra good or bad (hermetic). For example, walking is a low-stress activity (eustress). Running a marathon might be considered a high-stress activity (distress) if a lack of preparedness and a shortened rest and recovery period are not adhered to. Hermetic stress represents a special kind of stress where one goes slightly past the Goldilocks rule (not too much, not too little) just to the point of over stress but never crossing.

Physical Stressors

Physical stressors are easy to identify in the world of the concrete. A short list includes the following:

- Physical traumas such as a broken leg
- Physical environment we bathe in
- Diet including processed foods and factory-farmed animal products
- Movement or lack thereof
- Toxins
  - o Biotoxins or toxins that are alive such as yeast, bacteria, fungus, mold, and parasites
  - o Exotoxins or environmental toxins that are not alive coming from the outside-in which can be further broken down into natural and manmade

- Allergens
- Contaminated and polluted air and water
- Drugs and vaccines
- Alkylphenols such as hygiene products, food packaging, and household cleaners
- Organochlorides such as DDT and PCBs
- Volatile organic compounds (VOS) such as gasoline, paint fumes, and exhaust fumes
- Organophosphates such as pesticides and insecticides
  o Endotoxins or toxins that are not alive coming from inside-out, such as waste products made by various biochemical pathways in the body (e.g., free radicals) and our gut bacteria

Nonphysical Stressors

Nonphysical stressors are less identifiable but just as contributory as their physical counterparts. They include:

- EMFs or electromagnetic pollution from cell towers, microwaves, X-Rays, electronics, and the like
- emotional, mental, relational, and spiritual influences
- cultural indoctrination (memes)
- trans-generational influences from the collective unconscious

The Stress Response

Regardless of the stressors, they collectively elicit a stress response or adaptation within the body. When bad stressors (sedentary lifestyle, environmental toxins, poor diet, and toxic relationships) exceed our body's stress resiliency threshold or window, we will see, as an effect, ill health, stunted growth, starved potentials, and aberrant physiological changes such as chronic inflammation, chaotic energies, and incoherence.

But with good stressors (exercise, eating healthy, and self-care practices) we will see nourishing, healing, and regenerative changes that, cumulatively, actualize our human potential and create coherence within the body.

Hormesis: When Bad Stress is Actually Good Stress

Hormesis is best understood and defined by its opposite, the traditional dose-response curve. The traditional curve tells us that the more you take of a substance, the greater the effect and vice versa (e.g., drugs and alcohol). By contrast, hormesis is the phenomenon whereby small things produce greater than expected changes and effects.

Well-known examples include vaccines and homeopathic medicines. In this light, small amounts of a potentially noxious substance (if given at higher doses) create larger than expected positive and protective results. These smaller doses help to inoculate and strengthen one's adaptability for a future noxious encounter.

Hormesis presents us with one of life's paradoxes. Namely, certain bad stressors, in small amounts, are advantageous and can increase survival, reverse aging, and increase longevity. In other words, intermittent exposure to extreme stressors (rather than chronic exposure) can unexpectedly turn a so-called bad stressor into a good stressor.

A well-known example is exercise. Initially, the stress load (e.g., weightlifting) causes muscular tears and inflammation. Hours and days later, however, the body responds with compensatory changes that make the muscles stronger and your cardiovascular system more efficient.

From the works of David Sinclair to Italian-American biogerontologist and cell biologist Valter Longo and many others, it appears hormesis activates very specific longevity genes (e.g., mTOR, Sirtuins, and AMPK) that move us through the healing continuum from degeneration to autophagy to cellular regeneration.

Some of the key metrics these longevity genes are tracking include amino acid levels (higher than normal protein levels), caloric intake, sugar levels, and environmental extremes, including oxygen deprivation and temperature changes. Translating this into practical application, we are encouraged to change our daily eating habits from an overburdened caloric, processed foods, and animal-based high protein diet (e.g., standard American diet) to a whole food plant-based approach that stabilizes our sugar levels and decreases our overall lifetime caloric burden.

Let's look at a few hermetic examples. Starvation is destructive to an organism. Intentional, intuitive, and controlled fasting, however, is one of the greatest antiaging and longevity tools known to man and womankind. We move away from an endless barrage of snacking and meals to allow the body to move through the healing continuum more efficiently and with greater frequency. Adversity and trauma, for some, can be redirected into fuel for growth, purpose, and resiliency. Finally, extremes of heat or cold will kill us, while optimal exposure (e.g., infrared saunas and cryotherapy) can be health-promoting.

In short, chronic exposure to bad stressors that extend past our ability to adapt or recover is destructive to our health (e.g., an injury versus exercise). On the other hand, optimal, intermittent, controlled, and deliberate exposure to certain extremes of bad stressors turns on autophagy, stem cell production, antiaging, and longevity genes. As the saying goes, what doesn't kill us makes us stronger and more adaptable.

Remember, we have needs for certainty (comfort) and uncertainty (discomfort). Our society is built on comfort. We have enough food, shelter, live in air-conditioned buildings (temperature is always the same), and our risk of dying, as compared to our ancestors, is minimal. Living a life that shelters us from intermittent hermetic inoculations that help to strengthen and challenge our window of tolerance and adaptability will inevitably make us fragile, brittle, more vulnerable, and keep our longevity genes in a state of dormancy.

Nature has set up hormesis to be reciprocal. For example, eating plants that have been optimally stressed can cause the plant to respond by producing larger than normal amounts of phytonutrients (plant chemicals) referred to as stress mimicking nutrients (e.g., resveratrol, berberine, and quercetin). The nutrients of optimally stressed foods convey their beneficial effects on the consumer when eaten, mimicking a similar effect to that of, for example, exercising and fasting.

Finally, there is a special class of toxins not defined or recognized by hard science. Although these toxins are often overlooked or discredited, their contributions to our health should not be dismissed. In short, they carry energies of karma (cause and effect) and include:

> • Macrometaphysical: toxins that are tangible or detectible through scientific inquiry (For example, it is well documented that animals, at the time of slaughter, have higher than normal levels of the stress hormone cortisol within their body. This increase can create a cascade of aberrant physiological changes within the animal, which, in turn, are passed on to the consumer.)

- Micrometaphysical: toxins that are intangible or unde-
tectable through current scientific inquiry (They are
intangible subatomic or para-atomic energies with negative hormetic effects. In other words, it would be unwise
and naïve to think that the torment, torture, and mass
confinement imposed on sentient creatures and imple-
mented through modern-day factory farming practices
have no consequences or ripple effect.)

Identification of Stressors: Excess, Deficiencies, and Incoherence

Using and building upon ancient wisdom, we can identify stressors
by looking at the following three components: excesses, deficiencies,
and incoherent energies.

If we look at physical influences, we can easily identify excesses
and deficiencies in the overconsumption of food and the deficiencies of individual vitamins and minerals. In the world of nonphysical
influences, we have everything from the deficiencies in the universal
human needs (safety, security, love, self-esteem) to the excesses of
our monkey mind, the weight of our emotional baggage (fear, pain,
anger, hatred, jealousy, and guilt), and overconsumption of media
(TV, newspaper, radio, and social media).

The concept of imbalance or incoherence denotes, in a broad
sense, all the energies running through the dimensions in need of
coherence. The ancient wisdom traditions tell us that life exists in
duality, as inseparable and contradictory opposites such as light-dark,
male-female, up-down, love-fear, life-death, being-doing, and old-
young. It's as if the pairs of equal opposites attract and complement
each other. The yin yang symbol, an ancient concept in Chinese

philosophy, helps to illustrate this point. Each side has within its core element a small piece of the other. An increase in one brings a corresponding decrease in the other. Neither pole is superior. Finding coherence is the goal.

The greatest level of coherence occurs when we activate The Alignment Continuum, creating coherence between our soul's awareness, our mind's attention, our heart's intention, and our actions and behaviors. In doing so, our triune brain (plus the angel lobes) syncs up and catapults us to new and higher levels of potentiality.

In summary, stress is the cause of all disease and health promotion, broken down into physical, non-physical, good, and bad stressors having any of the following characteristics:

- Excesses
- Deficiencies
- Incoherent energies

The Antidote: Removal, Nourishment, and Coherence

Once we identify the things of excess, the things of deficiency, and those out-of-alignment elements of incoherence, treatment can be viewed as a simplified application of:

1. Removal or transcendence of excesses
2. Nourishment of deficiencies (Nutrients, in this context, are redefined as anything that nourishes our physical, emotional, relational, mental, and spiritual bodies. This includes intangible universal human needs and the more conventional definition of nutrients that emphasize only the physical aspects of food, such as macronutrients and micronutrients.)
3. Coherence and fulfillment of incoherent or imbalanced energies such that we integrate, transcend, and include all aspects of the PERMS continuum

CHAPTER 16

The Unifying Theory of Genetics (UTOG)

The collective unconscious contains the whole spiritual heritage of
mankind's evolution born anew in the brain structure of
every individual.

-Carl Jung

Now that we understand the basics, we will turn our attention to
various nuances of the health equation as we further elucidate causes
and effects. Here is a more expanded version of the health equation:

Causes (Nature + Nurture) = Effects (Systems, Mediators, Signs,
Symptoms, Diagnoses)

The true cause of all diseases can be thought of as the dance
between nature and nurture. Classically, nature has been confined to
the inheritable factors or traits stored in our DNA (classical genetics),
the great Book of Life, handed down to us from parents to offspring
at the moment of conception. Nurture (epigenetics), on the other

side, represents the environment that this genetic blueprint bathes in, such as our diet and lifestyle (e.g., the PERMS).

It may be helpful to view nature as analogous to a book of matches. Nurture, on the other hand, represents all the physical and nonphysical environmental factors (toxins, nutrition, pollution) that could potentially come into contact and strike the match. The new paradigm tells us that the factors that strike the match (epigenetics) rule over previously held genetic determinism. We can no longer abandon our cocreative responsibility, feeling as if we are mere victims of our inheritance. In fact, the single greatest contributing factor in how our genes are expressed lies, simply and emphatically, in our daily choices.

The dance of nature and nurture (the environment striking the match) produces physical and energetic changes in the organism, referred to as systems and mediators. In our continuing analogy, these components are represented as fire. The systems include all the macro events in the body, such as various cells, tissues, and organs working together (cardiovascular system, the endocrine system, the nervous system). The mediators represent the more micro-events such as substances produced and used by cells for communication (hormones, cholesterol, inflammation, blood sugar, oxygen, and other biomarkers) which can often be quantified through objective diagnostic testing.

In the final part of the equation, the mediators and system-wide changes give rise to our phenotypic expression or outwardly appearing signs, symptoms (fatigue, pain, headache), and diagnoses (diabetes, autoimmunity, cancer). These elements are analogous to the smoke produced by the lit match.

The pathogenic model focuses its attention on the smoke and singularly chosen mediators (e.g., cholesterol), while the salutogenic model focuses on systems and causes. In review:

- The match represents nature or our genetics.
- The factors that strike the match represent nurture or the environment.
- Both, the match and that which strikes the match, represent the cause.
- The fire represents mediators (e.g., physiological damage such as cholesterol, glucose, and inflammation) and body systems (e.g., cardiovascular and nervous).
- The smoke represents signs, symptoms, and diagnoses.
- Both the fire and the smoke represent effects.

Where We Are Going

The unifying theory of genetics is an expansion of the physical environmental factors, targets, and mechanisms. It adds nonphysical factors, targets, and mechanisms that extend beyond the body (metagenetics) and transcend the body (transgenetics).

We will continue to use classical genetics as our framework and, at the same time, present new concepts that serve to transcend atomistic "physical" thinking. We will be discussing the field of epigenetics and the newly proposed emerging fields that are best described as metagenetics (beyond our genes) and transgenetics (transcending our genes).

To summarize what is to follow, it is helpful to think broadly about what exactly is being contrasted—namely, the old and new paradigms.

The old paradigm states that nature consists of physically inheritable factors (genes and chromosomes) that were presumably given to us at the moment of conception from our parents. Nurture, on the other hand, represents the sum of all the nongenetic environmental factors influencing the DNA.

The new paradigm extends nature past the DNA to other physical and nonphysical components of the mind-body complex. The DNA, for example, no longer serves as the sole recipient and transmitter of genetic inheritance. Nurture, in the new paradigm, extends environmental influences to nonphysical factors throughout one's entire life cycle: transgenerational, preconception (time before conception), periconception (time around conception), conception, in utero, and post-utero (infancy to childhood to adolescence to adulthood). In short, the new paradigm includes both the physical and nonphysical dimensions of existence.

Epigenetics

Epigenetics means above, upon, or over and refers to all the accepted physical influences acting on the physical components of our DNA through the well-established biochemical processes such as DNA transcription, translation, and gene expression. In other words, environmental influences working on the DNA determine which genes are turned on and which ones are turned off through various biochemical objectifiable mechanisms.

It may be helpful to think of our genes as analogous to a great big "choose your own adventure" book. These childhood books allowed one to choose a new ending or storyline by turning to a specific page. In this analogy, our genes are analogous to the actual physical book. Perhaps, we inherited a chapter on autoimmunity? A chapter on cancer? A chapter on depression?

In the past, science embraced the idea that if we inherited one of these chapters (genes), we were then destined to become victims of the information held within the pages of that specific chapter (our inheritance). We now know that how the book is read, what story is chosen, what new story is written, what pages are omitted, what pages become faded over time, and what order the pages are read are all determined by epigenetics (e.g., the choices we make).

Some of the most convincing research that lends credence to overturning the old paradigm of genetic determinism exists in population migration studies. For example, in a study published in *Cancer Epidemiology Biomarkers and Prevention*, the results showed that breast cancer risk was 50 percent lower in foreign-born Hispanics than in their US-born Hispanic counterparts. Risk increased, however, with increasing duration of residence in the United States, decreasing age at migration, and increasing acculturation. In other words, migration studies show a direct correlation with increased rates of certain cancers as migrants move from low-risk countries to high-risk westernized countries. If it were all in the genes, the location where you lived would not matter.

In 2001, the results of the Human Genome Project were announced to the world with unexpected results and mixed reactions. The findings would forever change our understanding of genetics. The goal of this international scientific research project was to identify and map the genes within the human genome (our DNA).

Genes can be thought of as instructional codes for protein synthesis. At the time of the research project, it was believed that the body made approximately 100,000 proteins. The working hypothesis and expectation was a 1:1 ratio of genes to proteins (e.g., the body should have at least 100,000 genes). However, what they found was in stark contrast.

Our human genome has approximately 20,000 to 25,000 genes. This is the same number as found in mice and roundworms. To put this in perspective, grape plants have 30,000 genes and the water flea, Daphnia pulex, has 31,000. In addition, we also share 98 percent of our DNA with chimpanzees, 36 percent with fruit flies, and 25 percent with a grain of rice. This obviously was a huge blow to scientists and those who embraced speciesism or the specialness, dominion, and uniqueness of humans.

Scientists assumed, and pharmaceutical companies dreamed that they would find a gene for every disease—an obesity gene, a diabetes gene, a heart attack gene, and so on. Scientists and biotech companies were devastated as the story unfolded and emphatically stated that there was not a simple one gene, one disease correlate. There must be more to the story– and, of course, there was.

The debunking of the one gene, one disease correlation is analogous to a piano player (epigenetics) playing a piano (our DNA). The scientists were studying the piano but not the piano player. The expression of health-promoting genes or disease-promoting genes is more like a melody or chord rather than a single note. If we, for example, eat healthy, exercise, and bathe ourselves in a nurturing environment, then a Mozart-like health-promoting symphony is created.·On the opposite spectrum, if we engage in unhealthy eating, a sedentary lifestyle, and bathe ourselves in a toxic environment, then the combination of notes "played" would be disease-promoting, childish, nonmusical, incoherent, or amateur at best. The problem with the Human Genome project stemmed from the very questions they were asking. In other words, it's impossible to find Mozart's symphony in just one piano key.

Although epigenetics has been a momentous leap forward in our understanding of genetics, the key takeaway is that both the "causes and effects" are pigeon-holed in the physical dimension of existence, with a few references to the contrary. The classically accepted epigenetic physical factors refer to the foods we eat, the water we drink, the air we breathe, past surgeries, whether we obtain adequate sunshine (vitamin D), the prescriptions or supplements we consume, whether we were born through natural childbirth or surgical C-section, sleep hygiene, and exposure to toxins.

The story of our genes and DNA can no longer be thought of as the sole key to unlocking the mysteries of who we are and disease prevention and treatment.

Metagenetics and Transgentics

Before we begin this discussion, it will be helpful to clarify the factors that will be contrasted:

- Environmental factors are the external inputs or influences coming towards the human body, such as diet, air quality, and water intake.
- Targets are the areas in the human body where these environmental factors are received or targeted (classically seen as the DNA).
- Mechanisms refer to the reactions or effects produced from environmental factors interacting and working upon their target (e.g., the classically held mechanisms of biochemical DNA transcription and translation).
- Targets and mechanisms include the full spectrum of how information is received, transformed, and assimilated.

Metagenetics

The prefix "meta" means beyond. In this context, we are discussing concepts that lie beyond the physical environmental factors (e.g., diet and lifestyle), targets (e.g., DNA), and mechanisms (e.g., DNA translation and transcription). We are transcending and including epigenetics but adding the following:

- Nonphysical environmental factors such as needs satiation (safety, security, love, belongingness, meaning, contribution), limiting beliefs, and other subjective interpretations. Although there are no "physical traces" to these well-accepted influences, most people would find it hard to deny their influences on our overall life satisfaction, health, aging, and longevity. Nonphysical environmental factors also include information influencing our body as carried by sound, light, EMFs, and other waveforms from the electromagnetic spectrum.
- Nonphysical targets or the entire spectrum of mind and body, which includes but is not limited to the DNA. Nature includes the entire human body, from its most gross (tangible) to its most subtle energies (intangible).
- Nonphysical mechanisms produced by the body beyond the simplistic biochemical model (DNA transcription and translation and the "lock and key" cell receptors model).

Discussing all these metagenic factors, targets, and mechanisms is beyond the scope of this book. I will, however, point to a few ideas that I hope will clarify any ambiguity.

From the studies of Fritz-Albert Popp, a German researcher in biophysics, and others, emerged the startling discovery that all biological organisms emit light (bio-photons). The biophoton theory and other experimental research showed that DNA in living cells store, receive, and release photons. These light particles help to transmit information within and between cells. The DNA is, in fact, one of the body's largest warehouses of biophoton emissions. It's as if the DNA is acting like a master tuning fork sending out information (frequencies) to various atoms, cells, tissues, and organs, allowing for instantaneous communication. Examples of common everyday technologies using light (e.g., red light therapy and lasers) are well documented to stimulate cell healing, reduce inflammation, and more.

In addition to biophotonic energy, the human body responds to sound (bioacoustical). Consider well-known examples such as the application of therapeutic ultrasound to an injured area, diagnostic ultrasound to create pictures of the developing fetus, use of sound waves to break up kidney stones (e.g., shock wave lithotripsy), or the simple act of listening to our favorite song or a guided meditation.

Completing the list of nonphysical influences and attributes, the body is made up of quantum subatomic particles which are "extra-sensory" in nature (bioquantum), produce and respond to chemicals (biochemical), and emit and respond to electro-magnetic impulses (bio-electromagnetic) such as those produced by our heart, brain, and nervous system. Research from the Heart Math Institute has quantified the presence of an electric field produced by the heart, extending ten feet from the gross physical body. One can imagine or may have experienced this phenomenon as we recall a time when we may have entered a room and sensed an immediate problem or the idiom, "You could have heard a pin drop."

The human body receives, senses, communicates, and expresses through complex networks and mechanisms, which I refer to as "quantum-sensing." Quantum is used to signify the nonphysical, extrasensory realms, while "sensing" is used to signify our current classical physical understandings (touch, taste, smell).

Thus, quantum-sensing is the transmission and receiving of information through various energies and mediums consisting of but not limited to the following: biophotonic, bioacoustical, bioelectro-magnetic, bioquantum, and biochemical. From a commonsense per-spective, there are approximately fifty to one-hundred trillion cells in the human body, each undergoing an average of 200,000 separate reactions per second. Some estimate 37 billion billion reactions a second occurring in the body at any given time. The coordination of your entire body feeling a state of instantaneous joy cannot be explained by biochemical processes alone.

One final example and research area lie in the exploration of fascia, microtubules, and the crystalline structures found in our bone matrix. Collectively, they make up our connective tissue matrix and are composed of a triple helix of protein molecules wound tightly around a central tubule. These structures spread out like the branches of a tree, terminating into a small network of filaments or antennae to each and every one of our 50-100+ trillion cells. They exist, literally, in every crevice of the human body. Some researchers have purported that quantum-sensing information can be carried instantaneously throughout this complex network in addition to the master tuning fork analogy of our DNA.

Transgenetics

The prefix "trans" means transcending. Thus, transgentics refers to influences, targets, and mechanisms of "inheritance" that literally transcend the physical body. For example:

- Nurture expands to include the entire life cycle of an individual: transgenerational (influence of past generational shadows), preconception (before conception), periconception (time around conception), conception, inutero (the life of the aquatic interdependent fetus), and post-utero (childhood to adolescence to adulthood).
- Energy fields of other people and animals
- The collective unconscious, archetypes, and morphogenic field modes of psychological transmission
- Cultural memes defined as an idea, behavior, or style that spreads through initiation from person to person within a culture. Memes are regarded as cultural analogs to genes in that they self-replicate, mutate and respond to selective pressures. Memes, in some ways, are just another semantic play on the collective unconscious and morphogenic fields.
- Evolutionary impulses seen literally everywhere in existence and described by Integral Theory, such as the impulses of Eros, Agape, agency, and communion.
- Miasms (an old homeopathic term), describing units of energetic, nonphysical inheritance.
- Spiritual patterns of karma, patterns of death and rebirth inherited through the cycles of samsara and nirvana as discussed by the world's perennial wisdom traditions.

Summary

The expanded ideas of meta- and transgenetics are simply an attempt to add language to something that I believe most of us already accept—namely that nonphysical factors have an influence and a real impact on our overall well-being and health.

CHAPTER 17

Pathogenesis and Wound Development

It is one thing to process memories of trauma, but it is an entirely different matter to confront the inner void—the holes in the soul that result from not having been wanted, not having been seen, and not having been allowed to speak the truth.

-Bessel A. van der Kolk

All of us have wounds. As previously discussed, the primal struggle creates a needs dynamic that starts in childhood and continues to our dying day. In this brief section, we will explore how wounds become encoded and sclerotic (hardened) within the body's subconscious mind, cells, tissue, fascia, and biofield.

During our formative years, we are exposed to "little t" and "big T" traumas. Whether or not the wound digests itself or becomes encoded depends on the intensity (high or low) and duration (acute, sudden, gradual, or ongoing). Big T traumas have been studied extensively and are called adverse childhood experiences (ACEs). The original study by the CDC and Kaiser Permanente in 1997 looked at abuse (physical, emotional, and sexual), neglect (physical and emotional), and household challenges (divorce, incarcerated parent, substance abuse, domestic violence, and mental illness). Since then, other ACEs have been studied, including poverty, discrimination, racism, and more. ACEs are traumatic events that occur in childhood (0-17 years) and are directly linked to chronic health problems, mental illness, substance abuse, relational issues, and job opportunities as that child becomes an adult.

Wound creation occurs as the body-mind complex internalizes the dysfunctions of the primary caregivers (traumas) and encodes them with strategies it felt were appropriate at the time. This encoding includes complex interactions of needs dynamics, triggers, emotions, and reactions. It has been suggested that traumas are stored as dysfunctions in the biofield first (e.g., the subtle energy blueprint), which then direct or inform our physiology.

Interestingly, the traumas in the first few years of life create wounds and imprints that are more biological than psychological. In other words, impulses, sensations, symbols, perceptions, raw emotions, and images come online first and serve as the primary tools for encoding. We can call these early childhood wounds our "core primordial beliefs." They are characteristically rudimentary, preverbal, binary, and elementary childhood complexes tied to specific needs without the complication of "story." This primal software, which is still running our life, is hard to "locate" or intuit as the preverbal encoding mechanisms are stored deep within the subconscious mind-body complex. Words, rules, concepts, beliefs, and mental models develop later.

Initially, our core primordial beliefs were simple strategies for survival and needs attainment. If they could talk or had "language," they would be straightforward and binary such as *I am, you are,* and *the world is.* Examples include, *I am safe* versus *I am not safe, I am loved* versus *I am not loved, the world is friendly* versus *the world is unfriendly,* and *whatever I need is available* (precursor to the abundance mindset) versus *nothing is available* (precursor to the scarcity mindset).

In today's pop culture is a metaphysical theory correlating our physical symptoms with childish mechanisms and causes. For example, if you have eye or ear pain, you may not be looking at your life correctly or listening to your true authentic voice. However, are these correlates nonsensical and childish? Is there a thread of truth contained within?

Since the initial conflicts or wounds cannot be stored explicitly or verbally, they are stored implicitly and somatically (within the body). This encoding, therefore, is biosymbolic, where the symbology (meaning) is found within the body's biology. How this happens, scientists don't quite understand. We can, however, hypothesize.

There are basic physiological processes accepted, identified, and categorized within the body. They include transport, assimilation, structural integrity, communication, defense/repair, energy production, and elimination. If the initial conflict or wound was correlated with protection and safety, it's not farfetched to think the primal protection mechanisms were brought together with barrier and defense physiology such as skin, mucosa, and inflammation. Other ideas hypothesized include the following correlates: loss of meaning with immune compromise and inability to create healthy boundaries (e.g., not being able to say "no") with autoimmunity (immune system attacking self).

Why This Is Important

Trauma leads to wounds. Wounds, in turn, are encoded at the level of consciousness the person had at the time of the trauma. For example, a child encodes their wounds with pre-verbal complexes and adults with verbal and nonverbal complexes. The sclerotic nature of the wound holds the consciousness, mental structures, and age that existed at the time of trauma. In adulthood, wounds become triggered, consciously or subconsciously, and emerge as an embodiment of a child's reactive pattern that shows up in adult's clothing.

Our brain can replay our wounds by projecting the past onto the present. What once served us may no longer be protective or nourishing. Most of our habits started out as simple and functional. Today, however, they have morphed into something complex and dysfunctional. Faking an illness at a young age to avoid going to school to confront a bully could play out in adulthood in various social settings causing dysfunctional introversion. These old scars and wounds are about what happened in the past, yet they are busy running our lives and often distracting us from the present moment.

Children, of course, are dependent on adults to care for them. If an adult is psychologically wounded, unaware of their own need's dynamics (e.g., how to meet their own needs), and not ready to parent, they will, inevitably, pass their wounds onto their children, who will, in turn, pass them onto their children. Some of the most primal wounds are abandonment, rejection, betrayal, shame, and injustice.

Since we all have wounds, it is vital to bring them to the light of awareness. We must identify our core wounds so we can understand them, know what triggers them, and can change our relationship with them. In this manner, wounds and trauma can either inoculate us for greater resiliency or make us more vulnerable. If one does not heal old unresolved wounds, they become triggers, perhaps a vice or a virtue.

Some of the greatest sources of trauma today are undigested emotions, and frustrated or unmet needs. Emotions have a beginning, middle, and end. Emotions, as discussed earlier, are intimately tied to needs acquisition. If needs remain unmet and emotions are not allowed to complete their cycle, they may get entangled, stuck in the middle, and linked to a chronic stress response cycle (wound) or a maladaptive physiological pattern.

PART 3

The Territory

Some people want it to happen, some wish it would happen, others make it happen.

-Michael Jordan

Here's where the rubber meets the road as we move from the theoretical to the practical. We will discuss the following topics:

- The Focus Funnel: the exact framework for treatment prioritization using the ingredients of awareness, sorting out, first things first, and second things second
- The key or fundamental practices to start your health and wellness journey including diet, movement, and self-care practices
- Advanced techniques for subconscious reprogramming, anti-aging, and longevity
- The Miracle Method: learn how to live and create a miraculous life
- Best practices in each of the dimensions

Chapter 18

The Focus Funnel

Simplicity boils down to two steps: Identify the essential.
Eliminate the rest.

-Leo Babauta

To preface this section, I will be using inspiration from the metaphysical text, *A Course in Miracles* and the Serenity Prayer by Reinhold Niebuhr. It asks us to concentrate our time, attention, intention, and energies on those things we have control over and to surrender to those things to which we do not. The most widely distributed version is:

> *God, grant me the serenity to accept the things I cannot change, courage to change the things I can, and wisdom to know the difference.*

We can further granulate the things we can and can't control by adding the concept *first things first*, introduced by Stephen Covey in his book *The 7 Habits of Highly Effective People*.

First things first, from our context, represents a process of identifying and then prioritizing the most important and nurturing practices (eating healthy, exercising, loving more, forgiving more) that make the largest contributions towards our happiness, well-being, inner peace, fulfillment, and overall health. It asks that we commit to organizing our life around that which is most valuable rather than on the minutia of activities that create a mundane life of quiet desperation—the valueless (second things second).

Combining the Serenity Prayer with the ideas of miracle-mindedness, we have, the Miracle Prayer.

The Miracle Prayer

> *Grant me the wisdom to distinguish between the things I can and cannot control.*
>
> *Grant me the wisdom to distinguish the valuable from the valueless.*
>
> *Grant me the wisdom to distinguish the nourishing from the non-nourishing.*
>
> *Grant me the wisdom to know who I am and who I'm not.*
>
> *Grant me the wisdom to distinguish love from fear and truth from illusion.*
>
> *Grant me the courage to embody this wisdom as I remove the blocks to the awareness of love's presence, make peace with my past, create a vision for my future, and live in the present, one moment and miracle at a time.*

First Things First, Second Things Second

With all the myriad of environmental inputs, the choices we have, and the treatment options available, we frequently find ourselves consumed by the energies of paralysis by analysis. So, we ask, "Where do we begin this journey?" and "What exactly should we focus our attention upon?" It's as if we desperately need a systematic, fluid, and nondogmatic map directing us when, how, where, why, and what to prioritize. The Focus Funnel is our answer. It consists of four distinct parts: *awareness, sorting out, first things first,* and *second things second.*

Starting with awareness, we are asked to become aware of our life–our thoughts, emotions, feelings, beliefs, behaviors, and circumstances (factually, without attached stories). Next, we begin to sort out the things we can control from the things we can't. In other words, it is just as important to know what to focus on as it is to "unfocus" on. Unfortunately, so many of us spend far too much of our precious time and energies on life's uncontrollable factors. In doing so, we create a psychological cancer that ultimately metastasizes, distracts, and contracts our precious awareness away from those things that matter most. The goal is to invest our valuable energies on the controllable and surrender (not forget, suppress, alienate, or repress) to the things we have deemed as uncontrollable.

The third and fourth steps in The Focus Funnel are applying the concept of *first things first* and *second things second* to the identified controllable factors. *First things first* represent our roots and fundamentals. A short list would include diet, exercise, and self-care practices. It is prioritization towards the lowest hanging fruit. It includes the activities, actions, behaviors, and choices that help provide the largest impact on our physical, emotional, relational, mental, and spiritual health.

First things first challenges us to identify the most important and nurturing activities (that we are either doing or not doing) that contribute to the majority of our happiness, well-being, inner peace, and health. These are the areas, habits, and activities we want to highlight as our nonnegotiables. Once identified, our goal is to laser-focus our awareness, attention, intention, and actions on them.

Most individuals live a life in complete opposition to this principle as they laser-focus their time, energy, and money on the minutia of activities that matter least. It's as if the majority of our activities are useless, valueless, draining, and nonnurturing and include such things as watching TV, surfing our phones, and running errands.

In today's health care arena, the mindset is often *second things first* and *first things never.* Imagine an all-too-common example of a doctor reviewing a patient's blood work, "I'm sorry to tell you, but your labs indicate a diagnosis of diabetes. I'm prescribing you a blood sugar lowering medication." This scenario represents our current healthcare system whereby pharmaceuticals are prescribed prematurely with no discussion about the use of noninvasive methodologies (e.g., diet and lifestyle) first.

I am also reminded by the daily onslaught of well-intentioned but misguided patients who have come into my practice over the years inquiring about specific supplements, biohacks, and dietary and fitness trends to help their X-Y-Z condition. The contradiction, however, is apparent. They are simultaneously searching for a panacea while, at the same time, engaging in destructive habits, such as eating unhealthy, smoking, consuming excess alcohol, and more.

Focusing on second, third, and fourth things keeps us blindsighted and in a cloud of unnecessary confusion. Our attention should instead be hyperfocused on the big picture, *first things first.* Getting lost in the details of a specific diet book or exercise video without focusing on the *first things first* is often a distraction, a form of avoidance, and a recipe for failure.

Every one of us can begin, without complicating the matter, to eat more whole foods, eliminate processed foods, nurture our closest relationships, love more, and forgive more. The key is to create healthy habits and replace the unhealthy ones. Remember, you can't build upon a habit that has not yet been started.

As a reminder, when treatment is applied holistically, we create synergy, coherence, and multiplication. For example, diet, exercise, and self-care practices, when combined, will produce greater effects than each one alone. Einstein is quoted as saying, "The most powerful force in the universe is compound interest."

The Focus Funnel

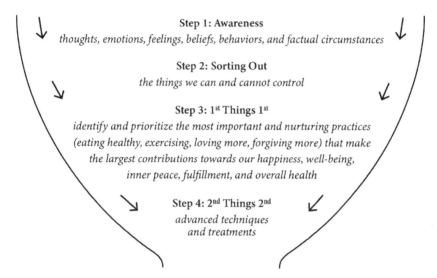

Step 1: Awareness
thoughts, emotions, feelings, beliefs, behaviors, and factual circumstances

Step 2: Sorting Out
the things we can and cannot control

Step 3: 1st Things 1st
identify and prioritize the most important and nurturing practices (eating healthy, exercising, loving more, forgiving more) that make the largest contributions towards our happiness, well-being, inner peace, fulfillment, and overall health

Step 4: 2nd Things 2nd
advanced techniques and treatments

The Focus Funnel

The Focus Funnel mirrors a concept referred to as minimalism. The minimalist ideal, contrary to some interpretations, has nothing to do with minimizing physical possessions, although this is often the outcome. Rather, it is the art and science of releasing the baggage of excess that burdens our spiritual growth, evolution, and contributions. It is about living a life centered on that which is valuable (rather than on the valueless) and working diligently to rid oneself of life's heavy excesses that distract us from living.

Psychologist Oliver Burkeman describes the drive for efficiency and productivity as a kind of trap. We believe we have too little time and too much to accomplish. Time is seen as a container where every minute must be filled. Ironically, the more we fill up the minutes and hours, the less accomplished we feel. We may even find ourselves doing more of what is less important. Business coach Paul Watts summarizes this perfectly, "You can't be effective without being efficient, but you can be efficient without being effective."

In this light, The Focus Funnel attempts to identify the most fundamental dimensional practices and factors within each area of the health equation (causes, mediators, systems, signs, and symptoms) that deserve our time, energy, and attention.

Factors

- Causes or dimensional practices (see below)
- Systems: detox, regeneration, gut/immune, and communication
    - Detox: cleaning the old (autophagy) and eliminating or decreasing the body's toxic burden (biotoxins, environmental toxins) while supporting all organs of elimination (liver, kidney, skin, lymphatics)
    - Regeneration: enhancing and supporting genetic signaling mechanisms that move us along the healing continuum from degeneration to regeneration, surviving to thriving, and allow activation of anti-aging and longevity gene expression (e.g., stem cell production) while, simultaneously, dampening their antagonists

o Gut/immune: healing and repairing the gastrointestinal system to help increase the efficiency, quality, and quantity of absorption (ultimately maximizing energy production called cellular metabolism and respiration), restoring the microbiome, establishing proper gut/brain signaling, strengthening the immune system, and decreasing inflam-aging

o Communication: restoring maladaptive conscious and subconscious programs to ones that are more nourishing and constructive

- Communication includes everything from our nervous system (brain and spinal cord), endocrine glands (hormones), and neurotransmitters to the quantum-sensing mechanisms discussed earlier. The goal is to create coherence (e.g., aligning brain, heart, and respiration) for the coordination, healing, and regeneration of every cell, tissue, organ, and co-habitant (e.g., friendly bacteria) within the body. Communication strengthens our stress resilience, window of tolerance, and overall adaptability. Our ultimate level of communication, however, is aligning to our higher Self and taking the hero's journey to self-actualization and self-transcendence.

• Mediators: inflammation, sugar imbalances (e.g., diabetes), oxygen deprivation (e.g., anemia), polydysbiosis (acute, chronic, or hidden infections in one or more areas of the body), and mitochondrial dysfunctions

- Signs/symptoms: addressing those symptoms whereby their amelioration will infuse one with the greatest level of motivation, energy, and momentum

It is beyond the scope of this book to outline the holistic and functional medicine protocols and supplements needed for every disease. We can, however, tackle most health-related challenges with a true, trusted, and tried methodically shared approach. In other words, the practices in the sections to follow can be used initially as a starting point and foundation for all your health-related concerns. Over time, the compounding and individual natures of these practices will indirectly lend a helping hand to heal every sign, symptom, mediator, system, and diagnosis.

Dimensional Practices

- Classical genetics, along with epi-, meta-, and transgenetics
- Environmental
  - o Removal, avoidance, or minimizing exposure to physical and non-physical toxins, experiences, and traumas
  - o Creating a nourishing environment to encourage the expression of your highest Self, states of equanimity, and signposts to trigger healthy habits and routines reflecting one's needs, values, dreams, and goals

- Physical
  - o Diet and supplements
  - o Movement and exercise
  - o Rest and recovery
  - o Elements: air (breath), fire (the Sun, vitamin D), water, earth (grounding and earthing practices), and ether (soul-based embodiment practices)
- Emotional Intelligence (EQ or emotional quotient), a set of practices, skills, and intuitions that help us:
  - o Recognize, discern, understand (emotional gifts), use, and manage our emotions in nourishing ways for self and others. This can be thought of as responding rather than reacting or self-awareness for self-management.
  - o Connect and trace emotions back to universal human needs.
  - o Move through and digest (rather than repress or deny) unpleasant emotions.
  - o Cultivate pleasant emotions and internal states of peace and equanimity.
- Mental Intelligence
  - o Conscious practices that help us:
    - clarify our needs, values, dreams, and goals
    - reflect and upgrade our stories and beliefs to ones that are nourishing, meaningful, and purposeful

- cultivate mindfulness so we can focus our most powerful muscle, attention, on the valuable, make peace with our past and future, and strengthen present-moment awareness
  o Subconscious practices that help us:
    - identify, evolve, and upgrade hidden software programs such as limiting beliefs and maladaptive strategies that are no longer serving us
- Relational Intelligence
  o Higher Self: understanding, self-fulfilling, communicating, expressing, and receiving needs
  o Subpersonalities: needs assessment and integration to allow the ego or subpersonalities to become a servant to our higher Self
  o Others: creating a growth environment for others to understand, self-fulfill, communicate, express, and receive their needs
  o Mother Nature (vitamin N): practices that help one to plug back into life's interconnectedness, find solace, cultivate awe, generate energy, wisdom, and alignment to yearly, seasonal, circadian, and ultradian rhythms (chronobiology)
- Spiritual practices for self-realization, integration, transcending and including, and alchemizing the energies of being and doing
- Multidimensional practices that combine and compound various disciplines or dimensions to reset maladaptive patterns (e.g., traumas and various mental-emotional complexes) to a state of coherence

Individuality and Where to Start

The Focus Funnel is not a dogmatic approach. Rather, this is a highly individualized journey. Any practice as found within any of the dimensions is fair game to add and start with. Choose the practices that work best for you based on the following:

1. Subjective: intuition, interest, accessibility, opportunity, necessity, and overall level of motivation
2. Objective: although objective, tangible results (e.g., blood work) have been the gold standard, they must be balanced and viewed holistically with all the factors listed
3. Health advantages: comparing long versus short term benefits and costs
4. Season of life

We will explore your seasonal assessment in the following chapter. For now, remember that our genetics, personality, and season of life will often dictate whether a particular practice or therapy is nourishing or toxic. For example, metaphoric summer practices include action and achievement, while a season of winter begs for rest and recovery. Problems arise when we use winter practices in a season of summer and vice versa. Consider the following mismatches:

- A loved one suddenly passes, and a person continues with their perpetual summer day-to-day hustle and bustle without taking time to metabolize their emotions, grieve, and welcome the temporary season of winter.

- A person engages in intensive exercise practices while, at the same time, ignores a severe musculoskeletal injury or severe adrenal exhaustion.
- Someone stays in a perpetual season of winter (apathy, addiction, and pathological depression) fed by endless nights of TV binge-watching, overeating, excess alcohol consumption, and avoidance of nature while, at the same time, spring and summer are knocking at their door offering the gift of rebirth.

So, where do we start? When answering this question, it is important to start simply. For example, I usually recommend beginning with diet, movement (e.g., power walking), and any other individual practice that nourishes the mind, body, and soul (generally referred to as self-care practices).

In other words, individualize and start with those things that most resonate with you, reflect your season of life, and activate your hero's journey. Once a firm foundation is established and the chosen practices become rooted, you can add and compound additional practices or therapies. When you fall off the track, return to the fundamentals, rerooting the two or three most important practices. It is best to acknowledge upfront that this cycle will, most likely, repeat over and over again. This is the essence of first things first and second things second.

In the chapters to follow, I will outline what I believe are eleven of the most important practices to choose from:

- Awareness
- Diet
- Movement
- Hermetic and detoxification practices
- Coherence exercises
- The Sandwich Method
- The Elemental Diet
- Emotional-relational practice
- The Manifestation Method
- Self-realization and spiritual practices
- The Miracle Method

It is important to continually assess your needs and strategies to pivot with the dynamism of your ever-changing life. This is best appreciated by understanding the difference between your functional and genetic constitution.

Functional Constitution

Our functional constitution can be defined as the culmination of physical and non-physical changes in the human body affected by poor diet and lifestyle or ever-changing experiences with the need for short- or long-term adaptability. For example, someone suffering from severe type 2 diabetes (high blood sugar) is unable to tolerate, in this current constitution, high sugary snacks like a banana. Their current functional constitution is "diabetic."

Genetic Constitution

Our genetic constitution can be defined as the culmination of physical and nonphysical changes in the human body unearthed after building a strong foundation of dietary and lifestyle excellence. The same person, for example, with diabetes, commits to six months of dietary and lifestyle excellence. In turn, this unearths their non-functional or true genetic constitution, which is, simply, "non-diabetic." In this constitution, they can handle a high sugary snack like a banana so long as they continue to eat healthy.

The Genetic/Functional Constitution Error

The mistake many laypersons and doctors make is treating an unearthed genetic constitution as if it were still a functional constitution. For example, someone reverses their diabetes, normalizes their blood pressure, and lowers their cholesterol levels but remains forever on medications. Another example includes an individual avoiding all the foods on their sensitivity panel years after their initial diagnostic. The error here is mistaking short-lived and functional food sensitivities for long-term genetic food allergies.

On the opposite spectrum, some individuals get trapped into treating a functional constitution as a genetic one. Imagine, for example, an individual who eats unhealthy, smokes, and does not exercise, adhering to the belief that they do not have diabetes and high blood pressure simply because they are taking medications for said diseases and their blood work and blood pressure numbers are "normal."

Diagnostics and Cause

As we begin to commit to the fundamentals (diet, movement, and self-care practices), over time, more first order, upstream, and proximal causative factors can be uncovered. In other words, when someone is unhealthy, initial stage diagnostics mirror back poor dietary and lifestyle choices by showing all the lower order, downstream, and distal mediators, systems, signs, and symptoms—our functional constitution.

However, after we address first things first and clear out the smoke, we are able to look at deeper textures of causation, find hidden root causes, and unearth or move closer to our true genetic constitution.

Commitment

There is no one recipe, secret, or elixir to fast track us along the healing continuum from surviving to thriving. One of our major blocks is our frequently backward thinking on how we are "supposed" to journey. Dan Sullivan, author, speaker, and founder of Strategic Coach, offers a useful framework to help. He calls it the 4C's—commitment, courage, capabilities, and confidence.

It all starts with commitment. Commitment is a mental shift away from wanting and toward deciding to boldly declare a 100 percent commitment. Anything less is an interest, not a commitment. As we commit, our faith and "why" become greater than the sum of our fears. It's as if we encounter an impenetrable wall stretched out as far as the eye can see. We have no idea how to climb it, go over, or around it. We take a leap of faith and throw all our treasured belongings (our knapsack) over the wall. This simple act signifies a contract that commits us to moving forward. It releases us from concentrating on the "how" or the pathological focus on the capabilities we must obtain.

As we commit, we take a step into the world of the unknown. The virtue of courage is summoned, helping us move past all uncertainty, fear, suffering, pain, and those desperate energies of trying to avoid uncomfortable feelings and emotions. One definition of courage states that courage is not the absence of fear but the awareness that something else ahead of us is more important. As we push forward, capabilities are obtained, learned, and mastered, providing us with the needed confidence to continue our journey step by step, inch by inch, and moment to moment.

Think how different this is from the approach so many of us take. Most people wait to feel a certain way before deciding or acting. Unfortunately, most people will wait a lifetime before they "feel" the emotions or feelings that will jump-start them into acting. Recall, in the 4C's model—the feeling or emotion (e.g., confidence) comes at the end, not the beginning. For example, consider a simple goal of wanting to eat healthier.

In the beginning, most people try to rely on an exhaustible resource we call willpower. They beat themselves up—shaming and blaming—when the confidence and energies are not available to fuel their desires. They concentrate on acquiring resources and capabilities—equipment, recipes, online classes, cooking techniques, and more. This often leads to paralysis, overwhelm, and catastrophically thinking, "I can't do this!" According to the 4 C's model, this is completely backward. Capabilities and confidence come later. The model begins with commitment, then courage (to move through uncertainty), then the acquisition of capabilities, and, finally, the effect—increased confidence.

CHAPTER 19

Awareness

The awareness that health is dependent upon habits that we control
makes us the first generation in history that to a large extent
determines its own destiny.

-Jimmy Carter

We have habituated thoughts, emotions, and feelings and perform
robotic-like actions and behaviors that are frequently incongruent
with our core values and needs. The reason for this discrepancy is
best understood by likening the parts of our mind, once again, to
the iceberg metaphor. The part of our mind responsible for decision-making (the conscious mind) represents the tip. The part of
our mind that controls, runs, and directs most of our behaviors and
actions represents the entire iceberg below the water's surface (the
subconscious).

As we turn the light of awareness on our unconscious programming (the iceberg below the water's surface), we can integrate and
align these habituations with our conscious mind and take another
step towards living a life by design. This integration allows us to "look

at, rather than through" our dominant lens of perception. In doing so, we begin to see that we have been wearing outdated and distorted glasses with a dim focus on a rather small segment of reality. This virtual reality, of sorts, has chained us and prevented us from discovering, participating with, and taking responsibility for our divine co-creative inheritance. We have permitted ourselves to be victims of our environment, subconscious programming, traumas, and destructive self-identities.

Recall the classic tale between two fish in the ocean—one who is aware and the other who is not. The aware fish asks the other fish, "How's the water?" The unaware fish looks perplexed and asks, "What water?" As we bring awareness to our emotions, thoughts, words, actions, feelings, and the myriad of glasses we use to narrate our experiences of the world, we will be able to choose more empowering and nurturing lenses and heroic responses that serve us on our journey towards self-actualization and self-transcendence.

It has been said throughout the eons in many ways and in many tongues, that "energy flows where attention goes." The core understanding suggests that whatever we focus our attention on will, as a matter of effect, become the most compelling and prominent story of our lives. It will consume our day-to-day thoughts as we hand over, consciously or unconsciously, our power and responsibility. So, we start with the concept of awareness simply because to understand where we want to go, we need to know where we are, what is hidden from us, our potentialities, and what exactly our attention has been keeping in the spotlight.

All of this can be thought of as the "streetlight effect," or a type of observational bias we all initiate in various aspects of our lives. This idea comes from a parable that describes a police officer who encounters a drunken man, searching desperately for his lost keys under a streetlight. The police officer decides to stop and help. After a few minutes, the police officer asks, "Are you sure you lost the keys in this spot?" The drunk man replies, "I actually lost my keys in the park." The perplexed police officer asks the man, "Why on earth then are we searching here under the streetlight?" The man replies, "This is where the light is."

Avoiding hell on earth requires us to look at the multitude of stories we tell ourselves and to be honest as we try to equate these so-called reasons for what they really are—excuses. We can no longer wait to make the heroic plunge from safety to growth, from surviving to thriving. Our somedays will run out someday, especially if we live in the "when...then..." metrics of existence—when I get that job, when I get a new relationship, when I get a bigger house, then and only then will I be happy and stand in the shoes of my most heroic Self.

Let's explore some awareness exercises.

❀ EXERCISE
Present-Moment Awareness

This exercise can be used at any time and it will help you to identify your present-moment embodiment. In other words, are you acting as your conditioned or highest Self?

- What am I thinking? Is it nurturing or toxic? Pleasant or unpleasant?
- What memories are showing up? Are they nurturing or toxic? Pleasant or unpleasant?

- What am I feeling physically? Is it nurturing or toxic? Pleasant or unpleasant?

- What am I feeling emotionally? Is it nurturing or toxic? Pleasant or unpleasant?

- What words, speech, and communication (to yourself and others) am I using? Are they nurturing or toxic? Pleasant or unpleasant?

- What am I experiencing? Perceiving? Is it nurturing or toxic? Pleasant or unpleasant? Am I resisting what is? Am I in flow with what is?

- What am I doing (eating, smoking, alcohol consumption, running away, running towards, distracting myself)? Is it nurturing or toxic? Pleasant or unpleasant?

- What family, societal, or cultural influences are present?

- What other perspectives are available?

❀ EXERCISE
Illness and Wellness Story

The stories we tell ourselves about who we are, how others are supposed to behave, and how the world works can be inspiring, useful, or disempowering. This exercise asks us to write down two of our most compelling stories and to make nourishing bold declarations. Examples include:

What is your illness story?

I commit to bring loving awareness to my false self or the number of ways I speak about myself (privately or publicly) that are shameful and disempowering. This includes: *I am lazy. I am stuck. Life is hard.*

Life is hopeless. I am too busy. I don't have enough time. I don't have enough money. I am too tired. I'm overworked. I can't change.

What is your wellness story?

I commit to making a declaration of my truth and defining my higher, true, and most heroic Self. This includes: *I am complete. I am loving. I am entitled to miracles. I am capable of following through with my vision and goals.*

❀ **EXERCISE**
Energy and Joy Audit

This exercise is simple but profound. On one side of a piece of paper, list your joy and energy builders. These are the things that light you up, give you mental or physical energy, and bring a joyful, content smile to your face. On the other side of the paper, list your joy and energy robbers. Sit in quiet contemplation as you review your list. Make a commitment and decide what you will add, eliminate, or release in the days and weeks to follow.

❀ **EXERCISE**
HALT

A common tool in rehab and twelve-step programs is the use of the HALT technique. It is an acronym for "hungry, angry, lonely, tired." It is a tool to remind addicts where they may be most vulnerable to relapse. We can use this tool for self-awareness and to identify any underlying, more proximal causes of our day-to-day stressors. I have added an additional question that revolves around our incessant need to remain forever comfortable, to experience only "positive" emotions and feelings, or to avoid all that is unpleasant and uncomfortable.

So, next time you're stressed or triggered, ask yourself if you're experiencing any underlying proximal causes:

- *Am I hungry?*
- *Am I angry?*
- *Am I lonely?*
- *Am I tired?*
- *Am I trying to avoid discomfort?*

❀ **EXERCISE**
Thirty Days Question Exercise

This exercise is from the book *Stop Living on Autopilot* by Antonio Neves.

- Based on your last thirty days of work, if your company had to decide whether to rehire you, would they? If yes, why? If not, why?
- Based on your last thirty days of marriage (or your most important relationship), would this person immediately recommit to you?
- If you are a parent, would your children want you to continue to be their caregiver based on the last thirty days?

- Based on your last thirty days, would you befriend yourself? Would you consider yourself authentic? Would you admire the man or woman you are?

❀ EXERCISE
Gravesite Exercise

What do you want your tombstone to say, and how do you want others to remember you?

❀ EXERCISE
A Day in the Life of You

Describe factually (don't embellish) a typical day in the life of you. This exercise asks you to become aware of the daily monotony you call your life. In doing so, it will bring awareness to what you are valuing, consciously or unconsciously. It is important to remember *how you live your day is how you live your life.*

- Take a mental inventory or write down the exact experiences, activities, actions, internal dialogue, speech, and habits that make up an average day in the life of you.
- Ask yourself, "Am I moving towards or away from who and what is most important to me? Towards or away from my highest Self?"
- Bring into your awareness your vision, dreams, and goals.
- List all the actions and behaviors you can do right now that lead you toward your vision, dreams, and goals.

- List all the actions and behaviors you are engaging in right now that lead you astray and away from your visions, dreams, and goals.
- Be honest and ask yourself how much of your day and time is spent moving towards or away from your vision, dreams, and goals.

❈ EXERCISE
Dimensional Analysis

Look at the various accounts or dimensions that wholly encompass the entirety of your life, and be completely honest as you grade your level of fulfillment or satisfaction in each area on a scale of zero to ten (zero is unfulfilled and ten is complete fulfillment).

- Health (e.g., diet and exercise)
- Intrapersonal relationship (your relationship with yourself):
  - Character: Are your actions and behaviors aligned with your core values?
  - Self-Care
    - engaging in any activity that provides soul nourishment, internal peace, guiltless "feel good" emotions, and healthy pleasures
    - learning, growing, and cultivating new skills
    - creative expression such as hobbies, singing, dancing, and the like
    - your emotional and intellectual life
- Interpersonal Relationships
  - Romance

- o Social (friends)
- o Family
- o Parenting
- o Circle of Influence (surrounding yourself with people that inspire and allow you to grow)
- Professional (work, career, calling)
- Financial
- Experience (including recreation, fun, adventure, bucket list, travel, culture)
- Environment (the space where you spend time, at both work and home)
- Spirituality or Contribution
- Other

❀ EXERCISE
Awareness of Your Core Programs, Needs, and Values

- Identify your core needs and limiting beliefs (see Chapter 4).
- Identify your values by asking yourself, who and what is most important to you (see Chapter 1).
  - o Pick any area of life from the dimensional analysis above. Ask yourself what you want (it can be grand or trivial) in this dimension of your life? What's important about that? What will having this do for you? Why? Why? And so on. Each layer should elicit deeper reflections, ultimately arriving at a list of values.
- Identify any resistance and turn it into a value (see Chapter 1).

- Identify your most experienced emotions. Identify your most used reactive behavioral patterns (fight, flight, flee, avoidance, befriend). What are they trying to tell you? Are they moving you towards or away from your universal needs (see Chapter 5)?
- Look back over your life, identify past wounds or adversities that influenced and continue to influence your very being and belief systems.
- Look back over your life, identify growth points or areas in your life that were associated with positive experiences that influenced and continue to influence your very being, personality, and belief systems?
- Identify the most common complex secondary elements running your life. Make sure to include awareness of your sub-personalities—one of our most important contributors (see Chapter 7).

❀ EXERCISE
Seasonal Assessment

For everything there is a season, a time for every activity under heaven. A time to be born and a time to die. A time to plant and a time to harvest.

-Ecclesiastes 3:1-11

We all participate and experience various seasons in our lives. Some individuals may carry the world's weight, darkness, and heaviness upon their shoulders (season of winter), while others are motivated, driven, and on-purpose (season of summer). Understanding your current season of life could be one of the most helpful tools in balancing the struggles between the energies of being and doing. Just like our health, our lives move cyclically (albeit in a more chaotic-looking circle) from fear to safety to growth. The cycles can be seen in both the macrocosm of our life (infancy to adulthood) and the microcosm of a particular year. Taking a step even further and allowing ourselves to drop down from our previous "bird's eye view," we can now see the cycles repeat once more in the macrocosm of a day to the microcosm of a single moment.

Each stage or season comes with its own lessons, gifts, darkness, needs acquisition, trials, and tribulations. As you read over the following seasonal descriptors, reflect on your own life to see if you resonate with any of the stages. In short, our lives revolve around times of healing and being, of doing, and of transformation. Trying to resist a season amounts to needless suffering—such as an individual trying to "do" when they should "be" in a season of healing and surrendering.

Winter / Healing / Dark Night

This is the season of gestation. It is a time for nourishing oneself, a time for recovery, a time for pause, a time for rest, a time for hibernation, a time for healing, a time for reflection, a time for making meaning, and a time to embrace the transformative process that is occurring—the butterfly of the next season. This season encourages us to dream, imagine, and reflect. Possibilities abound, but action is not required—the dreams are incubating. In short, this is the season of being.

The darkness of this season represents one's plunge into the dark night of the soul. This is the metaphorical crucifixion. One's heart is heavy. Confusion, anticipation, fear, grief, and anxiety abound. You are about to leave home, along with all the security and safety of the womb. Birth, however, awaits. What will the new season bring? Who will I become? *A Course in Miracles* states, "Those who are certain of the outcome can afford to wait and wait without anxiety." One must trust in the energies of creation or the soon-to-come birthing process. We must simply be, surrender, and patiently wait. All the trials and tribulations of this season are, in fact, internal ones. It is okay to wait until you are ready. Just make peace with what is true right now. Eventually, a time will come when one just knows, and the pain of staying exceeds the pain of moving forward—the season of spring.

Spring / Birth / Transformation / Discovery

This is the season of birth, resurrection, and discovery. It is here where courage becomes stronger than the fear and darkness of winter, allowing for the rebirth of the true Self. This is the time to take your first few steps into the great unknown. The possibilities, dreams, and musings of winter can now begin their ascent to actualization, to manifestation. We begin to trust in both the power that created us as well as our journey and growth into individuation and autonomy. Imagine a parent holding on to their child's hand while at the same time knowing the days are numbered, and they will soon need to let go. This season, therefore, has one foot in being and one in doing.

The darkness of the season lies in resistance and attachments. It is important that we embrace this season of life by letting go of the old and making room in our hearts and minds for the creative power to continue its ascension. This season is about saying *yes* to life by saying *no* to past habits, beliefs, attachments, and resistances that no longer serve us.

We have allowed the seeds of winter to spring forth, so this is no time to cut the bamboo shoots that have sprouted.

Summer / Achievement

This is a time for achievement, a time for growth, a time for cele-bration, and a time for manifestation. Fear dissolves, and we feel liberated by the transition into autonomy and individuation. There is no conflict in this season—this is a time to get stuff done! This is the season of doing.

The darkness of the season is materialism, abandonment of the spiritual, habituation without meaning, chasing nonessential goals, and becoming attached to outcomes rather than processes, experiences, or the present moment. The light of achievement, in contrast, is done for both the joy of doing and the harvest that will come from the fruits of labor. These ideas are not mutually exclusive. One need not sacrifice happiness to some later date.

Fall

The time has now come to shed one's skin for a metaphorical death. We can imagine emptying our chalice so that the great nectar of life can once again fill us. The wine is ready to be shared. This is the self-transcendent season where we find ourselves transcending our finite self for something greater than ourselves. We understand life's interconnectedness. "Giving is receiving" is engrained within our souls. The harvest from summer is plentiful and ready to be shared with all. We feel a sense of completion and a sense of accomplish-ment. However, we have a bit more to do before winter arrives. Fall's sense of doing arises from a place of nonresistance for what is about to come next—the new season of change, the metaphorical death. This season, therefore, has one foot in doing and one in being.

Seasonal Questions

- Where am I? What stage of life am I in? What season am I in?
- Is this a time for healing your physical body? Mental body? Emotional body? Past traumas?
- Is this a time for discovery? For allowing things to incubate? A time to dream? A time for idea-making?
- Is this a time to reinvent yourself?
- Is this a time to put words into action or to get off the couch, so to speak?
- Is this a time or season to give back? To take care of others?
- Is this a time to just *be*?
- Is this a time to *do*?

Addictions

As we move forward on this journey, it's important to reflect and expand our definition of addiction past substance abuse (e.g., drugs). Our most influential addiction is the one we have to our conditioned or past self. This is a complex addiction made up of our thoughts, emotions, feelings, habits, and behaviors.

We can literally become addicted to anything, physical or non-physical. Addictions come in so many flavors. For some, it's a named diagnosis, the news, depression, or sexual pleasures. The addictive chemical cocktails produced by the body-mind reinforce our incarceration to a past reality. We can either find ourselves in a never-ending battle trying to escape or, worse yet, the addictions stay hidden for a lifetime.

Here is the most important aspect to keep in your awareness—the chemicals produced for choosing the wrong thing reward us (in the moment) and, conversely, penalize us (in the moment) for doing the right thing. For example, as the alcoholic drinks alcohol and the diabetic eats sugar, they are both initially rewarded but will, of course, suffer long-term consequences.

As one reprograms the mind and engages in more nurturing behaviors (e.g., eating healthy), the addictive feedback loop and pleasure reward circuitry begins to reverse. We return, to our rightful inheritance, to a healing system that begins to reward us, chemically speaking, for doing the right thing and penalizes us for doing the wrong thing. The time for the transition is unique and individual. I'm reminded of common everyday phrases such as *It only takes thirty days to break a habit.* From my experience in working with thousands of patients, it can be thirty days, ninety days, six months, and so on. Be patient, be consistent, and your reward circuitry will eventually align with your highest Self.

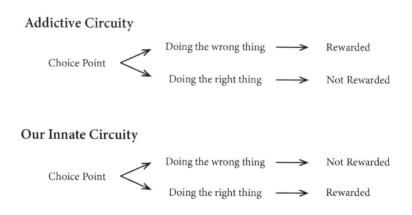

Addictive Circuity

Choice Point

Doing the wrong thing ⟶ Rewarded

Doing the right thing ⟶ Not Rewarded

Our Innate Circuity

Choice Point

Doing the wrong thing ⟶ Not Rewarded

Doing the right thing ⟶ Rewarded

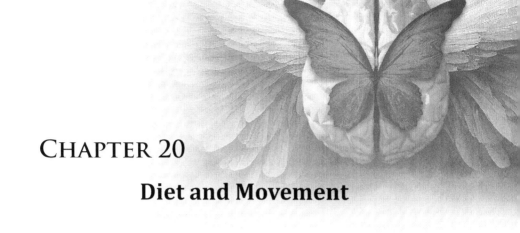

Chapter 20

Diet and Movement

Exercise is your King, and nutrition is your Queen.
Together they create your fitness kingdom.
-Jack Lalanne

Diet

We begin our journey of diet with a brief discussion of stars. You might be thinking, *stars?* Yes, stars! The story of food energy is the story of stars.

The universe is in the star-making business. Stars and life are synonymous. When a star is birthed, it makes elements, planetary systems, and provides the energy for all of life. Stars begin their creation story as vast clouds (nebulae) made up of mostly hydrogen. Gravity and nuclear fusion act on the cloud and create a central core surrounded by a disk of cooler material. Eventually, the core will become the star, and the disk will turn into its corresponding planetary system.

A star can last for billions of years. As it goes through different stages of maturity, the elements, as found in the periodic table, are manufactured. A star's death begins as the core nuclear fuel becomes exhausted. Various fates include white and black dwarfs, supernova explosions, and black holes.

Back on Earth, green plants learned to capture the energy of one of these stars (our sun) through the magic of photosynthesis. This amazing process stores potential energy as chemical bonds of sugar within the leaves and stems of a plant. Animals, in turn, eat the plant. Within the animal, complex processes, including digestion and cellular respiration, help break down the chemical bonds, releasing the stored energy as ATP (adenosine triphosphate)—the energy from stars.

Primary, Secondary, and Tertiary Nutrients

We obtain nutrients through primary, secondary, or tertiary sources. Primary sources include plants in their natural state. Secondary nutrients include animal products. Tertiary sources include processed foods (animal or plant) that are often three, four, and five times removed from the original primary or secondary source.

In addition to directly capturing the sun's energy through photosynthesis, plants also uproot, from the soil, all other elements (calcium, magnesium) previously produced by stars millions to billions of years ago. Through various chemical processes, they covert these inorganic rocks from the soil into organic elements that can be consumed and then used by the animals that eat their leaves, stems, and roots. Animals, in turn, accumulate and transform these nutrients into their flesh (cells, tissues, organs).

Ill health and degenerative diseases are directly proportional to the amount of secondary and tertiary nutrient sources a person eats. Optimal health and the prevention of disease, on the other hand, are directly proportional to the amount of primary sourced nutrients one consumes.

The more light we consume (primary nutrients), the more light we make, and the more vitality we express. The less light we consume (secondary and tertiary nutrients), the less light we make, and less vital energy is available to keep our bodies healthy.

The Longest Lived

Populations that eat a whole foods plant-based diet (think fresh vegetables, sweet potatoes, and beans versus soy hamburgers, cookies, and pasta) are virtually free of degenerative diseases including diabetes, heart disease, chronic fatigue syndrome, obesity, cancer, hormonal disorders, liver disease, gastrointestinal diseases, and autoimmunity.

Our previously discussed health equation—causes and effects—reminds us of the many other contributing and causative factors to health, such as strong familial bonds, beliefs, movement (e.g., non-traditional exercise), and purpose. A whole-food, plant-based diet, however, is a consistent thread among the diverse centenarian populations of the world.

The longest-lived have superior life and health spans. In other words, they don't only live longer (longevity) but experience a healthier quality of life (aging). They can be found living with more fulfillment, vitality, and grace. It's not just about adding years to our life; it's about adding life to our years.

We can look to some of the largest nutritional studies and longevity research to date, including the China-Cornell-Oxford Project (e.g., The China Study), The Seventh Day Adventist Health Studies from Loma Linda University, and the Blue Zone's research (the name given by National Geographic researcher, Dan Buettner) in specific communities where people generally lived active lifestyles into their nineties. All the evidence points back to the most tried and true nutritional recommendation over the last century—eat your vegetables!

"Dis"ease

All organisms exist at various levels on the great food web of life. The first and lowest level contains the producers, green plants. The higher levels include the animals with the largest biomass or size. Toxin accumulation and magnification mirror the position an organism holds within the food chain. At the top, bioaccumulation and biomagnification of environmental toxins (pesticides, herbicides, GMOs) and bio-toxins (yeast, bacteria) are the greatest. Conversely, at the bottom, they are the lowest. For example, plankton have less mercury than salmon, salmon less mercury than tuna, and tuna less than swordfish.

Primary sourced nutrients (the bottom of the food chain) contain the most amount of nutrients (referred to as nutrient density), while secondary and tertiary sourced nutrients (the top of the food chain) are the most nutrient-poor.

A high toxic burden (found with meat and processed-centric diets) along with decreased nutrient density correlates with all-cause mortality. These diets (the cause) turn on chronic protective and survival mechanisms (effects) to deal with the rising inflammation, sugar levels, and infections. The body's terrain begins to move from a health-promoting alkaline and oxygen-rich environment to an acidic and oxygen-starved one. This, in turn, may lead to abnormal cell growth, immune compromise, and incoherent macro (e.g., glands and hormones) and micro (e.g., cellular) communication.

Recall our healing continuum—degeneration to maintenance to healing to regeneration. If the toxic, acidic, dysbiotic, and inflammatory burden is elevated, the stress response mechanisms keep us on the degenerative side of the equation.

There is nothing more intimate than the adage, "You are what you eat." Consumption of food is more intimate than sex. The food you eat literally becomes incorporated into the cells, tissues, and organs of your body. There are approximately fifty to one-hundred trillion cells in the body. We produce around three hundred billion new cells a day. In fact, about 98 percent of all the atoms in the human body are replaced every year. For example, you get a new stomach lining every four to seven days, skin every month, and so on.

- If you put junky food (dead decaying flesh, processed and fast foods) into your body, you will make a junky body.
- If you put healthy food (fresh fruits and vegetables) into your body, you will make a healthy, more vibrant, and energetic body.

In summary, processed foods and animal foods contribute to decreased longevity, advanced aging, and all-cause mortality. Here are some of the most important hallmarks:

- Inflammation
- Dysbiosis
- Elevated sugar levels
- Environmental and biotoxin accumulation
- Abnormal cell growth or the inability to clean up damaged senescent cells
- Acidic and oxygen-starved environments
- Loss of energy for healing and regeneration

Characteristics of a Health-Promoting Diet

An optimal diet for decreasing degenerative diseases and promoting health and life span includes the following characteristics:

- Whole food plant-based or primary sourced nutrients
- Eating foods found in nature, not laboratories, that have undergone minimal processing (Acceptable forms of processing include procedures that enhance nutrient bioavailability such as fermenting and sprouting.)
- Eating foods that maintain the natural synergisms of nutrients working together referred to as their holo-nutrient wisdom
- Eating an abundance of biogenic, sun-ripened, and enzymatic-rich foods such as green leafy vegetables, raw foods, and sprouts
- Foods with high nutrient density (elevated levels of vitamins, minerals, and other phytonutrients) rather than nutrient-poor and caloric dense foods (e.g., cookies and soda)
- Foods that are hermetically stressed and grown in natural environments that eliminate the use of anti-nutrients (xenobiotics, biotechnology GMOs, herbicides, pesticides) and idyllic monocropping
- Eating foods based on physiological and spiritual needs rather than wants and taste preferences
- Foods free of metaphysical toxins (Dr. Will Tuttle states, "Until we live our prayers for peace and freedom by granting peace and freedom to those who are vulnerable in our hands, we will find neither peace nor freedom…The price we must pay for love and freedom *is* the ice cream cone, the steak, and

the eggnog we casually consume. We conditioned mentally to disconnect our food from the animal who was mindlessly abused to provide it, but the vibrational fields created by our food choices impacts us profoundly whether we pretend to ignore them or not.")

- Foods individualized for your constitution
- Intermittent and long-term fasting strategies, along with a lifetime of optimal caloric intake that promotes movement on the healing continuum towards regeneration

Where to Start?

1. Start with self-honesty. To begin, you don't need fancy diagnostics testing (e.g., food sensitivity testing) or a new diet book if you are still eating processed foods and factory-farmed animal products. Start with eliminating these foods. Start with making a commitment to a whole foods plant-based diet.
2. Healthify and plantify your current meals. This can be achieved, simply, by adding more whole food plants to your current dishes. The plate method is helpful: imagine 50 to 75 percent of your plate loaded with your favorite whole plant-based foods (e.g., vegetables).
3. Shoot for five to ten or more servings of fruits and vegetables on most days.
4. Concentrate on nutrient density using green smoothies, salads, and easy whole food plant-based one pot meals.
5. Snack on real food such as avocados, vegetables, fruits, nuts, tubers, and seeds.

> 6. Add intuitive fasting weekly, monthly, and seasonally (see Chapter 21).

Processed Foods
as a treat or condiment, a few times a week
*Cookies, candies, sodas, pastries, fake meats, and all other non-intact
grains (e.g., flours) such as breads, pasta, bagels, and cereals*

Fasting
daily, weekly, monthly and seasonal
*Highly intuitive process that uses intermittent and prolonged
fasting techniques such as water and freshly squeezed juices*

Fats, Nuts, Oils, and Avocados
1-4 servings
*1 serving = 1/4 or small handful of nuts,1-2 tablespoons of seeds,
1 teaspoon of oil, 2 tablespoons of nut and seed butters, 1 cup or 8 ounces of
nut and seed milks, and 1/3 medium avocado*

Herbs, Spices, Mushrooms, & Super Foods
daily, no specific serving size
*Mushrooms such as white button, porcini , and shitake
Spices and Herbs such as ginger, garic, onions, basil, and oregano
Super Foods such as algae, spirulina, chlorella, wheatgrass, and fresh juices*

Intact Whole Grains
1-2 servings (1 serving= ½ - 1 cup dry or ½ cup cooked)
*Emphasis on gluten-free grains such as rice (basmati, wild, red, yellow), quinoa, oat,
buckwheat, millet, and amaranth. Grains containing gluten include wheat, rye, and barley*

Beans, Peas, and Lentils
1-2+ servings (1 serving = 1 cup cooked)
*Choose traditional and organic soy products such as edamame, tofu,
tempeh, and miso rather than processed variations (e.g., soy hot dogs and hamburgers)*

Fruits
1-4+ servings (1 serving = ½ cup cooked or 1 cup raw)
Include an abundance of berries such as goji, strawberries, and blueberries

Vegetables
5-10+ servings (1 serving = ½ cup cooked or 1 cup raw)
*Aim for 5+ servings of green leafy vegetables and sprouts with an additional 5+ servings of starchy
(potatos, yams, squash, yuca, and plantains) and/or non-starchy land or sea vegetables on most days*

Intuitive Eating and Individualization
Based on subjective and objective measures
*Examples include: eating with the seasons, food-combining, food allergies, food sensitivities, greater or
lesser amounts of a given food group, and varrying proportions or ratios of fats, carbohydrates, and proteins*

Universal Human Needs
*Physiological (food, air, water, sunshine), safety, security, pleasure, play, self-esteem, love and belongingness,
self-actualization (growth), self-transcendence (contribution)*

Example Weekly Menu

Day 1, 2, 3, 5, and 7

Breakfast: Low Glycemic Smoothie or The Fruit and Green Smoothie

Lunch: Hearty Salad

Dinner: All-You-Need-Dinner Recipe

Snacks: nuts and seeds or fresh vegetables and hummus

Days 4 and 6 (intermittent fasting days, eating within a 4-hour window)

Dinner: All-You-Need-Dinner Recipe

Snack: avocado

Recipe Examples

Snacks

Fruit

Avocado

Fresh vegetables and hummus

Nuts and seeds (trail mix)

Low Glycemic Smoothie

The Basic Formula

- Greens: romaine lettuce, spinach, kale, parsley, cilantro, etc.
- Citrus: lemon and/or lime
- Other veggies: cucumber, zucchini, or celery
- Fruit: apple, pear, or banana
- Other (optional): nuts, seeds, avocado, herbs, specialty powders, etc.

Example: Blend the following ingredients: 1 small head of romaine lettuce, 2-4 stalks of celery and/or 1 cucumber, juice from 1-3 lemons/limes (to your desired taste preference), 1 medium pear or banana, water, ice (optional), small piece of ginger (optional), turmeric (optional), ½ cup fresh parsley (optional), ½ cup fresh cilantro (optional). Easiest to drink with a straw.

Fruit and Green Smoothie
The Basic Formula
- Greens: romaine lettuce, spinach, kale, etc.
- Fruit: berries, bananas, cherries, etc.
- Other (optional): nuts, seeds, avocado, herbs, specialty powders, etc.

Example: Blend the following ingredients: large handful of frozen blueberries, large handful of frozen strawberries, 1 medium banana, greens (1-2 handfuls of spinach), and water to desired consistency.

Hot Cereal
Cook one or two servings of whole grain (no instant or quick varieties) quinoa or oatmeal to package directions in water or a plant-based milk (i.e., coconut milk). Before the grains are cooked all the way through, add cinnamon and/or any other sweetener/flavoring of your choice (vanilla, maple syrup, etc.). Top with a combination of nuts, seeds, or fresh fruit.

A New Kind of Cereal
Mix the following ingredients together: ripened fruit (mashed manana or chopped pear), tablespoon of nut butter (almond, cashew, etc.), and any other ingredients such as cinnamon, raisins, nuts, or seeds.

Hearty Salad

Put 3-5 cups of greens in bowl, "massage and scissor" down to manageable handfuls. Add avocado, organic canned beans of choice, sunflower seeds, and freshly squeezed lime. Mix, serve, and enjoy!

All-You-Need-Dinner Recipe:

Ingredients: sautéed or roasted veggies with grains, beans, tubers, or mushrooms

Make it Happen: Cover ½ to ¾ plate with sautéed and/or roasted veggies along with any of the following:
- Baked sweet potatoes topped with cinnamon and coconut oil
- Red skinned potatoes drenched in dill, rosemary, and olive oil
- Beans (any)
- Grains: basmati, quinoa, etc.
- Mushrooms

Exercise and Movement

The importance of exercise should not come as a surprise to anyone. Over the days, months, and years to follow, it is imperative to include the right combination of aerobic, strength, flexibility, and activities of daily living (ADL) exercises.

Aerobic

Aerobic exercise, exercise with air or oxygen, is an activity that promotes endurance, increases heart and breathing rate, and is performed over a sustained period. Examples include walking, jogging, rowing, and swimming. There are many ways to add this to your daily and weekly regimen. A quick and easy place to start is to power walk every day for thirty to sixty minutes.

Emotional Charge

One of the most important reasons for engaging in aerobic-type exercises is to prevent cardiovascular disease, the number one leading cause of death globally. Allow this to fuel your inner emotional enthusiasm for aerobic exercise.

Anaerobic

Anaerobic exercise, exercise without air or oxygen, is an activity that promotes strength. It consists of short, intense bursts of physical activity such as weightlifting. The goal of weight and resistance training is to engage every major muscle group a minimum of one time a week. This all depends on your individual rate of rest and recovery.

Strength training can be accomplished in two broad ways. The first is a form of circuit training where you engage every muscle in a single workout session. You would then allow for appropriate rest and recovery and repeat every three to seven days. Another common practice is to isolate various muscle groups during each workout session. For example, back and biceps on one day, chest and triceps on another, and shoulder and legs on another.

Emotional Charge

One of the greatest predictors of longevity is the ability to hold onto muscle mass as we age. Increased muscle mass correlates with increased bone density which preserves our skeletal system—the body's foundation. The emotional charge for engaging in anaerobic strength training practices, therefore, is to increase our longevity.

Flexibility

Flexibility training involves the active or passive stretching of hypertonic or tight muscles from overuse or poor posture. It is important to have a weekly stretching routine to preserve spinal and extremity ranges of motion.

Other additions in this category can include forms of spinal decompression (e.g., inversion table) to help maintain the integrity and function of our precious spinal anatomy.

Emotional Charge

To build an emotional attachment to flexibility, one of the most overlooked and neglected areas of health, it is best to equate flexibility with aging. Aging well is the ability to tie our shoes, reach for a cup in the cupboard, dress ourselves, and so on as we get older. In short, it's the ability to remain independent and autonomous.

ADL (Activities of Daily Living)

ADLs include your day-to-day activities or the time spent during nonscheduled exercise sessions. We must live an active rather than sedentary lifestyle and avoid the trap of confining "exercise" to scheduled exercise sessions. ADLs include gardening, taking the stairs rather than the elevator, walking five to ten thousand steps a day, and so on.

This area also includes awareness and postural hygiene practices when we sit, stand, and sleep to help prevent spinal degeneration.

Emotional Charge

Historically, people with the longest lives did not have a formal exercise practice. Life was exercise. Thus, ADLs are truly the most important category because it's where we spend the majority of our time contributing a significant portion to aging, longevity, and the prevention of disease.

CHAPTER 21
Detoxification and Hermetic Practices

Almost everything will work again if you unplug it
for a few minutes, including you.
-Anne Lamott

Hermetic and detoxification practices, when used appropriately, help augment and fast-track our movement on the healing continuum (degeneration to regeneration). They turn on dormant antiaging and longevity gene expression that catapults our body to higher levels of self-actualization and self-transcendence. For more information, see Chapters 14 and 15 for a refresher on the definitions of the healing continuum and hormesis to help understand the "why" behind the practices to follow.

Hermetic and detoxification practices help counteract almost all the aberrant physiological processes previously discussed, including inflammation, dysbiosis, abnormal cell growth, environmental and biotoxin accumulation, and immune dysregulation.

Detoxification practices help purify the cells, tissues, organs, blood, and lymph. They decrease and eliminate the body's overall toxic burden and free the body of self-poisoning or autointoxication (a process that occurs when the toxic load of the body is greater than the body's capacity for elimination). Detoxification sets the stage for the next level of healing as previous energies, tied up in maintenance, repair, and elimination, are now free to be used for regenerative purposes.

The hermetic practices to follow are optimal, intermittent, controlled, and deliberate stressors that turn on the innate powers of the body to heal. We approach but do not cross the needed exposure threshold to activate the antiaging and longevity genes and the physiological processes of autophagy, regeneration, and stem cell production.

Both these practices work together—one complementing the other.

Fasting

Fasting is one of the most important health tools and secrets for self-renewal, aging, longevity, and reversal of chronic disease. It is an evolutionary tool built inside the DNA of every cell, tissue, and organ in the body. Fasting strips away our daily concerns about food preparation and asks us to come face to face with our most vulnerable Self as we confront hidden emotions, sensations, beliefs, and feelings.

During a strict noncaloric "water fast," our body moves rapidly through the healing continuum. Metabolically speaking, the body's energy source shifts from sugar (the food we eat) to fat (our reserves). This shift, if done appropriately, is one of the most important tools in unleashing the power of our innate intelligence to heal from "above-down and inside-out."

On an average day, we use the sugar from the foods we ingest as our main energy source. Our digestive system helps take large macromolecules (carbs, fats, and proteins) and breaks them down into smaller components such as glucose (from carbohydrates), fatty acids (from fats), and amino acids (from protein). During an average day, the glucose or sugar from carbohydrates is the body's prioritized fuel currency. Imagine, however, if the body could take a break from all this hard work for a short period of time. What would happen?

Fasting Day by Day:

Twelve to twenty-four hours (Day 1): The body begins to use stored sugar (called glycogen) found in our liver and muscle tissues. The body is "transitioning" into a fasting state so it can begin the magic of cellular clean-up, repair, and cellular regeneration.

Twenty-four to seventy-two hours (Days 2 and 3): Once these sugar reserves (glycogen) are depleted, the body switches to fat for energy utilization (note: the timing depends on a person's glycogen reserves and activity levels). Ketogenesis (ketone production), autophagy, and cellular regeneration begin in their elementary forms.

Seventy-two to one-hundred twenty hours (Days 3-5): The body is in a complete and steady-state of fat energy utilization (nutritional ketosis). Autophagy (cellular clean-up), cellular regeneration, and stem cell production are ramped up, and we achieve antiaging and longevity benefits, unlike any other healing method.

Fasting: Beyond the Physical

In addition to physical benefits, fasting conjures up emotional, spiritual, and mental "toxins" that we are challenged to purge, surrender to, reconcile, and make peace with. During the first few days of a fast, our desires, sensations, and craving begin to heighten. We are forced to stay in the present moment a bit longer than we're accustomed to.

Why?

We are no longer able to use our number one drug of choice—food—to suppress or numb down our feelings and emotions. In other words, the carpet is pulled back, and we are confronted with years of shadows that we conveniently swept under the rug. The parts we kept in the dark come to light, and we begin to see our most vulnerable self.

Fasting Practices

We will be using fasting as an umbrella term that includes any of the following practices or similar iterations:

- Water-only (supervised): a days to weeks water fast performed under doctor supervision at a fasting clinic
- Water-only (unsupervised): one to three days, drinking water and consuming no food
- Intermittent: punctuated and deliberate fasting windows during the day or week
- Low-Calorie Nutrient Feasting (LCNF): examples include fresh green vegetable juicing, fresh fruits and vegetables, smoothies, and soups/broths for an extended period
- Low-Calorie, Fat-Based, Water-Only Fast or Low-Calorie Water Fast (LCWF): water-only fast combined with five hundred calories per day (approximately) of mostly high-fat foods

I recommend you speak with a medical professional to help guide you on to what program is best suited for your functional and genetic constitution, health goals, and current level of health. Much of this depends on how well you've taken care of your body, how many miles you've driven, accidents you've encountered along your journey, ability to recover or heal, metabolic state (catabolic versus anabolic), and more.

I believe everyone should have a weekly, monthly, and quarterly plan that is highly individualized and based upon the previously discussed tenets of The Focus Funnel: intuition, interest, accessibility, opportunity, necessity, and overall level of motivation. Here is an example:

- Weekly: Intermittent Fasting
  - o Beginner: start eliminating snacks throughout the day
  - o Intermediate: start eliminating a handful of meals throughout the week
  - o Advanced: a three-day approach, eat in a constricted feeding window of four to six hours (e.g., Monday, Wednesday, and Friday, you would eat from three to seven p.m.)
- Monthly: Water-only or LCFM Fasting
  - o Beginner: a one-day water-only fast throughout the day with a small snack (a handful of nuts) and high-fat, low-calorie meal in the evening (vegetable broth and avocado)
  - o Intermediate: a one-day water-only fast with freshly squeezed lemon or lime
  - o Advanced: a two to three day water-only fast with or without freshly squeezed lemon or lime

- Quarterly: Green Juicing
  - o Beginner: two to three days
  - o Intermediate: four to five days
  - o Advanced: seven days

Heat, Cold, Oxygen Practices

There are many ways to expose yourself to extremes of heat, cold, oxygen saturation, and oxygen deprivation. All these practices act like a hermetic stress and activate anti-aging and longevity gene expression. Here are just a few:

- Heat therapies: infrared sauna, Swedish sauna, and infrared mats
- Cold therapies: cold showers, ice baths, outdoor swims, and cryotherapy machines
- Hot/cold contrast: alternating hot and cold treatments
- EWOT: exercise with oxygen therapy
- HBOT: hyperbaric oxygen therapy
- Hypoxic Oxygen Training: formal exercise (high-altitude training) or specialized breathing techniques (e.g., Wim Hoff) alongside decreased oxygen intake for a controlled and specified time
- Occlusion bands: special bands that occlude blood supply while exercising

A beginner's practical application could look as follows:

- Infrared sauna: three times a week
- Cold showers: three times a week for thirty to sixty seconds
- HIIT: high-intensity interval training
- High altitude simulation (adapted from the book *The Oxygen Advantage* by Patrick McKeown):
  - o Walk for a minute or two, breathing in and out through your nose
  - o Exhale and hold your breath until a moderate or strong desire for inhalation arises
  - o Take short breaths for fifteen seconds
  - o Continue walking and repeat the cycle eight to ten times

Whole Body Detoxification

Detoxification is about the elimination of excess. This includes everything from our diet, emotional and relational burdens, information consumed (e.g., media), and much more. As we let go of the excess, remove the valueless, surrender, and detox, we create space.

With this new space, we are now open to receive. Visualize yourself as a receptacle or chalice that has been emptied and is now open and able to receive nourishing water, air, food, habits, and more. Here is a short list of practices to be added to your detoxification practice:

- Upgrade your hygiene products (toothpaste, mouthwash, makeup, lotions) to nontoxic varieties.
- Upgrade your cleaning supply products (soaps, detergents) to nontoxic varieties.
- Upgrade your air quality through air purification systems, house plants, and spending time outside.
- Aid organs of elimination through detox supplements and specialized lymphatic techniques, including jumping on a trampoline, lymphatic massage, and skin brushing.
- Upgrade your water quality through water purification systems.
- Eliminate toxic and non-nourishing media, including newspapers, magazines, TV, social platforms.
- Upgrade or reestablish social relationships and boundaries through eliminating, pruning, and reframing interactions with acquaintances, friends, family, and social media.
- Make peace and digest emotions.
- Nourish spiritual practices by eliminating the valueless and making room for those things of ultimate concern.

CHAPTER 22

Coherence Exercises

Coherence suggests that there is harmony, unity, and integrity
between your vision and mission, your roles and goals, your priorities and plans, and your desires and disciplines.

-Stephen Covey

The next set of practices correlate in many of the dimensions. Any
of these core coherence practices can be used as a standalone method
or combined in various ways for unique expressions and effects (e.g.,
The Core Miracle Method). All practices share a united goal to move
you away from maladaptive programs to ones that are more nourishing. They help you connect to the present moment, your experiences,
your body, your emotions, and beyond.

Two of the most important practices—mindfulness and meditation—are often used interchangeably. They share similarities but are
unique.

Mindfulness can be thought of as a quality, whereas meditation,
in the Western context, is a practice. Jon Kabat-Zinn, an American
professor of medicine and author of *Wherever You Go There You Are,*
defines mindfulness as the awareness that arises through paying

attention, on purpose, in the present moment, non-judgmentally. Using this definition, mindfulness can be summoned anytime and with anyone—when cleaning the dishes, walking outside, conversating with a friend. Mindfulness is about directing our attention to our experience, contacting the present moment, and cultivating a sense of equanimity.

Meditation is an umbrella term and is often associated with a host of practices (including mindfulness). Other types include progressive relaxation body scans, loving-kindness, guided, and visualization. From a more spiritual perspective, meditation is best thought of as a state of being, an uncovering, an exploration, a fulfillment of experience, and contact with our true Self. This type of "meditation," self-realization, is a topic we will explore specifically in Chapter 27, Self-Realization and Spiritual Practices.

Present-Moment Awareness and Mindfulness

***

✿ EXERCISE
Do Nothing

***

We begin with one of the hardest practices—do nothing! It may sound a bit too simple or even ridiculous. It is, however, a worthy practice to consider. In our busy "doing" life, we often do not allow the time or space to pause and filter out chaotic energies and noise.

The practice is straightforward and easy to follow. Sit quietly, eyes open or closed, and do nothing for one to five minutes (e.g., a few times a day). During this time, become a witness, observing your experience or whatever arises moment to moment without judgment. At first, the practice may cause anxiety as your mind races to tell you everything you could be doing. Over time, however, you can reinforce and build the ever-present muscle of "being and aware-ness," allowing you to unwind, quiet the noise, and reconnect to the stillness that lies hidden within.

❋ **EXERCISE**
Just Do That

This is another simple but difficult exercise. It can be performed at any time of the day and with any experience or activity. It's a call or movement away from multitasking to a more concentrated sin-gle-pointed focus.

Whatever activity you're engaging in (washing the dishes, talking to a loved one, taking a shower, cleaning the house), soak in this one activity or experience. Be mindful, present, and learn to control your attention like shining a flashlight on the task at hand.

❋ **EXERCISE**
Noticing

The next step is to simply notice, take time, and become curious about your internal and external environments. As you do, begin naming, out loud or internally, what you see, hear, smell, taste, or feel.

One of the best practices is the *See, Hear, Feel* technique devel-oped by American mindfulness teacher Shinzen Young. It consists of deepening three attention skills (concentration, sensory clarity, and equanimity) as your awareness focuses on six areas: see-in, see-out, hear-in, hear-out, feel-in, and feel-out.

- Concentration is the ability to focus on what you choose (following one's breath or listening to the chirping birds outside).

- Sensory clarity is the ability to track and explore our senses. It involves paying attention to the clarity, textures, and flavors of any sense experience. Often, these sensory clarity experiences are not something we are usually attuned to. As an example, if an angry thought arises, follow the awareness down into the body, noticing associated sensations in your chest and skin.

- Equanimity is the ability to allow sensory experiences to come and go without push and pull. Each experience has a natural birth and death with a punctuated space in between. Attuning to this process without fighting, disowning, rejecting, and resting is equanimity.

- See, Hear, Feel
  - See-out refers to what you see in the environment.
  - See-in refers to what you see inside your mind's eye (e.g., visual images).
  - Feel-out refers to physical sensations (including taste and smell) from the environment, such as the wind in your hair, the temperature of the room, the way the chair feels on your back, and so on.
  - Feel-in refers to physical sensations (including taste and smell) that relate to internal states such as the grumbling of your stomach and various emotional and feeling states.
  - Hear-out refers to what you hear in the outside world.
  - Hear-in refers to internal sounds such as the conversations in your head.

- The Practice:
  - Sit in a comfortable position with eyes open for a while, then closed. For five to ten minutes, begin to identify what you see, hear, and feel in your internal and external environment.

❀ **EXERCISE**
Awe

Awe contains mixed feeling states such as joy, overwhelm, and fear. It is a perception of vastness and can be perceptual (e.g., a beautiful sunset) or conceptual (e.g., listening to speech or reading a great book). This is a simple but profound practice that involves two steps:

1. Turn your attention towards an experience, big or small. It is easiest to focus on an experience you appreciate and find awe-inspiring, pleasurable, enjoyable, or value (a conversation, a bird chirping, a sunset, an activity).

2. Breathe in and out of the experience, literally and metaphorically, by savoring, slowing down, amplifying associated feelings, and discovering or connecting to the beauty or essence underpinning the material realm.

Breath Work

Breath is life. Life is breath. In fact, the English word for spirit comes from the Latin word spiritus, which translates as breath. It works to serve us, keeping us alive, and, paradoxically, can run anxiety-like maladaptive patterns. In short, our daily breathing patterns are short and shallow (from the chest), activating the overused sympathetic fight and flight mechanisms of the autonomic nervous system.

Even though the breath, most of the time, runs automatically, it can be consciously controlled to produce healing state changes. Depending on the context and what is needed, we can use our breath in various ways to calm, relax, heal, or energize our body-mind. For example, deep diaphragmatic breathing with longer exhalations is one of the best ways to activate the parasympathetic, rest, recovery, and healing physiology of the body. Here are a few simple but profound techniques to add to your daily practice. Please note, these are suggestions, and inhalation, exhalation, and rest periods need not be dogmatically followed.

❁ EXERCISE
The Relaxing Parasympathetic Breath

---

1. Breathe in through your nose for a count of five, expanding your chest and belly.
2. Hold your breath for a few counts.
3. Exhale through pursed lips (as if you were breathing through a straw) for an extended period longer than your inhalation (e.g., a count of ten).
4. Hold your breath for a few counts.
5. Breathe normally for a few rounds.
6. Repeat the entire process five to ten times.
7. Perform throughout the day as often as needed.

❁ EXERCISE
The Energizing Breath

---

1. Ten to twenty breaths: two seconds forceful inhalation and two seconds forceful exhalation

2. Ten to twenty breaths: one second forceful inhalation and one second forceful exhalation

3. Ten to twenty breaths: half second forceful inhalation and half second forceful exhalation

---

❋ **EXERCISE**
Balance (Right and Left Brain) and Concentration Breath

---

1. Close your right nostril with your fingers, and slowly breathe in and out one to two times through your left nostril.
2. Close your left nostril with your fingers, and slowly breathe in and out one to two times through your right nostril.
3. Repeat ten times.

❋ **EXERCISE**
Heart-Respiratory-Brain Coherence

---

1. Begin with awareness and conscious breathing, neither slowing nor speeding your breath.
2. Place both hands, palm facing into your chest, over your heart.
3. Breathe in and out at a controlled, comfortable, and slow pace allowing your focus, attention, and breath to converge at your heart center. Connect here for five to ten breaths.
4. Next, keep one hand over your heart and place the other on your forehead.
5. Breathe in and out at a controlled, comfortable, and slow pace allowing your focus, attention, and breath to converge

in an expanded space between your heart and head. Connect here for five to ten breaths.

6. Throughout your practice, try to recall and embody a nourishing, positive, or meaningful memory or experience. Savor, amplify, and drink in the positive associative emotions, feelings, and mental pictures. Some of the most meaningful and powerful emotional states to connect with are compassion, love, gratitude, forgiveness, and the embodiment of your future or highest Self.

Heart-Respiratory-Brain Coherence "Flavors"

- Eyes can remain open or closed
- Hand placement is optional
- Can stay with the heart the entire time
- Use of eye patterns to integrate right and left-brain hemispheres, such as eye gazing (moving your eyes, not your head) to the right and left during intermittent breathing cycles
- Add the sentiment of love and benevolence to yourself and others. This is a type of scripting based on the Buddhist *Metta* or *Loving Kindness* meditation practice. These mantras can be added at any time to the practice above. Repeat the words below, starting with yourself, as you connect to your breath and heart space. Next, extend this loving mantra to your inner circle, friends, and family, then to strangers, people with whom you experience difficulty, humanity, all beings, and, finally, all of manifestation:

> *May I be filled with love.*
> *May I be peaceful.*
> *May I be safe and secure.*

May I be healthy.
May I stay connected with love.

❀ EXERCISE
Grounding or Earthing

This is Vitamin N (Nature). We don't need science to tell us there is something special, something nourishing, something reciprocal, and something healing about connecting with Mother Nature. The benefits of walking on the beach or gardening, for example, cannot be quantified. They are felt experiences.

The scientific term for this is Earthing or grounding. Some identifiable objective benefits include immediate coherence, discharging non-nourishing electromagnetic pollution (e.g., cell phones), and charging the body, like a battery, with negative electrons and harmonizing frequencies (e.g., Schumann resonance, 7.83hz). This healing charge infuses our cells with voltage and helps to neutralize and decrease free radicals and inflammation. Practices include:

- Going outside (be still, observe, and listen)
- Walking barefoot on your lawn, at the beach, or in a nature preserve
- Working in the garden with your hands
- Lying on the grass
- Connecting with animals
- Connecting with plants
- Biohacking with Earthing or Grounding mats

❀ **EXERCISE**
Meditation

Meditation is grounded in the ordinary, the mystical, and the spiritual. For some, it conjures up visions of ancient seers sitting in the lotus position for hours and days in caves, but this form or style of practice is not the only way to do it. Meditation, at its core, should be personal. There is no right or wrong way to practice. The effect, not the form, should be your focus. Listed below is a simple mediative practice that can be individualized in various ways:

1. Sit quietly and comfortably in an environment that offers few, if any, distractions.
2. Let your eyes be opened or closed.
3. Choose an anchor: your breath, your body (e.g., body scans), a candle (flame), a mantra, your heart space (e.g., loving-kindness meditation), an emotion, a quote, a song, or a guided mediation.
4. Stay present with your anchor, and every time your mind drifts, slowly guide it back, lovingly without judgement, to your chosen anchor.
5. Integrate any breathing technique you desire.

CHAPTER 23

The Sandwich Method and The Elemental Diet

Most of us wouldn't think of beginning our day without washing the accumulated dirt from the day before off our bodies. Yet far too often we go out into the day without similarly cleansing our minds. And our minds carry more pollution than our bodies, for they carry not only our own toxicity but the entire world. At the beginning of the day, the mind is most open to receive new impressions. One of the most important things we can do is to take full responsibility for the power of the morning.

-Marianne Williamson

The Sandwich Method

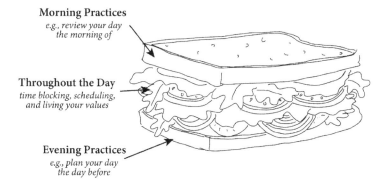

Morning Practices
e.g., review your day the morning of

Throughout the Day
time blocking, scheduling, and living your values

Evening Practices
e.g., plan your day the day before

The Sandwich Method is a nondogmatic approach to starting and ending your day with direction, confidence, nourishment, coherence, and healing. Too often, we commit to a certain practice (e.g., morning gratitude journal), find ourselves skipping a day here and there, shaming ourselves, and, ultimately, stopping with the practice altogether.

The Sandwich Method is the anecdote to monotony. It fosters diversity of practice and allows you to cultivate practices aligned with your intuition, intentions, best or worse days, mood, and energies. The Sandwich Method represents the pinnacle of self-development advice: plan your day the day before, review your day the morning of, and prioritize what matters most by time blocking and scheduling your values in between. The Sandwich Method is best summarized from the Marianne Williamson quote above.

The Sandwich Method

1. Carve out as little as one to five minutes or more (ten to thirty minutes) at the beginning and end of your day (your daily sandwich).

2. Find a place of solace or refuge. It can be anywhere, such as sitting in your bed or outside on the lawn. Dedicate this sacred time to feeding and nourishing yourself.

3. Prior to any formal practice, make a list of nourishing activities or experiences (five to ten items). Depending on your mood, energies, intuition, or your day's quality, choose the practice that best speaks to you in the moment. Allow flexibility and avoid making this a rigid practice. Examples include:
   - Planning your day the night before
   - Prioritizing what matters most by time blocking and scheduling your values

- Reviewing your vision, goals, and values
- Listening to a guided meditation
- Breathwork or coherence exercises
- Prayer
- Listening to a favorite or inspiring piece of music
- Reading an inspiring book
- Journaling or simply contemplating various questions such as: *What am I grateful for? What one thing must occur today to make this a great day? Who do I have to become today? What thoughts, emotions, and actions must think, feel, and take today? How did I respond today? How did I show up today? What lessons did I learn today?*
- Sitting in silence
- Looking in the mirror and saying, *I love you*
- The Elemental Diet (see below)
- The Manifestation Method
- Self-realization practices
- And more…

The Elemental Diet (Earth, Air, Fire, Water, and Ether)

According to the Indian Ayurvedic tradition, the elements of life are earth, air, fire, water, and ether. The Elemental Diet is a way to feed these primal elements and an opportunity to expand your definition of nutrients to anything that nourishes the mind, body, and soul. The Elemental Diet is a way to reconnect and plug back into what feeds us, gives us life, and provides us energy. It is an opportunity to break the pattern of disconnection that occurs throughout the day, morning, or evening when we plug into our electronics, phones, or the news.

Many ways to implement these elements in your daily, morning, or evening practices are available. Throughout the day we can choose just one or two elements, such as stepping outside (Earth) or taking a deep diaphragmatic breath (air) to quiet our overactive nervous system.

Here is an example of how to combine these elements in a simple but profound way to start your day:

- Air: Wake up and fill your body with ten to fifteen deep diaphragmatic breaths.
- Water: Reach for your water, drink, and rehydrate.
- Fire and Earth: Within ten to fifteen minutes of rising, go outside, and let the sun's rays hit the photoreceptors of your eyes to stimulate AM hormonal production. Touch the earth with your hands or bare feet to allow Mother Nature's radiating love (e.g., negative electron antioxidants) to fuel your body, mind, and soul.
- Ether: Connect with your values (who and what's most important to you), needs, goals, and dreams. Add any spiritual or religious practices that help you to connect to that which lies within and beyond you.

Chronobiology

Chronobiology is the art of synchronizing our actions and behaviors alongside the natural rhythms and cycles of the elements, sun and moon, seasonal variations, circadian rhythms (twenty-four-hour cycle), and ultradian cycles (biological rhythms with periods shorter than twenty-four-hours, minutes to hours). Chronobiology is about our relationship with Mother Nature. Here are just three examples:

- Sleep cycles
  - It is important to respect the twenty-four-hour circadian rhythm and practice appropriate sleep hygiene. This could include digital sunsetting in the evening (decreasing light exposure, eliminating electronic usage, and participating in calming, relaxing activities) and, upon waking, obtaining adequate sunlight and participating in nourishing morning rituals. If your schedule works against these natural rhythms, it may be helpful to look into various biohacking aids such as blue-blocking glasses.
  - Seasonal variations could include attuning to increased sleep during the winter months and decreased hours during the summer months.
- Eating and exercising for the seasons
  - A rather rudimentary example could be engaging in more aerobic activities and eating more cooling foods, fruits, smoothies, and sprouts during the spring and summer months and engaging in more strength training and eating more warming foods, soups, and fats during the winter months.
- Daily ultradian rhythms
  - An example would include honoring task-energy delegation. The human body tends to move through multiple sixty- to ninety-minute ultradian cycles throughout the day—a physiological period of activity followed by a short period of recharge. For optimal health, it is best to work with rather than against this natural inherent rhythm. We must try and take cues from our body when we find our concentration

and energy beginning to fade. Practically speaking, you may choose to work on your most important tasks for sixty to ninety minutes, then recharge, take a break, stretch, or go outside before starting back. Just imagine how many people, during an eight-hour work shift or a task-oriented day, push through these natural cycles and avoid all recharging sessions (e.g., making deposits into our energy-vitality bank). Years of this type of repetitive behavior will cause increased energy-vitality bank withdrawals, eventually moving you from wired and tired to complete exhaustion.

- Balancing being-doing, rest-recovery, and appreciating or embracing whatever "season of life" is showing up for you in this moment.

CHAPTER 24

Emotional-Relational Practices

Love and compassion are necessities, not luxuries. Without them, humanity cannot survive.

-Dalai Lama, XIV

Emotions, needs, and relationships are intimately connected. Recall, the primal struggle is the term given to the inherent universal human motivation for need's fulfillment and emotional expression. The story of our life revolves around how our needs are met, unmet, or frustrated.

Emotional Dimension

Self-actualizing in the emotional dimension involves understanding the true nature of our emotions and how they can be appreciated, honored, and used as catalysts for growth, transformation, and right action. Emotions call upon us to consider a momentary pause before making reactionary fear-based responses. Psychologists refer to this practice as emotional intelligence.

It is best summed up by the quote from an Austrian psychiatrist and Nazi-concentration camp survivor Victor Frankl, who stated we should strive to "…put a space in between stimulus and response." In doing so, we can summon a more loving, fruitful, constructive, and heroic response.

One of the greatest practices in the emotional dimension is to experience, name, and consciously acknowledge our emotions as they arise from moment to moment. We are asked to include the pleasant and the unpleasant emotions without judgment, denial, or avoidance. We are asked to practice nonresistance. The goal is not to eat emotions away, numb them with drugs, or drown them in mind-less hours of TV bingeing. Rather, we are asked to recognize their unique signatures, allow them to burn, show us their gifts and life lessons, and lovingly burn out.

We can use our emotions for either health or disease. The choice is ours. The first step is self-awareness. This leads to self-management. Both of these processes help us avoid pathological fusion (e.g., getting lost and becoming the emotion).

The emotional dimension calls us to lovingly engage in the pleasures and joys of life without shame or guilt. It calls on us to cocreate and participate in the generation of the so-called positive emotions such as joy, peace, equanimity, happiness, and excitement. We must allow ourselves to relish in the ecstasies of various experiences and activities (from the simple joy of mindful eating, play, sensuality, and sexuality) in our day-to-day existence rather than pushing these pri-mordial drives to some future date for fulfillment. The archetypes of the caregiver and martyr must be balanced with nourishing care, compassion, and attention to ourselves. At various moments or sea-sons in our life, we are asked to become child-like (not childish).

Relational Dimension

This dimension includes the relationship with ourselves, our children, our loved ones, our friends, our "enemies," Mother Earth, sentient creatures, and beyond. Technically, everything exists in relationship. Nothing stands independent from the great web of life.

Self-actualizing in this dimension includes fostering mutual care, mutual empowerment, mutual understanding, mutual purpose, mutual respect, compassion, and dialogue (rather than "monologue"). It is about creating value in ourselves and our daily interactions with others. The move from the emotional to the relational dimension bridges the gap between one's personal power and the extension of love. It's a move from autonomy to communion.

Self-actualizing in the relational dimension starts with our most important relationship—the one with our true Self. Our intrapersonal relationship is about integrity, values, and character. It beckons us to turn our virtues and values from Pollyanna-like wishes into tangible habits, actions, and deeds. According to Brene Brown, research professor at the University of Houston and author of *The Gifts of Imperfection*, integrity can be defined as choosing courage over comfort, choosing what's right over what's fun, fast, and easy, as well as practicing, rather than professing, one's values.

The relational dimension calls us to practice, cultivate, and embody an intrinsic rather than extrinsic locus of self-worth. It asks that we avoid using the temperature of others as a means of determining our self-worth. Our goal is to cultivate love and self-worth from within, not without. This is the beginning of unconditional love, the cornerstone of the relational dimension. If we betray or trespass against ourselves, we will betray and trespass against others.

The relational dimension embraces the virtue and skill of empathy. It involves the art of understanding, really trying to know another person, and perspective-taking or learning to "walk a mile in another's shoes." Empathy brings the wisdom gained from the emotional dimension and builds on it. Empathetic listening includes being present, quieting the chaotic noise in our heads, creating a welcoming space, and opening our hearts. Empathy invites us to connect with and understand the true needs of another person. The art of empathetic communication involves naming our emotions, lovingly expressing our needs, and never assuming others have magical fortune-telling powers to know our desires, needs, and wants.

The relational dimension is not about codependency, being right, imposing values on another, speaking first, and so on. Love, rather, is synonymous with acceptance, not agreement. Love involves creating and establishing healthy boundaries in all relationships, including ourselves. It is important to evaluate and periodically prune our interpersonal relationships. Which ones need to be released or let go of? Which ones are calling us to surrender or accept things just the way they are? Which ones require new boundaries? Which ones require boundaries to be redrawn?

One way to think about this is to categorize relations in terms of the seasons. In this respect, some people come into our lives for a reason, a season, or a lifetime. Trying to change a seasonal relationship into a lifetime relationship or vice versa must be met with caution, a sincerity of heart, and a balance of what best serves us as well as others.

The quality of our encounters is based on what we are willing to give and what we are withholding from another. Contrary to how many of us play the game, the quality of our encounters is not reliant on how others show up or interact with us. Our experience with others depends on how we show up and respond. *A Course in Miracles* states, "Only what we are not giving can be lacking in any situation." It is helpful to remind ourselves that we are responsible for what we think, say, and do. Sometimes, for example, the best gift you can give someone is to let them learn their lessons on their own time. Your job is to love them, accept them, and respect them for who they are. Our job is not to change them but rather invite them to change, create a healthy environment, and lead, as best we can—by example.

The relational dimension calls on us to evaluate our projections. Remember, our projections act like mirrors, reflecting unflattering personal qualities we cannot see in ourselves but have no problem identifying in others. As we begin to look within and uncover these unconscious shadow elements, we are gifted with an opportunity to transmute and transcend the shadow of toxicity into the light of nourishment. The ego projects. Love extends.

The relational dimension asks us to reinterpret our relationship with other sentient beings. It asks us to extend care, compassion, and concern to all sentient creatures. The old paradigm sees animals as inferior, as things, as property, and something we can use no matter the cost. Our awakening Kosmocentric consciousness rejects these ideas and embraces animals as part of the interconnected web, with their own interests and their own God-given rights for freedom and autonomy. We engage in relationships and respect and extend love toward those who share this earth.

Emotional and Relational Intelligent Practices

Emotional and relational intelligence embraces self-awareness for self-regulation. Below is a checklist of skills, attributes, and practices to help grow and evolve in these dimensions. Start with a few areas that speak to you. Perhaps, these are the areas you're struggling with or simply lack awareness of:

- Engage in emotional literacy or naming our emotions and the emotions of others.
- Understand our emotions by tracing them back to universal needs or primordial elements.
- Identify our needs (conscious and subconscious) independent of emotional weather patterns.
- Identify our values.
- Practice emotional diffusion by witnessing emotions (e.g., mindfulness).
- Respond rather than react for more heroic actions and decision-making.
- Learn to communicate and express our needs and emotions by sharing from the heart. Use appropriate language (such as I am, I feel, and I need) and state facts (without victimization, judging, blaming, comparing, or shaming) rather than opinions.
- Become self-aware before engaging in conversation. Am I ready for dialogue? Monologue? Am I retreating? Am I angry? By asking these questions first, we can move from self-awareness to self-management.
- Learn to stay open with a loving desire to connect and understand others' needs.
- Empathetically listen, allowing others to truly feel as if they have been seen and heard.
- Self-fulfill our needs.
- Learn to receive needs from others. Understand the universal spiritual principle, *giving is receiving* and vice versa.

- Create a safe space and growth environment for others to understand, self-fulfill, communicate, receive, and nourish their own needs.
- Cultivate positive emotions or states that are nourishing and growth-promoting. Engage in healthy pleasures (without guilt), embracing self-care, participle in sensual feel-good practices, and allow time for play.

Holy and Special Relationships

A Course in Miracles differentiates special versus holy relationships. Exploring this topic can help us embrace and move closer to a continuous practice of unconditional love.

The special relationship is a metaphor for singling out a person, object, or ideology to be the source of our happiness and fulfillment. It is based on the faulty notion that what we feel or seek in others is analogous to what we want or lack within ourselves. It is an illusionary mental construct that states we are inadequate or incomplete if we are not completed, complimented, or in union with another.

It represents codependency, addictions, enmeshments, and more. Special love relationships seek to be completed by another. We are trying to get that which we lack from another. It is based on conditions, "I will love you only if you meet my ego's needs." Most of the conditions and expectations we force on others are unconscious, unreasonable, and unattainable. The maxim of the special relationship is, "You complete me." The flaw in this approach is that if love is withdrawn—it will render you incomplete.

Holy relationships are unconditional and allow each person the opportunity to be heard, to express, to grow, evolve, and self-actualize. It's an acceptance of another without the need to change them. This type of unconditional love shines through when you are in the presence of someone who creates an environment of safety where shame, lack, and guilt are dismantled. They know you wholeheartedly, knowing everything there is to know about you, yet no judgment is given.

A Course in Miracles summarizes this beautifully, "An unholy relationship is based on differences, where each one thinks the other has what he has not. A holy relationship starts from a different premise. Each one has looked within and seen no lack. Accepting his completion, he would extend it by joining with another, whole as himself. He sees no difference between these selves, for differences are only of the body."

A holy relationship is about seeing the "god essence" in another—our shared divinity. We are reminded to lead from the heart. Here are a few more quotations to help remind us to lead from the heart:

- "When you meet anyone, remember it is a holy encounter. As you see him, you will see yourself. As you treat him, you will treat yourself. As you think of him, you will think of yourself. Never forget this, for in him, you will find yourself or lose yourself." *A Course in Miracles*
- "When you establish conditions on love, you experience the conditions, not the love." Paul Ferrini
- "Could a greater miracle take place than for us to look through each other's eyes for an instant?" Henry David Thoreau

Granulation and Perspective-Taking

Although this next technique could fit easily as a practice in the mental dimension, I have chosen to include it here as an emotional-relational practice because above and beyond its intellectual exploration, it gifts us with perspective taking, which is one of the greatest practices for understanding and connecting to others.

Multiple intelligences

Through all of life's dimensions, there exist various human potentials and intelligences. The idea of multiple intelligences began with the pioneering work of researcher Howard Gardner, who proposed in his 1983 book *Frames of Mind: The Theory of Multiple Intelligences*, that intelligence encompasses a much broader spectrum than the previously held IQ (Intellectual Quotient) highlighted in academia.

The field of multiple intelligence has grown over the years with debates on which intelligences to include, omit, or add. I have included the basic intelligences, reinterpreted others, and added two intelligences, interspecies and intraspecies that are critical and necessary intelligences to counter the hidden aspects of speciesism that pervade almost every aspect of society today.

- Physical intelligence: the ability to connect with physical practices (e.g., food selection and movement patterns) that nourish the body
- Emotional intelligence: self-awareness of emotions for self-management, digestion, and transcendence
- Mental intelligence: self-awareness of mental constructs for self-management, transcendence, and choice selection (e.g., choosing the most empowering, loving, constructive, and helpful stories, beliefs, myths, memes)
- IQ: or classical intellectual intelligence
- Moral intelligence: the ability to know right from wrong

- Intuitional intelligence: heightened and resonating connection to extrasensory information
- Spiritual intelligence: our personal relationship to the divine as well as questions pertaining to those aspects of life that are of ultimate concern
- Naturalistic, environmental, or Mother Nature intelligence
- Linguistic
- Logical-mathematical
- Spatial
- Musical
- Intrapersonal intelligence: our relationship to Self
- Interpersonal intelligence: our relationship with others who share close physical and/or emotional proximity
- Interspecies intelligence: our relationship with sentient living creatures outside our species
- Intraspecies intelligence: our relationship with humanity, those of the same species, not in close physical and/or emotional proximity

Granulation and Mutual Exclusiveness

We previously discussed the concept of mutual exclusiveness, one of the most pervasive self-actualizing pathologies. It is defined as self-actualizing in one dimension (physical, emotional, relational, mental, and spiritual) at the expense, mutual exclusiveness, or pathology of another dimension. We will now build upon this idea and present a more practical application.

I believe the concept of either looking at the dimensions or at their perspective intelligences allows us to shine a light on areas of our psyche, body, and spirit where we are healthy, where we are wounded, where potentiality still exists, where potentiality does not, and where pathologies may be lurking away from our conscious awareness. It is one of the most important tools for self-actualization.

As we look at the various intelligences in ourselves and others, we are called to bring awareness, unconditional love, understanding, and perspective-taking. This process will be referred to as granulation. Rather than seeing a person as a single line of intelligence, individual granulation expands our heart space and compassion to help explain the human condition and its many contradictions through a process of holism. In part, it is granulating an individual through the lens of multiple intelligences.

The goal of this process is not about achieving mastery (e.g., in each area of life or intelligence) or pointing out shortcomings. The goal or technique, once again, is about awareness, unconditional love, and understanding. This allows us to lay the foundation for right action or inaction.

Dominator and Growth Hierarchies

To understand the concept of granulation, we must unpack the definitions of dominator versus growth hierarchy. According to Ken Wilber and Integral theory, it is not hierarchies themselves that are bad. Rather, it is the inability to differentiate the two. As the name implies, dominator hierarchies foster domination, separation, disconnection, inequality, and racism and are responsible for most, if not all, wars. This is ethnocentric consciousness. Examples include the ancient caste and feudal systems where the inherited chosen ones rightfully took their position on the caste pyramid of moral superiority, allowing them to dominate those on the inferior or lower caste rungs.

A growth hierarchy, conversely, is void of childish hierarchies based on birth, race, and color. A growth hierarchy is a factual description of life and evolution. For example, it would be absurd to say that a forty-year-old man is better or superior to a two-year-old boy. They both have different levels of consciousness in a growth or evolutionary hierarchy. In other words, we can bring awareness and love to this simple fact (people grow from childhood to adolescence to adulthood) without clouding it with dominator-type hierarchical thinking or stories.

Hierarchies are everywhere—government, schools, workplace, and family dynamics. In our society, a spiritual and religious hierarchy assumes animal and physical inferiority. It values spiritual growth over physical, earth, or "root" growth. It demonizes the pleasures of the flesh (e.g., sexuality) in light of religious doctrine. However, life is a paradox. On the other side, modernity has clung to a disease-oriented physical hierarchy (focus on symptoms, achievement, drugs, and surgery) over cause and use of noninvasive dietary and lifestyle practices.

It is important not to elevate our external and internal heroes to some type of transcendental glory or, on the other side, take the internal and external shadow or villains and blacklist them without, first, bringing a sincerity of heart, empathetic understanding, and using the process of individual granulation to augment a heart-centered approach.

One of our greatest challenges and forever practices is that of unconditional love. Individual granulation offers us a way to separate a person's essence—the god within—from their acts, wounds, shadows, behaviors, persona, and masks. In short, we name to understand, to tame, and to transcend in both ourselves and others.

Let's look at a few previously used examples (in the section on mutual exclusiveness) to see how this process of granulation may be useful:

- An individual puts all their attention on lofty spiritual goals and dreams for humanity (the spiritual dimension) at the expense of their loved ones (relational dimension)
  - Granulation: high spiritual intelligence and low interpersonal intelligence
- An individual is highly intellectual (mental dimension) at the expense of being in touch with his or her emotions (emotional dimension)
  - Granulation: high mental intelligence and low emotional intelligence
- Someone displays Islamophobia, anti-Semitism, and various other forms of discrimination
  - These individuals can be quite high on almost any intelligence but all share commonalities of low moral intelligence.
- Imagine a spiritual guru with profound meditative awakening-type contemplative or meditative skills. He does not, however, treat his body as a sanctuary and struggles with one-on-one interactions or relations. He also possesses homophobic or xenophobic tendencies, which he argues are grounded in his religious doctrines. This is the concept we discussed and summarized through the insight, "not all transcenders are actualizers."
  - Granulating this particular guru, we can understand him better if we say that they have superior and increased spiritual intelligence, low physical

intelligence, low interpersonal intelligence, and low moral intelligence.

- An animal activist is unable to show compassion or empathy toward people of his or her own species—humanity—who do not share or hold his or her view
  - o Granulation: high interspecies intelligence and low intraspecies intelligence

A Personal Example

In looking deeper at the last example, I recall a time in my life when my expansiveness, empathy, and love towards animals (interspecies intelligence) grew leaps and bounds, and the veils of deceit were pulled from my eyes. I consider this time in my life a type of awakening experience. It's as if I lived metaphorically through three different days.

Day One was the "old me." I awoke in the morning, got dressed (put on my shoes, pants, and belt), ate breakfast, lunch, and dinner, and carried my outdated unconscious programs into the world. Day Two, I awoke, and "the ghost of Marley" reviewed my life, showing me the origins of my food choices (factory farms), the atrocities involved in the production of the very clothing I was wearing (e.g., leather products), and how animals were treated in circuses, zoos, and the entertainment industry. On Day Three, my soul's awareness would no longer allow me to participate in conscious animal exploitation. My life changed forever.

As I was shown the truth of animal exploitation and cruelty, I woke up, so to speak, to my participation and responsibility. Within one day, I began living in alignment with my outrage and sadness by committing myself never to use animals, eat animals, wear animals, or participate in activities (such as circuses) where animal exploitation occurred, explicitly or implicitly. This aspect of my life has now become so engrained within the caverns of my soul that I no longer have to think about it. With expanded awareness, we do better when we know better. Any behaviors or actions in direct opposition to my values are now seen as acts of self-betrayal.

As my care, compassion, and concern grew for those outside my species, it also carried shadow elements, albeit for only a short time, that grew less tolerant of those who did not share or "see" my view. In other words, my care, compassion, and concern for those within my own species became more and more judgmental. And in doing so, a pathology of conditional love and regression unfolded.

I believe it is important to avoid pigeon-holing and participating in "single-issue campaigns" that pathologically develop one line of intelligence (e.g., interspecies intelligence) at the expense of other dimensions (e.g., intraspecies intelligence). It is not that single issues (women's rights, racial inequality, animal exploitation, reforming the penal system, contributing to specific charities) should be stopped, reallocated, or considered inadequate in their pursuits. The issue, rather, is about their intentionality and effect. In other words, we must be on guard for lofty pursuits that simultaneously sprout pathologies in other lines of intelligence.

One particular concern is unconscious ethnocentric regression. As an example, imagine an individual who professes love, care, and concern for the universe, the animals, the environment, and humanity (e.g., Kosmocentric consciousness) and, at the same time, violently attacks those who disagree or who hold different values or beliefs. It's as if a moral unconscious superiority emerges that blinds them to the contradictions of their actions and values.

To avoid this self-actualizing pathology, we can use the initial emotions of sadness, outrage, anger, disgust, and pain to help push us forward into action. As we nurture these emotions, they transform alongside the level of consciousness that embraces them. At the pinnacle of our transformation, a Kosmocentric consciousness holds these emotions deeply within a context of love rather than fear. In doing so, these emotions can be used as exponential agents of change. No greater example of this transformation can be seen in and through the lives and actions of Mother Teresa, Gandhi, Jesus, and Martin Luther King.

CHAPTER 25
The Manifestation Method

What you think, you become. What you feel, you attract.
What you imagine, you create.
-Buddha

The mental dimension is complex with more subtlety than the physical, emotional, and relational realms. In many instances, it acts as a true bridge between the subtle and gross. Our thoughts become manifestations in the gross realm as they move from potential to actualization. For example, all the technology we see today was once a thought in the mind of a dreamer—electricity, TV, airplanes, computers, the internet, and a man on the moon. As one takes the more subtle mental constructs and adds tangibility through communication and action, the true creative powers become actualized, and we give credence to the saying, "Thoughts become things."

This dimension is about cultivating inner peace, equanimity, and virtuous thoughts and speech. It includes being vigilant against our ego's repetitive, robotic, and monkey-like mind. It is the practice of finding a still place of present-moment awareness to take sanctuary.

This is referred to as mindfulness (see Chapter 22 for exercises and descriptors).

Staying centered in the mind is a form of mental Jiu-Jitsu. The power of your attention literally determines the quality of your life. Directing our minds on how, when, and where to go is one of our greatest superpowers. Consider the following quote by Zicheng Hong, "Attention is the mind's feet; if you do not control your attention strictly, it runs into misleading pathways."

Most people have fallen victim to what one British-American anthropologist calls psychosclerosis, defined as "a hardening of the attitude which causes a person to cease dreaming, seeing, thinking, and leading." It is a hardening (sclerosis) of the mind (psycho) where one becomes unteachable, stops learning, stops growing, and pathological addictions and attachments are made to their own ideas, thoughts, and views.

To self-actualize in this dimension, we must begin a process of questioning, pruning, and upgrading our outdated beliefs, operating systems, personal philosophies, stories, and internal questions we ask ourselves.

Conscious Language

Your language reflects your reality. It reflects your level of consciousness and subconscious beliefs. Most of us don't take time to analyze the impact and consequences of the language we use to communicate to ourselves and others. If you wake up every morning dreading the day and going to work, you will, quite simply, dread the day and the time you spend at work. If someone asks you how you're doing and you reply, "busy," you will forever remain busy. As Henry Ford stated, "Whether you think you can, or you think you can't—you're right."

Any words that come after the words I am or similar correlates (I am unhappy, I am lazy, I have "x" disease) are particularly important. These words are so powerful that each statement becomes a declaration of being and an agreement you're making, consciously or subconsciously, about your limitations or lack thereof.

In addition to our narration and dialogue, the questions we ask ourselves are just as powerful. Tony Robbins states, "Quality questions create a quality life. Successful people ask better questions, and as a result, they get better answers." We can ask empowering and benevolent-type questions such as, "How can I help someone today? How can I become a better person from this experience?" These questions provide an opportunity to learn, co-create, and make a difference. On the opposite spectrum, we can ask limiting, judging, shameful, and destructive type questions such as, "Why does this always happen to me?" These questions leave us powerless, imprisoned, and in a state of victim consciousness. Einstein states it succinctly, "If I had an hour to solve a problem and my life depended on the solution, I would spend the first fifty-five minutes determining the proper question to ask… for once I knew the proper question, I could solve the problem in less than five minutes."

One last way to practice conscious language is to repeat and declare intentional affirmations or incantations (affirmations with emotions, strong vocalizations, and body movements) that keep our energies aligned and focused on who and what is most important.

The Manifestation Method

Instead of specific steps to manifestation, I think it's important to talk about the conditions (regardless of the order) that, if met, will help to guarantee, more times than not, our conscious intentions become a reality. For example, the more conditions we cohere together in the dimensions or embody in The Alignment Continuum (awareness, attention, intention, beliefs, thoughts, emotions, feelings, habits, and behaviors), the more "compounding interest" we experience, and more our chances of success and fulfillment increase.

As mentioned earlier, our subconscious, the iceberg below the water's surface, is arguably the strongest contributing factor directing our lives, with estimates as high as 95 percent or more. For this very reason, we are unable to simply state an intention, sit back, and expect life to happen to us. This is not the language of the subconscious. Any treatment plan that does not include subconscious practices is a form of malpractice in terms of actualizing our potential.

Our subconscious, just like the conscious mind, has its own language, needs, values, beliefs, goals, and habits. It prioritizes comfort, safety, and protection. It runs outdated childhood programs that no longer serve us. These programs, fed by the bedrock of limiting beliefs, exaggerate the effects of so-called negative experiences and interpret our conscious language as literal truth (e.g., it's raining cats and dogs).

To manifest, we must use this knowledge to reprogram the subconscious with the language it understands and responds to. This includes using our emotions, feelings, the intensity of experience, repetition, and imagery. For example, advanced subconscious language practices include autosuggestion, meditation, and hypnosis techniques performed in highly receptive alpha and theta brain wave states.

The world is energy. If we don't mold this energy through conscious intention, the subconscious will, by default, step in and run the past into the present. The manifestation process can be boiled down into three distinct areas: awareness, active participation, and non-resistance/surrender:

1. We become aware, as discussed previously, of our conscious and subconscious addictions to our old and outdated self-identity (beliefs, thoughts, emotions, behaviors). As we awaken, we begin to recognize that our current reality does not match our desired reality.

2. We actively participate by speaking the language of the conscious and subconscious mind-body. This step involves conscious clarity of our dreams and goals, corresponding action, and reprogramming the subconscious mind. In this step, we cocreate and align the conscious and subconscious minds.

3. We harness the power of nonresistance and surrender to balance the previous two steps. Nonresistance is a call to courage, trust, hope, and faith. It calls on us to embrace Nature's cycles and gestation periods. It's about respecting nature's laws and learning the art of being and doing. This step calls on us to contact our highest Self and to uncover the wellspring of inherent values and feeling states that reside within (a practice we will discuss in more detail in Chapter 26). Pursuit of dreams, goals, and desires from a posture of abundance, rather than lack, ensures greater success. In other words, take part in the inside-out revolution. To become wealthy, cultivate the feeling state of abundance from within. To love others, love yourself. To find peace, look within. Connecting with source energy (love, joy, peace, abundance) makes it easier to magnetize and attract outward circumstance to you.

Aha Moments

We grow in many ways. Conversely, we regress in just as many ways too. When adversity strikes, we can use this experience to either fuel or program ourselves for post-traumatic growth or post-traumatic stress. Some wait for the heart attack before making dietary and lifestyle changes (growth by fear and negative reinforcement). Some use willpower, make a declaration, and without hesitation begin to behave in alignment with said declaration. Some fuel their growth with joy or positive reinforcements such as, "I want to be healthy, so I can see my grandchildren grow into adults." However, I believe that one specific way of growing trumps them all.

Recall the difference between change and transcendence. The metaphor of change is likened to rearranging silverware placement on a table. The metaphor of transcendence, on the other hand, is likened to ice transforming, first, into water and then into vapor. Harnessing the power of transcendence and taking your health to the next quantum leap can be found in a psychological phenomenon called the *aha* moment.

The conscious, subconscious, and collective unconscious minds are constantly piecing together and interpreting bits of information, both physical and nonphysical. Some of this processing has, as its effect, the replaying of past programs. Other times, however, novel associations are created. During these times, some information can leak into our normal stream of consciousness and appear as an instantaneous insight—an *aha* moment.

Is there a way for us to take advantage of this transrational epiphenomenon? I believe, under certain conditions, we can. Although this research is in its infancy, one day in the future, scientists may be able to identify the techniques or preconditions to amplify this experience. We will explore three techniques, one in this chapter called "beta hooking," one in Chapter 26 under the heading self-realization, and finally The Miracle Method in the chapter of the same name. My hope is these techniques will lay a foundation to help accelerate and tap into this yet-to-be-discovered resource.

❀ **EXERCISE**
The Language of the Conscious Mind

After looking at the various areas of your life (health, finances, professional) in the awareness section, choose a few areas and use your conscious mind to answer the following questions.

What and Why?

- Vision (The What)
  - What precisely, with clarity, do I want in each life area chosen?
  - In one to two years from now, what changes must manifest for me to feel fulfilled and successful?
- Emotional Charge (The Why)
  - What precisely, with clarity, do I want to feel (rather than specifically accomplish) as I look down from the 10, 000-foot view on the totality of my life?
  - Why do I want this?
  - What is the purpose behind the vision?
  - Can I connect this vision with a need? An internal state I want to experience (e.g., peace)?

Who?

Everyone has a superhero waiting to be birthed. Remember when you were young and how, at times, you could instantaneously embody your favorite superhero? Remember how invincible you were—your mind unable to distinguish fact from fiction.

Todd Herman, the author of the *Alter Ego Effect*, says the power of using an alter ego and its rewards is not solely reserved for our childhood fantasies. Adults, he suggests, can harness this same power. In fact, at different moments and in various situations, we can all search our past and recall times when we wore capes and embodied personas to rise above our adversities, acting in heroic ways.

Chances are you're familiar with the tale of Clark Kent going into a phone booth to transform into the superhero, Superman. Who, however, is the alter ego—Clark Kent or Superman?

The Oxford Languages define alter ego as a person's secondary or alternative personality. Most people contemplating the above question answer with Superman rather than Clark Kent. The truth, however, is the opposite. In this context, the real you is your heroic and highest Self. Therefore, the goal is to choose, in any given situation, the higher and more empowered Self to step forward in a sea of hundreds to thousands of inner parts or subpersonalities. In essence, we are looking to create our future Self in all his or her glory.

- Identify Your Who
    - Who am I already at my deepest core?
    - How does my best Self start the day?
    - Who do I have to become? What are the needs, values, beliefs, habits, actions, and behaviors of my highest Self? What are my superpowers?

- ○ What is the name of my alter ego? What is the name of my highest Self?
- • Identify Your Villains and Obstacles
  - ○ What is holding me back from achieving my deepest desires? Write down any present or potential future obstacle or fear? Give a name to your obstacle, your villain.
  - ○ What current habits, actions, and behaviors are getting in the way?
  - ○ Become aware of your spoken language, internal dialogue, and questions. Are they empowering, nourishing, useful, or helpful? Or are they limiting, destructive, useless, and unhelpful? Pay particular attention to I am statements. Examples include:
    - ▪ I am…
    - ▪ I can't…
    - ▪ I should…
    - ▪ I must…
    - ▪ I have to…
  - ○ Try to identify the strongest, most influential, and deepest of limiting beliefs, stories, and narratives underpinning your language. Recall from our previous discussion that beliefs usually fall into three broad categories: beliefs about the world (it's a battlefield, playground, obstacle course), beliefs about others, and beliefs about ourselves.
  - ○ Read over the levels or stages of human consciousness (see Chapter 10), the wellspring and backbone of all language and beliefs. Can you identify with a specific level or center of gravity?

How?

- What is my strategy? What do I need to do to fulfill my deepest desires? What specific daily habits and practices do I need to cultivate and schedule?

- For each area of life chosen, create quarterly SMART goals that are specific, measurable (have identifiable success criteria that must occur for accomplishment, completion, or success), achievable or attainable (something that can be started now and tied to everyday habits, activities, and rituals), rewarding (have intrinsic rewards such as the fulfillment of a need or value), and time-bound (attached with a deadline).

- Day-to-day conscious language practice: Working, at first, with the beliefs about yourself, create more empowering and constructive questions and I am statements. For example:
  - *I'm busy* becomes *I'm productive today.*
  - *I have to pick the kids up and go grocery shopping* becomes *I choose to pick the kids up and go to the grocery store.*
  - *Look at all the wrinkles* becomes *I am grateful to have lived this long.*
  - *Why is my life such a mess?* becomes *What actions can I take today in alignment with who and what's most important to me?*
  - *I am a victim of my circumstances* becomes *I am powerful and responsible for the effects in my life.*

Speaking the language of the conscious mind is not enough. The next leg of this journey is to talk to the language of the subconscious mind and connect the two.

❀ **EXERCISE**
The Language of the Subconscious

Subconscious programming will be broken down into two broad training areas: the awakened or beta and the suggestible, hypnotic, or theta brainwave entrainment state.

Theta Training

There are many ways to initiate theta subconscious reprogramming. One effective way is to use well-known practices such as meditation (guided or unguided), music, visualization, neurofeedback, biofeedback, or hypnosis. Regardless of the practice, the intention of this training is threefold:

- State change: To help induce a more relaxed, noncognitive, or synchronized brainwave state, including theta, alpha, and gamma. Simple practices include breathwork, meditation, hypnosis, and brain-altering audio entrainment (e.g., binaural beats). Advanced practices include various biohack technologies that, for example, may layer or stack multiple therapies such as music, light, vibration, imagery, and voice.
- Reprogramming: Embedded within, before, or after your chosen state change practice are software upgrade reprogramming techniques to help your transformation to your higher Self, alter ego, or the personality that simply needs to show up to accomplish said vision or goal. Guided meditations with specific hypnotic suggestions, for example,

can occur simultaneously within your state change practice. Alternatively, one can simply review their vision, values, needs, goals, upgraded beliefs, or *I am* statements prior to or after any state change practice where the mind and brain are more open to suggestions.

- Beta hooking: Use a talisman (an object such as a stone, an unfamiliar smell, a written vision statement, an inspiring word or quote, or even the simplicity of your alter ego's name, your future Self, or highest Self) directly after your state change and reprogramming practices. The talisman will serve to ritualistically connect and hook you to your practice intention. In your awakened day-to-day beta state, you will use your chosen talisman to reinforce your new software upgrade. Over weeks and months, with consistent repetition, these connections will grow stronger, allowing faster response times. Perhaps, in the future, an *aha*-like moment can be achieved that instantly connects you to your higher Self or alter ego. Please note that when choosing a talisman, it is important to use something that holds great meaning. This hook, when seen, touched, recalled, or smelled in the awakened beta state, should hold the power to transform you from the ordinary to the extraordinary.

Beta-Theta Training

Although the reprogramming of the subconscious is usually associated with the suggestible theta rather than the awakened beta state, it's of vital importance to bridge and connect both worlds. The practices listed here are designed to do just that, allowing reinforcement and alignment of your conscious intentions with your new subconscious programming.

- Change your environment. Whether you know it or not, the environment constantly triggers and replays past subconscious programs. Pull into your driveway (trigger), and a burst of "have to" chores and problems grow stronger and stronger. Drive past your favorite restaurant (trigger), your stomach rumbles, and your mouth salivates. Look at your space (home and work), begin to reconstruct an environment that supports, reinforces, and strengthens the embodiment of your higher Self, your new identity, and reminds you of your values, needs, and goals. This could be accomplished through a simple physical reminder (inspiring quote or picture), the elimination of distractions, or a more nuanced energetic harmonization to one's environment, such as the ancient Chinese practice of Feng Shui.
- Anticipate villains or obstacles that may cause self-sabotage and create a plan B.
- Talisman practices
  o Non-trigger times during the day: Use your talisman alongside heart-centered coherence exercises or The Miracle Method to help infuse your talisman with the memory and experience of loving emotional and higher consciousness states.
  o Easy triggers: Use your talisman for easy wins to strengthen and reinforce your subconscious programming.
  o Challenging triggers: Use your talisman to help with the more daunting triggers that, in the past, conditioned you to use non-nourishing language and engage in unhealthy habits.

Summary

We have covered many practices and techniques. Let's summarize and simplify to help you get started:

- Clarify your vision, goals, and desires.
- Clarify your why or the emotional state, value, or need you wish to experience.
- Clarify your who. Who do I have to become? What are the needs, values, beliefs, habits, actions, and behaviors of my highest Self?
- Clarify your how.
- Give a name to your highest Self by creating an alter ego.
- Use a talisman to connect you with your highest Self and serve as reminder for the qualities and values you need to embody or uncover to achieve said vision, goals, and desires. During the day, practice conjuring your alter ego or highest Self. Start with easy wins and more challenging triggers later.

- For thirty days straight, induce a state change (meditation, theta music, breathwork, coherence exercises) and review your visions and goals directly after. One of the most profound techniques involves the self-realization and spiritual practices in the following chapter. The goal of these practices is to put you in contact with your highest Self and uncover the wellspring of inherent values that reside within. From this abundant posture, rather than lack, you will pursue your dreams and goals, allowing nonresistance to work her magic. In this final step, you balance being and doing and embrace courage, trust, hope, faith, and nature's cycles and gestation periods.

CHAPTER 26

Self-Realization and Spiritual Practices

The purpose of things in your life is not for you to love them but to
love the Self in all things.

-Krishna

What follows are profound practices to help connect you with self-realization, transcendence, and the spiritual dimension. Although presented as an intellectual process, this is, of course, experiential. Let's
try to invoke a small taste of spiritual embodiment by beginning with
the following exercise.

❀ **EXERCISE**
Your Council of Elders

This practice was highlighted in the book *The Awakened Brain* by Lisa
Miller and taught to her by one of her mentors, Dr. Gary Weaver:

1. Take five deep breaths in and out.

2. With eyes closed, imagine a table stretched out in front of you. This is your special table.

3. You are invited to ask anyone, living or deceased, who truly has your best interest in mind to join you. Once they are seated at the table, ask them, "Do you love me?"

4. Next, invite your higher Self. This is the part of you untouched by shame, blame, and guilt. The part of you that is much more than your accomplishments or regrets—the part of you that is more than what you have or don't have. Ask your higher Self, "Do you love me?"

5. Next, invite your higher power—whatever this means to you (God, Universe). Ask your higher power, "Do you love me?"

6. Finally, with everyone seated, ask them, "Is there anything you need to share with me or is there anything I need to know in this moment?"

❀ EXERCISE
Unconditional Living

The art of unconditional living combines the unconditional love practice of the relational dimension along with the unconditional forgiveness, dreams, and gratitude of the mental dimension. In short, we are called to love unconditionally (an act of love for both ourselves and others), make peace with the past (unconditional forgiveness), show appreciation for what is arising moment to moment (unconditional gratitude or present-moment awareness), and to cast unconditional, unrestrained, value-driven intentions, goals, and dreams, in alignment with our highest Self, into the ethers of the future for manifestation.

Unconditional Forgiveness

Unconditional forgiveness is a process of unlearning, uncovering, and rewriting our stories, beliefs, and trespasses. In much the same way that it is dangerous to look in the rear-view mirror when driving, it is equally as dangerous to allow the past to define who you are. Forgive yourself for trespasses you committed against others as well as trespasses you have taken against yourself (self-betrayal, self-hatred, guilt).

Forgiveness, from a spiritual perspective, has nothing to do with condoning behavior. It is an act that releases and transcends the hurt so we can grow and avoid karmic repeating patterns that continue to wound us and others. As the Buddha reminds us, "Each morning we are born again," and "Holding on to anger is like drinking poison and expecting the other person to die." Our role is not judge and jury. We are called to take responsibility for our reactions, stories, and judgments by rejecting the past to live in the present moment.

Unconditional Gratitude

Unconditional gratitude is about connecting with the present moment or that which is arising moment to moment. Gratitude helps us focus and appreciate our experiences, the people in our life, the mundane, life's simplicity, and life's complexity—from the awe-inspiring sunset to simply waking up another day. The present moment is often hidden, ignored, or neglected as our mind preoccupies itself with those things we don't have, our misgivings, the past, and the future. Unconditional gratitude, on the other hand, allows us to experience life rather than allowing her to pass us by. It involves doing what we love and love what we do.

It is easy to be grateful for the positive and the good in our lives. Unconditional gratitude, however, is nonjudgmental. It asks us to view events and circumstances as neither good nor bad. It is a recognition of so-called "bad" events, reinterpreted by our highest Self, whereby life is seen as a classroom and adversity as a doorway. Unconditional gratitude moves you directly into the experiential realm of "awe." For example, you are not only grateful for the flower, but you begin to touch the flower, smell the flower, and contemplate its majesty and the mystery of life.

You can practice unconditional gratitude and awe throughout the day by first expressing gratitude intellectually for any event, circumstance, or person and then taking the next step to "breathe in" the experience away from the intellect and towards the heart. In this way, we can experience gratitude through our five senses and align with extrasensory awareness. The gift of cultivating a more present-moment existence, unclouded by narration, opens the door to the profound. As Dan Millman, author of the *Way of the Peaceful Warrior*, states, "The quality of your moments produces the quality of your life. So, as thoughts come and go and the waves of the mind rush on, *carpe-punctum* or "seize the moment." It deserves your full attention, for it will not pass your way again."

Unconditional Dreams

Working with unconditional dreams is the practice of using mental constructs (e.g., visualization and goals) for manifestation on the physical plane. It is an understanding that "thoughts become things." Unconditional goal setting and future planning require balancing ends with the means, the journey with the destination. After we take the first step, we then practice extending love to the future, holding faith in our efforts, and surrendering to the outcome. Unconditional dreams and aspirations require us to reverse modern-day practices of goal setting away from extrinsic rewards to intrinsic rewards and desires that foster a deep sense of equanimity and peace as our destination. We can, for example, change the goal of something as simple as a tennis match from "I want to win the tennis match" to "I will play my best." Lastly, unconditional dreams are goals to be made manifest on the physical plane and are best when tied to needs (e.g., growth and contribution).

Unconditional Love

Unconditional love is about love, care, and concern for oneself and others. You simultaneously are in the light and see the light in others. You practice perspective-taking, using both/and thinking, and you see all experiences from all angles. It is about the art and practice of namaste and miracles.

Self-Realization

Self-realization is the journey to recover or remember our true essence. It is a movement from separation and fragmentation to wholeness (*I to We*). It is the part of us that is untouched by time, suffering, fear, or shame. It is the witnessing pure consciousness before fusion and attachment to the world of form and time (thoughts, body identification, emotions, subpersonalities, relationships).

To learn who we are, we must first learn who we are not. Ignorance, in this vein, can be defined as thinking ourselves to be that which we are not. As we disidentify or shed the various masks, parts, and shadow attachments, an ever-present awareness emerges or is remembered. In other words, that which you are searching for has always been there. It waits on welcome, not time. Unfortunately, we have lost connection to this loving presence. We become lost with the contents (our emotions, thoughts) on our movie screen.

Once we diffuse and release attachments, we may notice a calming, peaceful, non-judgmental, and witnessing background presence. This is our true nature that sits in the movie theater of life, watching the mind's projections (the movie projector) without losing itself or attaching to the contents on the screen. This presence is behind all experiences, emotions, and thoughts.

Before the mind attaches, our consciousness just is. For example, pure consciousness, *I am*, rests and is reborn in deep sleep. Upon waking, the body concept arises, and the mind attaches. The purity of *I am* turns into "*I am* a body." Moments later, the trouble deepens as we begin an endless array of attachments to our thoughts and to-do lists. We experience this every day. Although difficult to identify, it is possible to catch or watch this very phenomenon. Moments before you fully awaken from your night's sleep, there is a space of pure consciousness, the *I am*, immediately before body identification. This cycle repeats daily and can be thought of as a mini birth (awakening) and death of the ego (deep sleep).

Before you jump into the self-realization meditative exercises, it is important to read the descriptors that follow. They will help awaken a dimension of Self that often lays dormant, unthought of, or difficult to connect to. As you take this journey, notice the emotional-feeling state as you move from suffering to bliss to love. The question we are asking is simply, *Who am I?* This is the profound and simple practice put forth by the great Indian Hindu sage Ramana Maharshi.

As we explore these topics, we will use the great wisdom traditions and Ken Wilber's Integral Theory to help inform and redefine the ideas of suffering, bliss, and love.

Masks, Parts, and Shadows (Suffering)

For starters, we are not: the voice in our heads, our emotions, feelings, actions, behaviors, beliefs, job, work, career, goals, roles (mom, dad, sister, brother, caretaker), a particular religion, or all the countless other things we associate with, identify with, or become attached to.

We are not the areas in life where we seek praise, power, security, safety, and pleasure. We are not our codependent relationships. We are not the person who made a mistake or committed a crime. We are not our achievements or lack thereof. We are not the various sub-personalities that live in the mind (wounded child, the procrastinator). We are not even the most obvious of all identifications—the physical body. Our body is constantly changing. We no longer have the same body as our five-year-old self, our fifteen-year-old self, the self of yesteryears, or the self of just moments ago. Therefore, what is ever-changing cannot be the true Self.

All these false identifications, identities, and attachments will be collectively referred to as our objective self, persona, or mask. And it is this mask or version of ourselves that we most often show the world and present to others.

Let's take just one of humanity's most pervasive identifications—the thoughts in our head. In Michael Singer's book *The Untethered Soul*, an analogy is drawn between the voice in our head and an unwelcomed roommate. He begins by explaining the frequently unconscious fact that we all live with a "mentally challenged" and ill-equipped friend who takes residence and control within the confines of our very own head. The narration that takes place is a collection of scattered, incoherent, and rambling thoughts. And as we know all too well, the cornucopia of schizophrenic-like conflicting advice can leave us unfulfilled and in a state of anxiety. This dialogue goes on and on. For some, it never ends and never sleeps. Ultimately, it distracts us from experiencing the present moment as it incessantly focuses on narrating our life, recalling the past, projecting the future, and offering unwanted advice. Imagine an individual driving to work and the endless array of scattered thoughts:

> *I must get to work. When is the traffic going to move? What am I going to have for dinner tonight? Did I shut the lights off before I left the house? I wonder if that package will arrive today? Great, traffic started to move again. I am so tired. I wish I had gotten more sleep. Should I go to the gym tonight? No, I'll skip tonight and go tomorrow.*

Michael Singer suggests a thought experiment. Suppose this voice could take on a persona—an actual physical body—and could sit next to you all day like a friend or roommate. How would you respond? Most of us would try, desperately, to escape the ceaseless narration. We would try everything in our power to create boundaries—you are no longer invited to join me for my daily meals, no longer allowed to accompany me in the shower, or sit by me as I watch TV. The reality, unfortunately, is that we live with this person day in and day out and find it hard to escape their relentless and pathological narrations, identifications, and attachments.

It has been estimated that the average person has somewhere between twenty thousand to eighty thousand thoughts a day. These thoughts come from memes, dogma, cultural biases, and indoctrinated beliefs. Interestingly, most of our so-called beliefs are not truly ours. They have been implanted in us by and through society. Furthermore, most of our beliefs, thoughts, and emotions are negative and not in service to our higher needs. These thoughts and beliefs fixate on nontruths, our false self, the past, the future, and show little concern for the only time we have—the present moment.

These thoughts and beliefs run our lives on autopilot. Most importantly, they keep us busy and distracted from knowing the truth of who we really are. Mindfulness practices that quiet the mind are the first step. The spiritual dimension's practices, however, ask you to keep going and peel away, layer by layer, until you touch the essence of your true Self.

As we continue to peel the onion and strip away the top layer of our masks, we begin to contact the caverns of our shadows. It is here where we encounter aspects of ourselves that, at a distant time, we choose to hide from the world. The shadow elements contain deeper textures of our human nature that are not only hidden from others but from ourselves, as well. Shadows are everything we cannot see in ourselves. All that we deny in ourselves becomes part of the shadow complex. The relational dimension, as previously discussed, offers us a great tool (mirror)—for we project onto others those things we deny or bury within (our shadow).

Our masks, parts, and shadows represent some of the original coping mechanisms and strategies we consciously or unconsciously created on our journey from childhood to adulthood as our needs (safety, security, love) were either nurtured or unfulfilled. Our masks and shadows, of course, continue to evolve in the present moment as the cycle of needs acquisition repeats and plays itself out time and again.

Witness Consciousness (Bliss)

As we move further on our journey, continuing to peel away our masks and shadows, we eventually meet a part of ourselves that has been sitting peacefully and quietly, behind all experience, like a great sage. This part of our Self, like the shadow, is an aspect greatly misunderstood. It is oftentimes referred to as the witnessing Self. It is here where the subject (your true Self) is witnessing an object (your mask).

Our true Self witnesses all that arises (objects). We have thoughts, but we are not our thoughts. We have emotions, but we are not our emotions. We have feelings, but we are not our feelings. We perform actions, but we are not identified by them. We have diseases, but we are not our diagnostic labels, and so on. The wisdom traditions call this Neti Neti, a Sanskrit expression that means "not this, not that." If you want to know the true Self, you must first negate everything that it is not.

Whatever can be witnessed is an object and, therefore, not a subject. Whatever can be made object is not the seer, the witness, the subject, or your true Self. The true Self is the pure witnessing subject behind all experience. Our spiritual sight replaces our physical sight. Our spiritual voice replaces our physical voice. That which was at one time only experienced as a subject (e.g., we are a particular emotion) becomes an object to see, view, and observe. We stand as a witness to all that is arising, free of objects.

When witness consciousness becomes our center of gravity, we shine the light of awareness on all that is in front of us. As an observer, we are free of the limited and contracted identifications of who we are (thoughts, beliefs, subpersonalities). The voice of our highest Self is the universal and singular melody among the cornucopia of noises we have become accustomed to. It is soft, quiet, non-judgmental, and cocreative. It shows great patience and is always present and available. It can be glimpsed every time a choice or decision is made that moves us toward states of equanimity, love, and peace. As we become more deeply aware of the soul's signature song, we begin to drown out the chatter of the ego's subpersonalities. It's as if the voice of our highest Self (the sun) is always present, regardless of the chatter (the clouds in the sky).

Our goal is not to value what is valueless. It is to become as vigilant against as we are for the false self's chatter. This, of course, is no small task as the egoic voices (masks and shadows) often speak first and loudest. As we listen to voices of distress and disempowerment, we are using instinctive, ancient, reptilian, limbic, and habituated responses. Conversely, the voice of our highest Self moves us out of this habituated response and connects us with areas of the brain that evolved for higher consciousness.

When one sits in complete witness consciousness, a great freedom is felt each time we release object attachment (the world's problems, the effects, thoughts, emotions). We first separate subject and object. Then, witness the object. Then, realize we are free of said object. For example, *I have emotions, but I am not my emotions. I am free of my emotions.* As we do so, we begin to experience what the wisdom traditions call pure bliss, or "freedom from." You are the *I am* without anything to follow.

This sense of bliss allows you to exist in the eye of the cyclone, resting in a state of inner peace regardless of what is arising in and around you. You are at peace because the truth of your nature is eternal and cannot be threatened.

Bliss can be likened to the chalice of your body emptying attachments. The journey, however, does not stop here. Your empty cup, free of attachments, now waits to be filled by something far more expansive and profound. If one rests openly in this state, the great Kosmos may decide to revisit you, offering a rare opportunity to glimpse what lies beyond—unity consciousness.

Unity Consciousness (Love)

At last, if we peel just one more layer and take a step behind the witness, we may be gifted with an awareness of the groundless ground of all being. The Zen Buddhism tradition calls this "our original face," or the face we had before we were born. It is here where subject and object merge to become one.

The great mysteries of life are often found in paradoxes and polarities. Enlightenment, in part, involves the resolution or transcendence of life's contradictions. Recall that bliss (freedom from) involves the release of attachments and objects. Unity consciousness, on the other hand, like the prodigal son, calls for their return. There is not one single part of the Kosmos that is excluded. Everything is invited. The body's chalice had to release identification with the thousands of fragmented identities in order to fill back up with everything as an integrated whole (e.g., the ego and witnessing Self). The feeling-emotion state associated with unity consciousness is not bliss but rather all-encompassing love and fullness. *I am the ocean, my thoughts, my body, the thousands of subpersonalities, the Big Bang, creation, death, and life. I hold them lovingly without conflict.*

It is in this state that one feels a complete sense of oneness, love, unity, and interconnectedness. The original name to describe this state, cosmic consciousness, was coined by Richard Bucket. It describes a person who perceives the whole of the Kosmos as an integration.

Individuals who have experienced a unity-type of consciousness describe a mystical feeling of becoming one with the cosmic family rather than an orphan of the state. From the most practical and tangible, ideas such as nationalism, patriotism, and ethnocentrism are transcended. More intangible, however, it describes a process or state of existence whereby the witness (subject) of the previous section literally merges or becomes one with all that is arising (object). You no longer see the moon, the stars, and the sun. Rather, you are the moon, the stars, and the sun. Boundaries disappear as you realize you are part and one with all of manifestation. This is likened to our previous discussion on peak and plateau experiences. As Rumi states, "You are not a drop in the ocean. You are the entire ocean in a drop."

Unity consciousness can be thought of as the experience, not the intellectual understanding or description, of the words spoken by Jesus when he said, "The kingdom of God is within." Paradoxically, unity consciousness, according to the wisdom traditions, is not technically a state. It is reality, herself. The human plight, the unsolvable game of life, the great illusion—as it has been called—lies in our inability to recognize the truth of this unity. The great awakening occurs when we release our pathological identifications with the world of form and shift towards the world of the formless, eternal, infinite, and changeless.

Formless, Self-Realization Meditative Practices

❀ EXERCISE
Neti-Neti Traditional and Parts

---

1. Sit quietly and comfortably in an environment that offers few if any distractions.
2. Eyes are opened or closed.
3. Begin with the noticing practice of see, hear, feel (see Chapter 24).

4. Work with your sensations, perceptions, memories, emotions, feelings, thoughts, beliefs, desires, needs, wants, and dreams. Choose all or a few.

5. For each sensation, perception, etc., state:

   I have X, but I am not X. I have X, but I am not limited by X. I am free of X.

   I have emotions, but I am not my emotions. I have emotions, but I am not limited by my emotions. I am free of my emotions.

6. For each part or subpersonality, state:

   I have X, but I am not X. I have X, but I am not limited by X. I am.

   I have a wounded child part, but I am not this wounded child part. I have a wounded child part, but I am not limited by this wounded child part. I am.

❀ EXERCISE
A Meditation on Emptying: Who Am I?

---

1. Begin with Neti-Neti Traditional practice.

2. Visualize your very being as a big, beautiful chalice filled with dirty water.

3. As you release attachments (e.g., *I have emotions, but I am not my emotions*), imagine emptying this chalice of all its contents and impurities. You may begin to feel a sense of freedom or bliss that connects you to the witness or *I am* existing behind all things.

4. Contemplate the nature of Self. For example:

   If I lost my legs, would I still be aware? If I lost my arms, would I still be aware? If I had no thoughts or memories, would I still be aware? And what would be left? Who am I without my labels (e.g., mother, father, teacher) or fears? Where is the sense of my very being, my I am-ness, felt or located (e.g., head, heart)?

5. Optionally, look deeply at your reflection (especially your eyes) in a mirror and ask, *Who am I?*

6. Ask yourself intermittently and repeatedly in silence or with meditative music, *Who am I?*

❀ EXERCISE
A Meditation on Filling Up: I Am Neti-Neti

---

1. Begin with Who am I? meditation.

2. Connect with the feeling states of pure radiating love, gratitude, calmness, compassion, courage, clarity, creativity, curiosity, connectedness, presence, persistence, perspective, patience, and playfulness. For example, you can use simplified version of the Heart-Respiratory-Brain Coherence practice (see Chapter 24) or Your Council of Elders exercise.

3. As you connect with love, imagine your chalice filling back up with everything in existence. Everything is included, put back, purified, interconnected, and whole.

4. Scan your internal landscape for sensations, perceptions, memories, emotions, feelings, thoughts, beliefs, desires, needs, wants, and dreams.

   With your eyes closed, state:
   I have X. I have Y. I feel Z. I am X. I am Y. I am Z.

I have memories. I have thoughts. I feel anxiety. I am my memories. I am my thoughts. I am anxiety.

With your eyes open, look around and state:
I see X. I am X. I see Y. I am Y.
I see the tree. I am the tree. I see the sky. I am the sky.

Note: This practice is best experienced in an environment that brings a sense of beauty or comfort (e.g., nature).

❀ EXERCISE
Parts: Big Mind and Big Heart (adapted from the works of Zen Master Dennis Genpo Merzel and Internal Family Systems)

---

1. Sit quietly and comfortably in an environment that offers, few, if any distractions.

2. Eyes are opened or closed.

3. Notice an amalgam of sensations, perceptions, memories, emotions, feelings, thoughts, beliefs, desires, needs, wants, and dreams. Collectively, these objects may converge and reveal an association to a specific part or subpersonality. If you have trouble identifying a part, bring to your mind's attention the various roles you identify with (father, mother, doctor, lawyer) or a concern or problem you are facing and the subpersonality struggling with these issues. Examples of parts include:

   - Innocent child
   - Wounded child
   - Adolescent

- Adult
- Wise sage
- Critic
- Victim
- Controller or manager
- Big Mind
- Big Heart

4. Work with any or all parts that arise spontaneously or summon a few of the parts listed above. For each part, shift your body position to allow a ritualistic embodiment. Example internal dialogue:

Controller

What do you have to manage or control every day? My work schedule, the kids, groceries, everything.

How are you feeling? Tired, burned out, and anxious. There is simply no time left for me.

What do you fear would happen if you resigned your duties and stopped controlling or managing everything? Everything would fall apart. My life would be in pieces. There would be no order or structure. I would lose all security.

Critic

What are you critical of? In yourself? Others? The world? My appearance, my reactions, my habits, my behaviors, politics, world leaders, and people not doing what they are supposed to.

How are you feeling? This is a never-ending job. I'm tired of finding faults. I am tired of being so critical all the time.

What do you fear would happen if you resigned and stopped criticizing altogether? People would take advantage of me. I would not grow or improve.

Child

The child is associated with binary thinking, emotions, and feelings (I'm sad, I'm happy). Bring to mind an experience, concern, issue, or problem you are facing and ask, *What are you feeling?*

Adolescent

The adolescent likes to add stories narratives, reactive-type interpretations, and problem-solving. Your answers do not have to be rational; this is your adolescent, not your adult part. Bring to mind an experience, concern, issue, or problem you are facing and ask, *Why?*

Adult

The adult part offers more "grown-up" stories, narratives, interpretations, and problem-solving. Bring to mind an experience, concern, issue, or problem you are facing and ask, *Is there another perspective?*

5. Thank each part for working so hard. For example, thank the controller for never stopping even when they are tired. Thank the critic for motivating you to be the best possible version of yourself and for protecting you from being taken advantage of.
6. Take a few deep diaphragmatic breaths.
7. Summon the part of you called the "seeker of the way." This is the part of you that is always searching and seeking. Example internal dialogue:

What am I seeking? Understanding, enlightenment, peace, purpose, love, and connection.

What is my role? Do I ever rest? Am I ever satisfied? No, I constantly seek. I seek to find answers and ways to bring internal tranquility. I seek even though I know it is unattainable. I never stop seeking, this is my job. I am always searching for enlightenment.

8. Summon the part of you called the "non-seeker" or Big Mind. The non-seeker doesn't seek because within it is all that it ever needs. It doesn't need to seek love, it is love. It doesn't need to seek peace, it is peace. Breathe into the part of you that never seeks and is always content. Allow this space to grow. Example internal dialogue:

   How do I feel? Calm, peaceful, relaxed, and fulfilled. I am free of the burdens of incessant seeking. I am free of people pleasing and self-criticism. I see things as they are. I have no fear. I am.

   How big am I in this space? Are there limits? I am without beginning or end. I feel boundless, infinite, vast, and expansive.

9. Breathe into Big Mind and allow it to grow. As you do, Big Mind may begin to appear separate from your parts and concerns. Looking from the expansive space of Big Mind ask yourself:

   How do all my parts look? They are working very hard. They seem small. My problems seem insignificant.

10. Once again, look from the expansive space of Big Mind and ask yourself:

    How do I feel toward my parts? Extreme gratitude, love, and compassion for how hard they are all working to help and protect me.

11. The answer to this last question brings you in direct contact with Big Heart. Ask yourself:

    How are you different from Big Mind? I make distinctions and act from a place of compassion. Big Mind is simply aware and indifferent. When I see suffering, pains, and injustice I want to help. I want to do something.

12. As you connect with the compassion, love, and gratitude of Big Heart and Big Mind, tell your parts:

    All of you can work together. My mind, body, and soul have no conflict. There is only peace. You all have different roles to play but underneath it all, I am here. We are all connected for the same purpose.

13. Ask yourself, *What would be here now in this present moment if there wasn't anything to solve? If there wasn't a problem?*

14. Finally, you may choose to end with a modified version of the Council of Elders exercise.

❀ EXERCISE
The 3-2-1 Shadow Process

The 3-2-1 Shadow Process, adapted from Integral Life Practice by Ken Wilber, is one of the best ways to reclaim disowned aspects of yourself (see Chapter 7). This process can be done with people, experiences, events, circumstances, or things. For this exercise, we will use a person that triggered a heightened reactive emotional-mental state in you:

1. Choose a person that negatively charged you (i.e., emotions of anger or judgment) or positively charged you (i.e., elevating

someone to higher-than-normal levels of adoration) during the past week.

2. Hold them in your mind's eye, face them, and describe the details of your trigger or concern without minimizing or rationalizing, using third-person language (i.e., he/she said...).

3. Talk to that person, speaking in second-person language. Enter a dialogue and explain to them exactly what bothered you, what triggered you, and why you are upset. Ask them questions without expecting an answer.

4. Be that person by taking their perspective and entering first-person perspective. Use I am statements.

5. After completing the exercise, bring your awareness to these disowned qualities that may be hidden in yourself.

❀ **EXERCISE**
Polarity Thinking: Being and Doing

The universe is made up of a seemingly endless array of paradoxical forces. Starting with the most primitive, we have Spirit's directionality, transcend and include (Eros and Agape) alongside communion and agency. Polarities can be seen in the universe's expansion-contraction, life and death cycles, seasonal cycles, human emotions (happy-sad), and the human mind (formless) and body (form).

In Chinese philosophy, the yin-yang symbol is a masterful representation of embracing these paradoxes or polarities. The yin-yang symbol stands as a reminder that paradoxes are interrelated, complementary, and interdependent. We can look to the energies of being and doing to understand how polarities touch every part of our life.

- Being: inner purpose, rest/recovery, present-moment aware-ness, non-resistance, non-judgment, non-attachment, use of intuition, receiving, communion, safety, certainty, femi-nine-like energies, and more.
- Doing: outer purpose, movement, human drives or goals, action, self-interest, giving, agency, risk, uncertainty, novelty, change, transcendence, masculine-like energies, and more.

Since the universe is a polarity, we can avoid needless suffering by engaging and practicing the art of polarity or integral thinking. This is one of the most important practices in the cultivation of fulfill-ment, coherence, and internal states of peace and equanimity. Polarity thinking allows us to integrate, resolve, and transcend dichotomies.

Distinguishing Between Polarities and Polarization

Everyday polarities:

- Inside versus outside
- Dark versus light
- From versus formless
- Good versus bad
- Individual versus collective
- Subjective versus objective
- Heaven versus Earth
- Mind versus body
- Evolution versus devolution
- Masculine versus feminine
- Individual freedom versus collective responsibilities
- Globalization versus nationalism

So, what exactly are polarities?

For starters, they are not opposites. They are tensions or competing forces that exist in each experience. They are two sides of the same coin or interdependent parts of a greater whole. Polarities involve both-and thinking and lead to constructive solutions, ideas, and ways of being-doing.

The examples listed above are, in fact, examples of polarization, not polarities. The use of the word versus as found in between each pole or group of words is the culprit. Although this may sound like semantics, the context and meaning of the word versus implies either-or thinking, opposition, friction, and contradiction.

- Polarizing: either-or and right-wrong thinking
    o Selfish versus taking care of others
    o I'm stagnant or stuck versus growth
- Polarity: both-and thinking
    o Taking care of myself and taking care of others
    o Appreciation or gratitude for where you are and growth

The goal of polarity thinking is to move away from tension-filled polarization, positive or negative, to solutions that are constructive and nourishing. When we polarize, we create blind spots for ourselves and others. We think we see the whole. In reality, however, we are most likely favoring or disowning one pole of the polarity.

Polarity thinking allows us to see the sacred in our everyday life. It helps understand that sadness rides alongside joy. According to Susan Cain, author of *Bittersweet*, sadness is the very reason we experience joy and happiness. When we hold a newborn baby, share in the joyous nature of a puppy playing, or gaze our eyes at a breath-taking sunset, we experience joy and happiness because, consciously or unconsciously, we know this experience is fleeting (each moment is born and dies), one day they will be gone, and one day we will be gone.

Another example involves the poles of pain and pleasure. Pushing at the edges of pain and pleasure (jumping out of a plane, death of a loved one) makes you more alive and reveals something profound—something greater than yourself. Pain and sadness help us to connect, unites our shared humanity, fosters connection, and increases our empathy. When others bear their soul, we become honest and vulnerable. We begin to see past our ego to the divinity within.

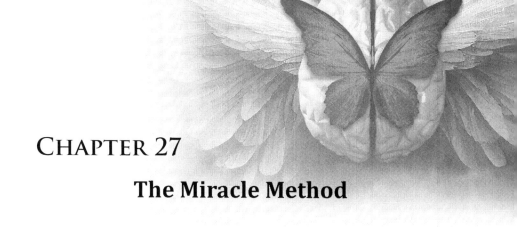

CHAPTER 27

The Miracle Method

Miracles occur naturally as expressions of love. The real miracle
is the love that inspires them. In this sense everything that comes
from love is a miracle.

-A Course in Miracles

The Miracle Method (MM) is an attempt to eliminate contradictions and mismatches between *who we are* and *who we wish to be*. It
is based on The Alignment Continuum, where we align our soul's
awareness, our mind's attention (both conscious and unconscious),
our heart's intention, and our body's inspired actions and behaviors.

The goal of The Miracle Method is not perfection. We are striving, quite simply, to be better than the moment prior.

Miracles require no steps, no methods. They occur spontaneously
anytime we reconnect with our higher Self. The steps to follow are
attempts to formulate that which can't be formulated. With that said,
the MM is an experiential process that ensures, more times than not,
you will succeed in the forever practice of creating miracles.

The MM is based, in part, on the triune model of the brain discussed earlier. Each practice helps to break the chains of pathological automations, reactions, misidentifications (with our ego), and emotional-mental fusion. The four-step process is a whole-brain practice of integrating our reptilian, mammalian, neocortex, and angel lobes. The specific techniques within each practice are not important. What is important, however, is finding the tools that resonate with you.

The MM can be likened to the spiritual practice found in Alcoholics Anonymous, "Let go and let God." It is one of the most important practices for living a life of peace. Miracles help us to recognize the divinity in and around us and the abundance of each and every moment. We must remember that it takes no effort to be who you really are and takes extreme effort (learned associations and programming) to be who you are not. This includes limiting beliefs such as the attachment we have to our body—designed for sickness and suffering.

We will use the acronym PATH to help guide us on CMM's four-step process. They include contacting the present moment, awareness, tracing and translating, and finally, contacting and connecting with your highest Self. This practice is amalgam of the ideas and theories laid out in this book:

1. Present Moment: Contact and connect to the present moment to help pause non-nurturing reactivity and less than heroic responses that arise from our reptilian and mammalian brain centers. It is here where we put a space in between stimulus and response or our endless array of non-nurturing reactions.

2. Awareness: Contact and connect to the "witness." It is here we can take a 10,000-foot view as we begin to observe our

lives without judgment. The gift of awareness allows us to see things as they are rather than as we think they are. In its most simple iteration, we name what we see and separate facts from opinions. In addition, this step helps to counter the pathological emotional-mental fusion arising from our mammalian cortex and neocortex, respectively. Recall that pathological fusion creates the misidentification of Self as an emotion, feeling, sensation, thought, belief, mask, shell, or shadow. As a counterpoint, awareness allows us to sit in the seat of pure witness consciousness as we put space between these misidentifications. This space between stimulus and response is connected to the infinite field and where our potential resides. Reaction collapsed the potential into a conditioned past habit. Response, on the other hand, allows us to collapse our potentials into an enlightened manifestation that rises above our past conditioning.

3. Tracing and Translating: This is a powerful mental and intellectual step that helps us tap into the brain's higher centers (neocortex and angel lobes) as well as the pure primordial powers of being and doing. Tracing, as the name suggests, asks us to trace our thousands of problems back to pure unity consciousness (*I to We*), the primordial elements (e.g., our needs), the tiny mad idea, or the simplicity of one problem, one solution. The second part of the process, translating, involves a movement from being (recognizing and surrendering to the one problem, one solution) to the energies of doing as we translate the primordial elements (tracings) into actionable values of living. From a practical perspective, this step is an exploration of your values, needs, and *who and what is most important to you*. It allows us to wake up from

the nightmare rather than trying to fix the nightmare of our thousands of problems. Simply ask, what need is unmet or frustrated? What values do they represent?

4. Highest Self: In reality, this is the only step needed. It is a full integration of physical and nonphysical brain centers. Here we move away from an intellectual and emotional understanding to a full embodiment as we contact and connect with our highest Self. As we do so, we respond heroically, shift from knowledge to wisdom, use nourishing discernment, and sit in a state of doing and being that transcends polarities and contradictions. The true Self is our home underneath the masks, shells, and armor we present to the world. Life is seen, quite simply, as love or a call for love. This step is the ultimate choice point–the choice to react from past egoic conditioning or to respond from our highest Self. From a practical perspective, this step asks us to embody and uncover our values (e.g., the qualities of the true Self). As we do, we begin to live "from or with" our values rather than states of emptiness, lack, and scarcity. Recall, it is far more effective to the manifestation process if we live in a state of fulfilment first before taking the necessary action or inaction.

The Miracle Method

P   Present Moment
Contact and connect with the
present moment

A   Awareness
Contact and connect with awareness
or the "witness"

T   Trace and Translate
Trace your problems back to human needs
Translate needs into personal values and
actionable daily habits

H   Highest Self
Contact and connect with your higher Self

Step 1: Contacting and Connecting with the Present Moment

The first step or goal is to contact the ever-present now moment and, if needed, release unwanted or undigested energies or emotions. This allows respite away from the reptilian and mammalian brain's automations, allowing us the opportunity to respond as our highest Self. There are a host of techniques that can be used. Here are a few ideas:

- When feeling stressed or experiencing unwanted feelings or emotions (fear and anxiety), pause, stop, and notice. Give yourself an adult time-out. If needed, use a mantra to remind yourself that "In the present moment, right here and now, I am safe."

- Coherence exercises (see Chapter 22): Practice present moment awareness, mindfulness, breathwork, grounding or Earthing, and heart-respiratory coherence.

- Releasing: A new field of treatment, broadly defined as somatic therapy, takes a novel approach to diffusion and the release of emotions, mental constructs, and traumas. Unlike standard mental health therapies (i.e., talk therapy), somatic therapy practices incorporate body-oriented modalities such as shaking, dancing, moving, and exercise to diffuse unwanted, stored bodily tension, trauma, and stress. One of its pioneers, Dr. Peter A. Levine, discovered thirty-five years ago that wild animals react, first, through the classic fight-flight mechanisms that, for example, increase stress chemicals and blood flow. The recovery process, however, involves the release of these same fight-flight mechanisms. For example, before the freezing response kicks in, wild animals complete the stress recovery cycle by tremoring muscular spasms and flailing of limbs. The shaking and tremoring help discharge stress chemicals, emotions, and unwanted traumatic energies that would otherwise get frozen in the body. All too often and partly due to culturally accepted modes of conduct, we humans feel we don't have the opportunity to diffuse, shake, dance, or release these unwanted energies. Levine created Somatic Experiencing bodywork to help patients experience and complete the discharge that was initially aborted decades prior.

Step 2: Awareness

Although awareness has many meanings, we will highlight, for the purpose of this discussion, its most salient characteristic as human consciousness embodied by the witness or seer.

Building on the practice of pausing, stopping, and noticing, we now take the first steps to diffuse from our emotions and mental constructs. Remember, the witness is you, a subject. Everything else is not you, an object. Anything you can name (see, hear, feel), quantify, qualify, or become aware of is an object and, therefore, not the witness. This includes our thoughts, emotions, feelings, sensations, personality traits, accolades, degrees, roles, and more. All these objects are witnessed by you as the subject and seer. They are things you sense or experience and in no way can be equated with who you truly are.

If we can hold on for ninety seconds without re-fusing or re-ruminating, we might be able to break free of our incessant emotional and mental loops. Brain scientist Jill Bolte Taylor, author of *My Stroke of Insight*, calls this the ninety-second rule: "When a person has a reaction to something in their environment, there's a ninety-second chemical process that happens; any remaining emotional response is just the person choosing to stay in that emotional loop." Two of the best practices to consider are:

- Neti-Neti Traditional and Parts (see Chapter 26)
- Name to tame to transcend: the art of taking an experience, naming it, and separating the facts from any opinions or judgements

Step 3: Tracing and Translating

Tracing

Tracing involves an intellectual exploration of our thousands of problems. In this step, we are asked to trace our problems or complex secondary elements back to their roots. Take time to look back over the primal elements and the concept of the primal struggle. Tracing involves identifying the cause behind our sea of endless problems. The goal is to identify the cause behind the problem as you explore:

- The human need involved
- The emotional landscape and its inherent meaning
- Your primal reactive pattern
- One problem-one solution doctrine

Example: *Someone says something to us. We react with anger and hostility. As the hours pass, we begin to feel an increased intensity in our emotional landscape. In turn, we go home and attempt to numb the pain, guilt, and shame with alcohol, binge eating, and Netflix.*

All these complex behaviors, thoughts, emotions, and reactions are secondary elements that we, collectively and erroneously, equate as our "problems." The truth lies hidden under these surface distractions. Our goal, therefore, is to trace the so-called problems back to the source of origin, our primordial elements.

Consider the example above; we reacted with anger, spiraled down into complex psychological musings (shame and guilt), and engaged in destructive behaviors simply because we may have felt unsafe. Our nervous system interpreted our friend's words as "danger," and then the primitive fight or flight programs mixed with past mental interpretations, stories, and beliefs. And because we did not take time to consciously reflect on our subconscious reactions, we continued to spiral downward, taking us miles and miles away from our true desire—the need for connection. The real problem in this scenario is how our needs for safety and connection were not met, not communicated, or frustrated.

Translating

With translating, we take the primordial elements and the one-problem-one solution doctrine and translate them into personal values and actionable daily habits. This step is an exploration of our vision, goals, strategies, and values. With the need uncovered, we can ask, "How do I satiate this need in a nourishing, loving, and empowering way?"

Step 4: Highest Self

This step in The Core Miracle Method is a practice of alchemizing, transmuting, and transcending all our fears (the metaphorical representation of pathological, maladaptive, toxic, and non-nurturing defense mechanisms, strategies, shadows, mental constructs, emotions, and behaviors) into ones that are more constructive, adaptive, nurturing, and healing (love).

It is a process of peeling away the onion layers or removing the proximal causes or effects to uncover and unearth root causes. Ultimately this process will lead us back to the decision-maker in the mind (cause), allowing us an opportunity to choose right versus wrong-mindedness, again and again, thought by thought, breath by breath, as we cultivate states of peace, equanimity, and love. Our goal is to make our ego a servant (wrong-mindedness) to our higher Self (right-mindedness). When this is accomplished, there is an instantaneous alignment in the present moment between our needs, values, awareness, attention, intention, and behaviors.

A Course in Miracles calls this moment the holy instant. In other words, we don't have to wait for every thought, emotion, feeling, and sensation to be aligned. Willingness to move towards the holy instant allows the holy instant to complete the process. As an analogy, we don't clean ourselves before entering the shower–that's the shower's job. The *Course* explains this poetically:

> *The desire and willingness to let it come precedes its coming... Come to it not in arrogance, assuming that you must achieve the state it's coming brings with it. The miracle of the holy instant lies in your willingness to let it be what it is...In preparing for the holy instant, do not attempt to make yourself holy to be ready to receive it. That is but to confuse your role with God's...You make it difficult, because you insist there must be more that you need do. You find it difficult to accept the idea that you need give so little, to receive so much...Never approach the holy instant after you have tried to remove all fear and hatred from your mind. That is its function...The necessary condition for the holy instant does not require that you have no thoughts that are not pure. But it does require that you have none that you would not keep.*

In this final step, every situation is seen as love or a call for love. As we embody miracle-mindedness, we surrender our self-identity and sit, without dichotomy, in a state of being and doing.

Recall that a miracle is a shift in awareness, perception, emotion, or behavior that moves us from fear (circumstances, anxieties) to love. The miracle occurs every time we create alignment with our highest Self (comfort to courage, choosing a better narrative, self-betrayal to a values-driven life, taking a deep breath, and more).

Comparing our highest Self and ego:

> • Ego: There are millions of problems, there is a hierarchy to our problems, and miracles are unavailable.
> • Highest Self: There is only one problem (fear), and it blocks the awareness of love's presence, there is no hierarchy of problems, and miracles are available at all times, waiting only on welcome.

There are many ways to contact our highest Self. Choose whatever options works best for you. Although some of the examples below may appear simple, think about their potential. Imagine how a person's state of being or life can change in just a single *aha* moment or decision. (See Chapter 22 for coherence exercises and Chapter 26 for self-realization practices.)

Empowering questions

- How can I move from fear to love?
- Is this true? Is it helpful? Kind? What would love do?
- What would be a more efficient, peaceful, or loving response?
- Do I choose conflict, to understand, or to be right over peace?
- How would my best Self respond?
- Can I see and hold other perspectives?
- What would you have me do, where would you have me go, and what would you have me say and to whom?
- What do I need to remove from my life? What do I need to say no to? What do I need to stop doing? What do I need to do less of?
- What do I need to say yes to? What do I need to continue doing more of?

- Can I do or not do whatever is called of me, peacefully?
- What nourishment am I missing from my life?
- For those things that I cannot control or remove, how can I transcend them? Surrender to them?
- Where do I need to create healthy boundaries? With myself? Others?
- How can I live a life by design?
- How can I avoid living in self-betrayal?
- How can I create more peace and equanimity in my life?
- How can I create more coherence (i.e., balance and harmony)?
- Do I know my values and needs? Am I living in alignment with them?

Affirmations or mantras

- At any moment, I can choose peace instead of this.
- At any moment, I can choose again.
- I choose to see my circumstances, problems, and obstacles as love or a call for love.
- I choose to respond rather than react from my core values and needs.
- I choose and desire miracles more than I desire pain and suffering.
- I am the unbounded witness behind my thoughts, emotions, and behaviors, free from the ego's stories, judgments, and expectations.

Conclusion

Love the one in you who is sad. Love the one in you who is scarred.
Love the one in you who is angry. Love the one in you who is
lonely. Love the one in you who hates herself. Love all the ones who
you are. Then you will know how to love the world.

-Elizabeth Gilbert

We have covered complex topics and provided tangible solutions.
There is no reason to wait to get healthy, contribute to the world, and
make a difference. We can all start by eating a little healthier, moving
a little more, loving a little more, and forgiving a little more. Don't
fall prey to a forever journey into the word of complexity that stifles
your potentiality.

Breathe.

Become aware of who you really are, the ever-present witness
consciousness.

Become aware of your ego's primal struggle and identify the universal need/s.

Align with your highest Self for action or inaction.

Ask yourself, "What would love do?" and remind yourself, "At any moment, I can choose peace instead of this."

Meditate on the delightful "Acornology" by Jacob Needleman, retold by Cynthia Bourgeault in *The Wisdom Way: Reclaiming an Ancient Tradition to Awaken the Heart*:

> Once upon a time, in a not-so-faraway land,
> there was a kingdom of acorns,
> nestled at the foot of a grand old oak tree.
> Since the citizens of this kingdom were modern, fully Westernized acorns,
> they went about their business with purposeful energy;
> and since they were midlife, baby-boomer acorns,
> they engaged in a lot of self-help courses.
> There were seminars called "Getting All You Can out of Your Shell."
> There were woundedness and recovery groups for acorns who had been bruised in their original fall from the tree.
> There were spas for oiling and polishing those shells and various acornopathic therapies to enhance longevity and well-being.
> One day in the midst of this kingdom there suddenly appeared a knotty little stranger,
> apparently dropped 'out of the blue' by a passing bird.
> He was capless and dirty, making an immediate negative impression on his fellow acorns.
> And crouched beneath the oak tree, he stammered out a wild tale.
> Pointing upward at the tree, he said, "We....are....that!"

Delusional thinking, obviously, the other acorns concluded,

but one of them continued to engage him in conversation:
"So tell us, how would we become that tree?"
"Well," said he, pointing downward, "it has something to do with going
into the ground and…and cracking open the shell."
"Insane," they responded.
"Totally morbid!
Why, then we wouldn't be acorns anymore."

Miracles await you!

References

Bourgeault, Cynthia. *The Wisdom Way of Knowing: Reclaiming An Ancient Tradition to Awaken the Heart.* John Wiley & Sons, 2003.

Bowlby, John. *A Secure Base.* Routledge, 2012.

Brown, Brené. *The Gifts of Imperfection: 10th Anniversary Edition: Features a New Foreword and Brand-New Tools.* Random House, 2020.

Cain, Susan. *Bittersweet: How Sorrow and Longing Make Us Whole.* Crown, 2022.

Campbell, Joseph. *The Hero with a Thousand Faces.* Bollingen Foundation, 2004.

Campbell, Joseph, and Bill Moyers. *The Power of Myth.* Anchor, 2011.

Childre, Doc Lew, and Howard Martin. *The HeartMath Solution.* Piatkus Books, 2011.

Covey, Stephen R. *The Seven Habits of Highly Effective People: Restoring the Character Ethic.* Macmillan Reference USA, 1997.

Csikszentmihalyi, Mihaly. *Flow: The Psychology of Optimal Experience.* Harper Collins, 2009.

Dana, Deborah A., and Stephen W. Porges. *Polyvagal Theory in Therapy: Engaging the Rhythm of Regulation.* National Geographic Books, 2018.

Diaz-Santana, Mary Vanellys, and Katherine W. Reeves. "Abstract B34: Breast Cancer Risk Factors and Screening Practices among Hispanics Subgroups in the United States." *Cancer Epidemiology, Biomarkers & Prevention* 24, no. 10_ Supplement (October 1, 2015): B34–B34. https://doi. org/10.1158/1538-7755.disp14-b34.

Eisenstein, Charles. *The More Beautiful World Our Hearts Know Is Possible*. North Atlantic Books, 2013.

Ekman, Paul, Wallace V. Friesen, and Phoebe Ellsworth. *Emotion in the Human Face: Guidelines for Research and an Integration of Findings*. Elsevier, 2013.

Frank, Adam J., and Elizabeth A. Wilson. *A Silvan Tomkins Handbook: Foundations for Affect Theory*. U of Minnesota Press, 2020.

Frankl, Viktor E. *Man's Search for Meaning*. Beacon Press, 2014.

Gardner, Howard. *Frames of Mind: The Theory of Multiple Intelligences*. Basic Books, 2011.

Henry, Todd. *Die Empty: Unleash Your Best Work Every Day*. Penguin, 2015.

Herman, Todd. *The Alter Ego Effect: The Power of Secret Identities to Transform Your Life*. HarperCollins, 2019.

Holmes, Jerry. *John Bowlby and Attachment Theory*. Routledge, 2006.

Houston, Jean. *The Wizard of Us: Transformational Lessons from Oz*. Simon and Schuster, 2016.

Huxley, Aldous. *The Perennial Philosophy*. Harper Collins, 2004.

III, Holmes Rolston. *Three Big Bangs: Matter-Energy, Life, Mind*. Columbia University Press, 2010.

Kabat-Zinn, Jon. *Wherever You Go, There You Are: Mindfulness Meditation In Everyday Life*. Hachette Books, 2009.

Koestler, Arthur. *The Ghost in the Machine*, 1968.

Krumwiede, Andreas. *Attachment Theory According to John Bowlby and Mary Ainsworth*. GRIN Verlag, 2014.

Lee, Thomas F. *The Human Genome Project: Cracking the Genetic Code of Life*. Springer, 2013.

Library, New World. *Wisdom of the Great Chiefs: The Classic Speeches of Chief Red Jacket, Chief Joseph and Chief Seattle*, 1994.

Longo, Valter. *The Longevity Diet: Discover the New Science Behind Stem Cell Activation and Regeneration to Slow Aging, Fight Disease, and Optimize Weight.* Penguin, 2018.

MacLean, P.D. *The Triune Brain in Evolution: Role in Paleocerebral Functions.* Springer Science & Business Media, 1990.

Mair, Victor H., and Lao Tzu. *Tao Te Ching: The Classic Book of Integrity and The Way.* Bantam, 2012.

Maslow, A. H. *A Theory of Human Motivation.* Simon and Schuster, 2013.

Maslow, Abraham H. *Religions Values and Peak-Experiences.* Rare Treasure Editions, 2021.

———. *The Farther Reaches of Human Nature.* Penguin Books, 1993.

———. *Toward a Psychology of Being.* John Wiley & Sons Incorporated, 1998.

Maslow, Abraham Harold, Richard Lowry, and Bertha G. Maslow. *The Journals of Abraham Maslow.* Penguin Books, 1982.

McKeown, Patrick. *The Oxygen Advantage: The Simple, Scientifically Proven Breathing Techniques for a Healthier, Slimmer, Faster, and Fitter You.* HarperCollins, 2015.

Miller, Lisa. *The Awakened Brain: The New Science of Spirituality and Our Quest for an Inspired Life.* Random House, 2021.

Millman, Dan. *Way of the Peaceful Warrior: A Book That Changes Lives.* H J Kramer, 2006.

Mitchell, Stephen. *Tao Te Ching Persona.* Harper Collins, 1992.

Moran, Brian P., and Michael Lennington. *The 12 Week Year: Get More Done in 12 Weeks than Others Do in 12 Months.* John Wiley & Sons, 2013.

Neves, Antonio. *Stop Living on Autopilot: Take Responsibility for Your Life and Rediscover a Bolder, Happier You.* Rodale Books, 2021.

Pagels, Elaine. *The Gnostic Gospels*. Random House, 2004.

Ph.D., Peter A. Levine. *In an Unspoken Voice: How the Body Releases Trauma and Restores Goodness*. North Atlantic Books, 2010.

Popp, Fritz Albert, and Qiao Gu. *Recent Advances in Biophoton Research and Its Applications*. World Scientific, 1992.

Pressfield, Steven. *The War of Art: Break Through the Blocks and Win Your Inner Creative Battles*. Black Irish Entertainment LLC, 2002.

Rosenberg, Marshall B., and Deepak Chopra. *Nonviolent Communication: A Language of Life: Life-Changing Tools for Healthy Relationships*. PuddleDancer Press, 2015.

Schwartz, Richard C. *No Bad Parts: Healing Trauma and Restoring Wholeness with the Internal Family Systems Model*. Sounds True, 2021.

Scribe, Helen Schucman. *A Course in Miracles: Combined Volume*. Foundation for Inner Peace, 2008.

Selye, Hans. *Stress in Health and Disease*. Butterworth-Heinemann, 2013.

Sinclair, David A., and Matthew D. LaPlante. *Lifespan: Why We Age—and Why We Don't Have To*. Simon and Schuster, 2019.

Singer, Michael A. *The Untethered Soul: The Journey Beyond Yourself*. New Harbinger Publications Incorporated, 2013.

Sullivan, Dan. *The 4 C's Formula: Your Building Blocks of Growth: Commitment, Courage, Capability, and Confidence*. Ethos Collective, 2021.

Taylor, Jill Bolte. *My Stroke of Insight: A Brain Scientist's Personal Journey*. Penguin, 2008.

Trayser, John Richard. *The Aces Revolution!: The Impact of Adverse Childhood Experiences*. Createspace Independent Publishing Platform, 2016.

Tuttle, Will. *The World Peace Diet*. Lantern Books, 2005.

Tzu, Lao. *Tao Te Ching*. Shambhala Publications, 2007.

Ware, Bronnie. *Top Five Regrets of the Dying: A Life Transformed by the Dearly Departing*. Hay House, Inc, 2019.

Wilber, Ken. *A Brief History of Everything*. Shambhala Publications, 2007.

———. *A Theory of Everything: An Integral Vision for Business, Politics, Science and Spirituality*. Shambhala Publications, 2001.

———. *Integral Meditation: Mindfulness as a Way to Grow Up, Wake Up, and Show Up in Your Life*. Shambhala Publications, 2016.

———. *Integral Psychology*. Shambhala Publications, 2000.

———. *Integral Spirituality: A Startling New Role for Religion in the Modern and Postmodern World*. Shambhala Publications, 2007.

———. *The Essential Ken Wilber*. Shambhala Publications, 1998.

———. *The Integral Vision: A Very Short Introduction*. Shambhala Publications, 2018.

———. *The Religion of Tomorrow: A Vision for the Future of the Great Traditions-More Inclusive, More Comprehensive, More Complete*. Shambhala Publications, 2017.

Williamson, Marianne. *A Return to Love*. HarperThorsons, 2009.

———. *The Law of Divine Compensation: On Work, Money, and Miracles*. HarperOne, 2012.

Young, Shinzen. *The Science of Enlightenment: How Meditation Works*. Sounds True, 2016.

Made in the USA
Columbia, SC
09 October 2023

24174275R00193